Criminal Justice
Recent Scholarship

Edited by
Marilyn McShane and Frank P. Williams III

A Series from LFB Scholarly

Road Rage

Maria L. Garase

LFB Scholarly Publishing LLC
New York 2006

Library of Congress Cataloging-in-Publication Data

Garase, Maria L., 1974-
  Road rage / Maria L. Garase.
     p. cm. -- (Criminal justice)
  Includes bibliographical references and index.
  ISBN 1-59332-139-2 (alk. paper)
  1. Road rage. 2. Automobile drivers--Psychology. 3. Traffic safety.
4. Aggressiveness. I. Title. II. Series: Criminal justice (LFB Scholarly
Publishing LLC)
  TL152.35.G37 2006
  629.28'3019--dc22

                                             2005037272

ISBN 1-59332-139-2

Printed on acid-free 250-year-life paper.

Manufactured in the United States of America.

Table of Contents

Acknowledgements

I would like to thank my parents Mary Louse and Joseph Garase for their support throughout this project.

Thanks to my reviewers: David Barker, Ph.D., Gannon University and Dawna Komorosky, Ph.D. California State University, East Bay. I appreciate all of your insightful comments and corrections.

Thanks to Gannon University, who gave me release time to work on this book.

I appreciate the time and efforts of my editor Leo Balk, who kept me on track and gave my technical advice.

I would also like to say a special thank you to Alida Merlo, Ph.D., who jumpstarted my writing career. She encouraged me to work on this project from the beginning, specifically when it was a dissertation topic.

CHAPTER 1

A Public Safety Concern

Feeling furious at the steering wheel is now a recognized part of modern life. Flashing your headlights, driving six inches behind the (crawling) car in front, gesturing from the window and shouting remarks about a driver's ancestry are virtually the law of the road. Yet it is still a shock to recognize the toll this takes in human life. (*The Economist*, 1997, p. 26)

"Road rage" is a problem on highways and roadways (Blake, 1998; Blanchard, Barton, & Malta, 2000; Deffenbacher, Huff, Lynch, Oetting, & Salvatore, 2000; James & Nahl, 2000; Murray, 2000; Willis, 1997; Wrightson, 1997). While road rage is not a new phenomenon, it was brought to the forefront in the early 1990s. The term road rage refers to an extreme form of aggressive driving that has been identified as "a risk factor for motor vehicle accident (MVA) morbidity and mortality" (Blanchard et al., 2000, p. 881). Road rage further has been defined as "an incident in which an angry or impatient motorist or passenger intentionally injures or kills another motorist, passenger, or pedestrian, or attempts to injure or kill another motorist, passenger, or pedestrian, in response to a traffic dispute, altercation, or grievance" (Mizell, 1997, p. 5). Many of the precipitators of road rage behaviors include repeated horn honking, red-light running, traffic weaving, tailgating, headlight flashing, excessive braking, verbal abuse, and obscene gestures. Aggressive driving or "road rage" has been blamed for numerous accidents, outbreaks of violence, and even deaths on the nation's roadways (Willis, 1997).

In the last decade, there has been increased media attention concerning incidents of road rage. Some of the most shocking incidents include situations in which drivers and/or passengers were shot, stabbed, run-over by the vehicle, or killed. In Massachusetts, Donald Graham became embroiled in a heated, ongoing traffic dispute with

1

Michael Bodgett (Mizell, 1997). After the motorists antagonized each other for several miles on the Interstate, they both pulled over and got out of their vehicles. At that point Graham retrieved from his trunk a powerful crossbow and murdered Blodgett with a razor sharp 29-inch arrow (Mizell, 1997).

Road rage incidents have also attracted international media attention. On February 11, 2000, in San Jose, California, Sara McBurnett, accompanied by her dog, Leo, was driving to the airport to pick-up her husband. Ms. McBurnett accidentally tapped the bumper of a black sport utility vehicle (SUV) that had swerved in front of her. Andrew Burnett, the driver of the SUV stopped, stormed back to McBurnett's car and began screaming. Without warning Burnett, who was apparently enraged, grabbed the dog and flung him into oncoming traffic. The small dog was seriously injured and later died (Harris, 2001). Burnett was convicted of animal cruelty and sentenced to a three-year prison term. The San Jose Superior Courtroom erupted in applause as Judge Kevin J. Murphy imposed the maximum sentence after saying that the defendant was a danger to the community (Harris, 2001). Not only in the United States, but also in many other countries (e.g., United Kingdom, Australia, and countries in Europe) researchers have reported significant increases in incidents of road rage (Parker, Lajunen, & Summala, 2002).

Prevalence of the Problem

The U.S. Department of Transportation (DOT) (1997) conducted a study in order to investigate the prevalence of road rage incidents. The research demonstrated that during the 1990s aggressive driving had risen fifty-one percent (Kowalski, 1998). *The Economist* (1997) noted that, since 1987 the number of miles of roads in the United States has increased by only one percent, but the number of vehicle miles driven has gone up by 35 percent. Furthermore, "the number of cars has increased by 27 percent and most journeys are taking longer than drivers think they should" (*The Economist,* 1997, p. 26). As a result, individuals have taken their frustrations to a new level. Wrightson (1997, p. 62) contends "when bad driving escalates into violence, men tend to resort to guns, knives, or baseball bats, while irate women are more likely to use the car itself as a weapon." Similarly, Mizell (1997) found that in 4,400 of the 10,037 known aggressive driving incidents, as indicated by nationwide official data sources, the perpetrator used a firearm, knife, club, fist, feet or other standard weapon for the attack. In approximately 2,300 cases, the aggressive driver used an even more powerful weapon—his or her own vehicle (Mizell, 1997).

The number and severity of aggressive driving incidents also have increased (Altman, 1997; James, 1997; Joint, 1995; Mizell, 1997; Vest, Cohen, & Tharp, 1997). According to the AAA Foundation for Traffic Safety, violent driving incidents increased every year from 1990 to 1995. These data were compiled from 30 major newspapers, reports from 16 police departments, and insurance company claim reports (Mizell, 1997).

Table 1: Aggressive Driving Incidents by Year (Mizell, 1997)

Year	Known Incidents of Aggressive Driving (January 1, 1990-September 1, 1996)
1990	1,129
1991	1,297
1992	1,478
1993	1,555
1994	1,669
1995	1,708
1996	1,201* (Jan. 1, 1996--September 1, 1996)
Total	10,037

The Foundation (Murray, 2000, p. 70) also reported "between 1990 and 1996, 218 people were killed as a result of road rage and another 12,610 were injured as a result of the 10,037 incidents—all because one or both drivers let anger get the best of them." In 1996, the Department of Transportation estimated that two-thirds of the 41,907 reported deaths resulted from automobile accidents attributed to aggressive driving (Martinez, 1997). Based on an estimate of road rage from James and Nahl (2000) there may be as many as 400 billion hostile exchanges between motorists in the United States in one year alone. As of August 2005, the Department of Transportation has not provided updated information as to the extent of aggressive driving.

Accompanying the increase in aggressive driving statistics, the public's concern over the issue has escalated. Willis (1997) conducted a survey of residents in Maryland, Washington, D.C., and Virginia, and found that forty-seven percent of these respondents reported that aggressive driving was their greatest concern. A follow-up study conducted by the American Automobile Association (2003) found that drivers noted that aggressive driving is a top threat on Washington, D.C., area roads.

Nationally, sixty-four percent (64%) of Americans believed that drivers in their own area were driving much less courteously and safely than five years ago (Willis, 1997). A National Highway Traffic Safety Administration (2000) survey of 6,000 drivers found that 60 percent of those interviewed believed that unsafe driving by others was a major personal threat to them and their families. Moreover, results show that aggressive driving is viewed as a serious problem for sixty-five percent (65%) of Canadians polled (N=1,207) (Beirness, Simpson, Mayhew, & Pak, 2001). This finding also was consistent with the Rasmussen, Knapp, & Garner (2000) research in which 75.8 percent of the American participants said drivers were more aggressive and dangerous than they were five years ago. In addition, Rasmussen et al. (2000) found that 19.1 percent of the respondents in the sample (N=407) reported that they feared being shot by another driver.

The public concern for aggressive driving and road rage behaviors has been translated into legislation in some areas of the country. Congressional testimony indicated that aggressive behaviors were involved in nearly 28,000 American highway accidents, according to Dr. Ricardo Martinez, head of the U.S. National Highway Traffic Safety Administration (Wald, 1997). Arizona was the first state to create and enact legislation specific to aggressive driving. The Arizona law created the misdemeanor offense of aggressive driving, which includes any event where a driver speeds and commits two or more listed traffic offenses (Aggressive driving is now a crime on Arizona highways, 1998). Eight other states (California, Delaware, Florida, Georgia, Maryland, Nevada, Rhode Island, Virginia) enacted similar legislation (Flango & Keith, 2004).

Although Pennsylvania did not enact legislation as of August of 2005, several bills have been introduced concerning road rage as a public safety concern. On March 21, 2001, House Bill 1096 was introduced and referred to the Committee on Transportation of the General Assembly of Pennsylvania. House Bill 1096, of Title 75 of the Pennsylvania Consolidated Statutes, §3737 Aggressive Driving, defines aggressive driving as:

A person commits the offense of aggressive driving if the person operates a vehicle in a manner which tends to harass, annoy or alarm another person and in a manner which endangers or is likely to endanger the safety of another person or property when the offense involves the commission of two or more violations of the following sections in a single act or series of acts in close proximity to another vehicle.

On June 13, 2001, House Bill 1740 was introduced and referred to the Committee on Transportation of the General Assembly of Pennsylvania. House Bill 1740, of Title 75 of the Pennsylvania Consolidated Statutes is amended by adding a section to read:
§6118 Toll-free Hotline

The department shall establish, advertise and maintain a toll-free hotline for motorists to report observations of road rage and shall provide courses or counseling for drivers who exhibit road rage.

Definition: As used in this section, the term "road rage" means an incident in which an angry or impatient motorist or passenger intentionally injures or kills another motorist, passenger or pedestrian, or attempts to threaten to injure or kill another motorist, passenger or pedestrian.

Although PA House Bills 1096 and 1740 have added legitimacy to the public's concern about aggressive driving and its potential escalation to road rage incidents in Pennsylvania, neither of these bills has been enacted as of August 2005.

Purpose of the Study

Road rage is a salient public safety issue as evidenced by the prevalence of aggressive driving incidents as well as aggressive driving legislation. All too often elected officials react to social problems by enacting legislation and exacting punishments on offenders who have already violated societal norms and laws (Merlo & Benekos, 2000). However, this approach does not provide an effective mechanism for preventing the behavior. Although the criminal justice system has historically adopted a reactive stance to public safety concerns, this study aims to adopt a proactive approach in searching for an explanation or a greater understanding of road rage behaviors.

Although the statistics coupled with the increase in public concern illustrate the prevalence of the problem, road rage behaviors have not been sufficiently studied. According to existing research, road rage has been examined only from a psychological perspective (Alm & Nilsson, 1995; Deffenbacher et al., 2000; Donovan, Umlauf, & Salzberg, 1988; Dukes, Clayton, Jenkins, Miller, & Rodgers, 2001; Ellison, Govern, Petri, & Figler, 1995; Ellison-Potter, Bell, & Deffenbacher, 2001; Larson, 1996; Novaco, Stokols, & Milanesi, 1990; Rasmussen et al., 2000). Specifically, road rage has been examined in relation to anger (Deffenbacher et al., 2000; Deffenbacher et al., 2002; Ellison-Potter et al., 2001), stress (Novaco, Stokols, Campbell, & Stokols, 1979; Novaco et al., 1990) and frustration-aggression models (Joint, 1995; McDonald & Wooten, 1988). The proposed study aims to investigate the likelihood that individuals may/may not engage in road rage behaviors from a criminological approach. Therefore, the purpose of this study is to examine a public safety issue that affects the public as a result of road rage behaviors. To date, no such research has been published in this area.

This research provides a greater understanding of the road rage domain as a criminological issue and explores Agnew's General Strain Theory (GST) (1992) in order to determine its viability as an explanation for road rage behaviors. The model to be tested incorporates Agnew's GST (1992), the role of anger as a mediating variable, and the role of coping mechanisms, specifically self-control and peers. It is important to note that the role of anger is a key component of GST, yet the majority of past research has focused on examining the relationships between exposure to strain and delinquency (Agnew & White, 1992; Hoffmann & Miller, 1998; Paternoster & Mazerolle, 1994). This is not to suggest that the role of anger as a mediating variable has been ignored; as some studies have investigated the relationship between strain, anger, and delinquency (Aseltine, Gore, & Gordon, 2000; Brezina, 1996; Broidy, 2001; Capowich, Mazerolle, & Piquero, 2001; Mazerolle & Piquero, 1997; Mazerolle & Piquero, 1998; Mazerolle, Burton, Cullen, Evans, & Payne, 2000).

Generally, the studies that examined whether anger mediates the effect of strain on delinquency found support for GST; however, these studies measured the role of anger as a "trait" based measure. Trait based measures of anger reflect relatively stable characteristics of individuals (Spielberger, Jacobs, Russell, & Crane, 1983; Spielberger,

Johnson, Russell, & Crane, 1985). Nevertheless, GST suggests that anger that occurs in response to strain is a key to the theory; thus, measures of "situational anger" that are directly linked to strain would represent a more valid test of strain. For this reason, the present study is unique in that it will utilize measures of both trait and situational anger. A measure of trait anger is used as a control variable, thus examining its potential influence on the strain and coping mechanism variables. A measure of situational anger is used as a mediating variable between strain and road rage. Further adding to the literature, the role of coping mechanisms (i.e., level of self-control and peer relationships) also will be investigated as the role of coping mechanisms also have been ignored in strain models.

In addition to assessing Agnew's strain theory as the theoretical framework, this study specifically employs Agnew's general strain theory with an adult population. Most research of Agnew's general strain theory (Agnew & Brezina, 1997; Agnew, Brezina, Wright, & Cullen, 2002; Agnew & White, 1992; Aseltine et al., 2000; Brezina, 1996, Brezina, 1998; Brezina, 1999; Hoffman & Cerbone, 1999; Hoffman & Su, 1997; Mazerolle ct al., 2000) used an adolescent population. Therefore, this project adds to the literature by using strain theory with an adult population. The study attempted to develop a comprehensive model of the antecedents of road rage behaviors among college students.

In addition to the theoretical advancement, the use of a self-report survey is also an instrumental component of this study. According to Stephanie Faul (personal communication, November 13, 2001), the director of the AAA Foundation for Traffic Safety, no data have been compiled on road rage statistics since 1996. The AAA Foundation for Traffic Safety study (1997a), which is the last known study that compiled data on road rage statistics, used information from accident reports, newspaper articles, and insurance records. Thus, the data presented are a conservative estimate of the prevalence of road rage behaviors in the nation.

While media sources are speculative at best, the prevalence of road rage incidents is not known in Pennsylvania. According to Corporal Almindinger and Corporal Minneon (personal communication, November 19, 2001) of the Pennsylvania State Police, there currently is no standardized mechanism to record road rage incidents in Pennsylvania. The road rage incident may be recorded in the official statistics as simple assault, aggravated assault, disorderly conduct, terroristic threats, and/or reckless driving. However, the simple and/or aggravated assault categories do not delineate if the incident occurred as a result of a traffic altercation. Therefore, not only has the number of road rage incidents been underreported, but also there is no uniform mechanism for recording such incidents in Pennsylvania. This study provides the first self-reported incidence of aggressive driving and road rage incidents among college students in Pennsylvania.

The present study is designed to broaden the existing knowledge of road rage and identify characteristics of aggressive drivers. Furthermore, it delineates the role of anger into situational and trait anger as it relates to the GST model. Lastly, it examines the viability of Agnew's strain theory with an adult population, uses multi-measures to represent the dependent variable, and suggests policy implications stemming from road rage incidents.

CHAPTER 2

Aggressive Driving

According to Marsh and Collett (1986) individuals have symbiotic relationships with their vehicles to the point where their entire livelihood depends on them and what they represent. Cars have become more than a means of going from one place to another; they have become a "second home." The car has essentially transformed the home environment. "Before the mid-1930s, the garage was usually a shed or some other utilitarian outbuilding, it was detached from the house and often out of sight" (Marsh & Collett, 1986, p. 11). But as the car came to rival the home as a symbol of prestige, its accommodation became a matter of increasing importance. Later, there was a tendency to integrate the garage into the home; which for many suburban homes replaced the function of the porch as the garage was the main mode of exit and entry to the home (Marsh & Collett, 1986). According to Marsh and Collett, (1986) this culminates into people humanizing cars and regarding them as having qualities and personalities in common with their owners (Marsh & Collett, 1986).

It has been noted that individuals have a relationship with their vehicles; thus, vehicles have personal value. "People can choose a car that is suited for them (e.g., color, style, make, model); the vehicle is able to express their status, lifestyle and personality" (Marsh & Collett, 1986). Furthermore, individuals have radically altered the environment in which they live in order to create societies where the automobile is a central feature. Even the auto-manufacturers cater to these individuals by promising vehicles that have more cylinders, more horsepower, and are far more ornate than is required for the purpose of safe and efficient travel (Marsh & Collett, 1986). Many of the vehicle names portray this as well; for example, names of cars include: Mustang, Cougar, Jaguar, Bronco, Firebird, and Thunderbird. These cars, by their very name, convey a sense of power and status about the driver of the vehicle. Therefore, the automobile satisfies not only practical needs but also the need to declare oneself socially and individually.

9

American society buys into these images of the car. Not only has the automobile been accepted by society but thousands of highways, garages, and parking lots have been built to accommodate vehicles; thus legitimizing the car's function as a mode of transport (Marsh & Collett, 1986). The vehicle provides individuals with a shield and a feeling of invulnerability for all manner of activities. There are many social activities that people engage in while driving in their vehicles (e.g., talking, smoking, eating, sleeping, reading). People even make obscene gestures and threaten total strangers, behavior that is not normally exhibited in other circumstances; yet this may occur because of the feeling of security of the inviolable territory--the vehicle (Marsh & Collett, 1986).

The imagery and symbolism of the vehicle suggest speed, excitement, vitality, and opportunities for independence (Marsh & Collett, 1986). Both cars and trucks have been used by drivers as instruments of dominance, thus the road has served as an arena for competition and control (Novaco, 1991). In this context, the car can be viewed as a weapon. Although there are a plethora of deadly consequences that result from vehicle usage, the term used to describe these ramifications is accidents. The term *"accidents"* is a suitably dispassionate term, which largely removes any sense of blame from both vehicles and their drivers (Marsh & Collett, 1986). The killings are taken for granted and seen as inevitable. March and Collett (1986, p. 152-153) further contend that

> [Individuals] can behave recklessly, aggressively and with criminal irresponsibility, and yet [they] are unlikely to be imprisoned even when [they] are caught. The lethal and injurious consequences of automobile use may not be 'intentional' in any simple sense, but neither are they totally accidental.

As such, the car can be seen as a potential means of expressing anger, aggression, and frustration (Marsh & Collett, 1987).

Defining Road Rage

As early as 1915, Engleman's Autocraft noted that "some automobilists abuse their rights and needlessly run over the rights of others" (IIHS, 1998). Although the public had voiced concern periodically, between

1915 and 1980, the public's demand for action has increased in recent years (Beirness et al., 2001; Joint, 1995; Mizell, 1997). In the late 1980s, drivers in the United States, apparently frustrated, in part, by increasing congestion, began fighting and shooting each other on a more frequent basis (Joint, 1997). According to Novaco (1991, p. 284) "between mid-June and the end of August [1987] there were approximately 70 shootings and one serious stabbing on southern California roads reported in newspapers." As a result of these reports of exceptionally violent and extreme cases of aggressive driving, the public and elected officials have focused their attention on "road rage" incidents (Beirness et al., 2001).

While the term "road rage" has been popularized by the media, it is important to recognize the definitional debate of what specifically constitutes aggressive driving and road rage behaviors. Most researchers (Connell & Joint, 1996; Grey, Triggs & Haworth, 1989; Hennessy & Wiesenthal, 1999; Martinez, 1997; Mizell, 1997) agree that aggressive driving encompasses a broad spectrum of behaviors ranging from extreme acts (e.g., shootings or malicious assaults) to less severe manifestations (e.g., roadside arguments, confrontations, and gestures). Ellison-Potter, Bell and Deffenbacher (2001, p. 432) define aggressive driving as "any driving behavior that intentionally (whether fueled by anger or frustration or as a calculated means to an end) endangers others psychologically, physically, or both." Similarly, Martinez (1997) contends that aggressive driving is any behavior that jeopardizes or potentially jeopardizes people or property.

Another definition purports aggressive driving to be "the operation of a motor vehicle without regard for other motorists' safety and is often the result of anger or frustration" (AAA Foundation for Traffic Safety, 1997a). Some examples of aggressive driving are speeding, tailgating, horn honking, red-light running, blocking the passing lane, and headlight flashing. The common threads of these definitions are that these behaviors are less extreme in nature, and, individually, they have been classified as traffic offenses.

Although the terms aggressive driving and road rage are often used interchangeably, they are not synonymous. Road rage has been defined as an uncontrolled anger that results in violence or threatened violence on the road; consequently, it is also viewed as criminal behavior (Rathbone & Huckabee, 1999). According to Ellison-Potter et al., (2001, p. 432) "road rage refers to the more extreme cases of aggressive driving, involving assaultive behavior with the intent of

bodily harm and possible homicide."   Similarly, Mizell (1997, p. 5)
has defined road rage as

> an incident in which an angry or impatient motorist or
> passenger intentionally injures or kills another motorist,
> passenger, or pedestrian, or attempts to injure or kill another
> motorist, passenger, or pedestrian, in response to a traffic
> dispute, altercation, or grievance.

From these definitions it is apparent that the primary delineation
between aggressive driving and road rage behaviors is the element of
violence or the threat of violence.   Moreover, these definitions
emphasize actual or potential danger from personal violence as the
result of traffic altercations and driver frustrations. Thus, road rage in
its broadest sense refers to any display of aggression by a driver (e.g.,
verbal and/or physical assault) that occurs as a direct result of a
disagreement between drivers (Joint, 1995). Some examples of road
rage behaviors which result from a traffic incident are: drivers
assaulting other drivers, drivers threatening to shoot other drivers,
passengers and/or pedestrians, and drivers destroying the property of
another driver.
        According to Harding et al. (1998), the term road rage has been
colloquially used to describe a wide range of negative, unpleasant, and
aggressive driving experiences. The popular concept of "'road rage'
involves spontaneous violence between strangers arising out of driving
interactions" (Harding et al., 1998, p. 223). Thus, this definition limits
a road rage incident to an incident that includes the threat of violence
and/or an actual physical assault as a result of the driving experience.
These instances of violence are characterized as being spontaneous or
impulsive rather than planned or delayed.
        For purposes of this study, the definition of road rage incorporates
elements of both the Mizell (1997) and the Harding et al. (1998)
definitions. Therefore, road rage is defined as "an incident in which a
motorist commits various infringements on the road that act to annoy,
endanger, or threaten to injure another motorist or passenger, or
damages the property of another motorist, in response to a traffic
dispute, altercation, or grievance." This definition is qualified further
to include violence or property damage between strangers that erupts as
a result of a spontaneous traffic altercation.   Thus, the definition

encompasses elements of violence or threats of violence as well as potential and real property damage to other motorists and passengers.

Road Rage Between Strangers
The road rage definition used in this study further qualifies a road rage incident in terms of the victim's status; it refers to violence between strangers. The research (Meadows, 2001; Wolfgang, 1958) on stranger-to-stranger violence suggests that some victims facilitate their own victimization by engaging in risky activities and by their lifestyle choices. Luckenbill (1977) found that violent encounters between strangers usually result from arguments, threats, or trivial matters, such as a dispute over a parking space, inappropriate lane changes, and horn honking. Similarly, Meadows' research (2001) also contends that trivial matters have the capability to escalate into physical confrontations that could lead to serious injury of one of the parties involved.

Lundesgaarde's research (1997) suggests that establishments where alcohol is served facilitate the likelihood for explosive encounters and assaults between strangers. This is especially salient if the tavern is located in disorganized or high crime areas, where the chance of stranger victimization increases. Miethe and McCorkle (2001) further contend that drug and alcohol use are often a major contributory factor in the onset of many violent and property crimes. "When the presence of others similarly situated is coupled with reduced inhibitions often associated with drug and alcohol use, a rather trivial comment or action may quickly escalate into a violent episode" (Miethe & McCorkle, 2001, p. 38). As a result, when an argument erupts and there is no management intervention or effort to diffuse the situation, the incident is ripe for a physical confrontation (Meadows, 2001). Similarly, the Cambridge-Somerville Youth Project Study (McCord, 1984) found that those convicted of Driving While Intoxicated (DWI) were more likely to report getting into fights and to be more likely to act rather than talk when angry. All of these above factors have been found to increase the chances of a road rage incident occurring.

The reference to strangers is an important dimension; it filters out individuals who may have a violent outburst due to a pre-existing relationship rather than a suddenly discovered dissatisfaction with each other's driving conduct. According to Harding et al. (1998, p. 224) "a central characteristic of road rage is that the aggressor's target is initially anonymous." Meadows (2001, p. 103) purports that the "anonymity of the highway as well as the privacy of the car can be stimulants for further actions." The relative anonymity, ease of escape, and mobility of the automobile offers some drivers the temptation to victimize others on the road (see Ellison-Potter et al., 2001). Although the target of the road rage incident is not known initially, it is important to note that only one of the targets has to be the driver of a vehicle. The road rage incident (Harding et al., 1998) may take place between (1) two drivers; (2) a driver and a passenger(s) of either vehicle; (3) driver and pedestrian; and (4) driver and a cyclist. Occasionally, it is passengers who take on the mantle of outrage.

The definition of road rage encompasses the dimensions of violence and anonymity of drivers (and/or passengers) and also it may include the threat or destruction of property. The term has also been characterized as "...not only the infliction of personal violence but also attacks on cars by thumping or banging and also such matters as obscene language or gestures, flashing lights, tail-gating, lane hopping, and queue jumping into parking bays" (Harding et al., 1998, p. 223). Because destruction of property is a potential result, it is important to note that not all road rage incidents occur on the road, some incidents may arise "off the road" in parking lots and continue on the roadways (Harding et al., 1998). However, violent altercations also have been known to take place in the parking lot stemming from a dispute over a parking space.

The literature on road rage has been examined in terms of aggression and violence between strangers. With respect to aggression, road rage behaviors are considered behaviors that result in personal injury and physical destruction. Research (Luckenbill, 1997; Lundesgaarde, 1997; Meadows, 2001) suggests that the central issues in stranger violence revolve around the defense and enhancement of reputation as well as an individual's status. For the individual perpetrator, violence is viewed as a necessary and justified response to what is perceived to be an injustice (e.g., inappropriate lane change, unnecessarily slow driving, construction, traffic), or some form of degradation or threat to the value of the self (Harding et al., 1998).

Although trivial at the outset, this injustice can culminate into a full-blown road rage incident. Luckenbill (1977) has outlined the process whereby, once initiated, arguments tend to follow a predictable course: (1) the victim presents to the offender a set of actions or noncompliance relevant to the offender; (2) the offender interprets the victim's actions as offensive; (3) the offender retaliates with a challenge or violence; (4) the victim retaliates or resists the offender's directions; and (5) both parties are committed to the confrontation. Similar to Luckenbill's research, Meadows (2001) suggests a paradigm for these situational events. These events are delineated into four categories: triggering event, argument, escalation, and assault.

The triggering event is the initial situation that precipitates an intrusion or insult of an individual (e.g., inappropriate lane change). The argument phase is the challenge to the intrusion or insult (e.g., inappropriate gesture or shouting at the intruder). The escalation phase is where the individual attempts to "save face" or "show off" to the others (e.g., driver speeds up, drivers are racing) (Meadows, 2001). The final phase of this paradigm is the assault, in which injury or death is likely to occur to one of the parties involved (Meadows, 2001).

Although Luckenbill's research (1997) suggests a process of escalation for a perceived injustice, it is important to note that not all injurious behavior and destructive acts will be perceived as aggressive; it is dependent on the subjective intentions and causality (Bandura, 1978). Bandura (1978, p. 13) contends that "most of the injurious consequences of major social concern are caused remotely, circuitously, and impersonally through social practices judged aggressive by the victims but not by those who benefit from them." Thus, it is important to examine the overall situation in terms of the individuals' perceptions of injustice and their susceptibility to escalating certain situations into full-blown aggressive incidents.

The initial anonymity of the individual coupled with the escalation of certain situations increases the likelihood of an aggressive incident. Given the perceived injustice by either one or both of the drivers, in order to rectify the situation, one of the individuals is likely to displace responsibility for his/her actions. In such cases, one or both of the individuals may not hold themselves accountable for what they do (Bandura, Underwood, & Fromson, 1975). It has been argued that these situations attribute blame to the victim, thus contending that victims are responsible for their own suffering as well as the extraordinary circumstances that are invoked as vindications for punitive conduct (Bandura et al., 1975). Furthermore, dehumanizing the victim is another means of reducing self-punishment for cruel actions; thus allowing the aggressor of the situation to escalate the situation into violence, but at the same time minimize his/her level of accountability (Bandura et al., 1975).

Situational Versus Dispositional Factors

Although these paradigms/processes of stranger violence are informative, research on aggression has demonstrated that situational factors and dispositional factors or situational and dispositional factors play significant roles in the manifestation of aggression (Ellison-Potter et al., 2001). Thus, environmental circumstances as well as personality traits are important factors to help identify whether individuals will engage in road rage behaviors. For example, "many individuals may anger more easily on the road than others, but will not manifest this anger through aggression unless the situation prompts it" (Ellison-Potter et al., 2001, p. 433). Some situational factors include events occurring outside of the driver's control, such as construction and lane obstructions; whereas, personality traits refer to the individual's predisposition toward aggressive behaviors.

Identifying the situational triggers of aggressive driving before they escalate into road rage incidents is pertinent to understanding why individuals engage in this form of impulsive violence. Harding et al. (1998, p. 231) identified five categories of precursors to road rage incidents: encounters with slow drivers; other drivers cutting in or overtaking; stereotyped sex roles-attributions of driving incompetence by males in relation to females; accidents between vehicles; and competition for parking spaces.

Research (Beirness et al., 2001; Joint, 1995; Mizell, 1997; Shinar, 1997) cites slow drivers as a source of annoyance for many potential road ragers. According to Harding, et al. (1998, p. 231) "the tacit situationally negotiated and predominantly masculine rules of driving legitimate a robust driving style aimed at reducing travel time, decisively negotiating barriers to movement and keeping traffic moving." Thus, road rage can be viewed as "punishment" by the offender for failure to conform to the tacit rules of the road.

Because many drivers take pride in their driving ability, this sentiment can easily escalate into a competition with other drivers. Drivers who are overtaken or "cut off" may view these actions as an insult to their driving ability (Harding et al., 1998). Consequently, the driver who is swerving and overtaking others regards his/her maneuvers as an indication of his/her superb driving ability. These situations give rise to status competitions among drivers, which are often associated with interpersonal violence in general. In these instances, it is sometimes difficult to determine who is the victim and who is the aggressor. In addition to the competitiveness of some drivers, male drivers have, in some cases, attributed driving incompetence to females. Moreover, male drivers have been known to assault female drivers that have violated the rules of the road, specifically for the failure to move decisively into traffic (Harding et al., 1998).

In terms of the competitiveness of the driving environment, the invasion of an individual's territory has been cited as a reason for driver aggressiveness. Territorial defense is a one of the prime reasons for aggressive behavior in people. The "maintenance of territorial integrity is a major motive for threatening displays, intimidatory behavior and straightforward violence by men" (Marsh & Collett, 1986, p. 156). When the "territory of the automobile is invaded, or when some other car tries symbolically to dominate it, the perceived threat is sufficient to evoke almost primeval reactions in even the meekest of motorists" (Marsh & Collett, 1986, p. 156). Many defensive reactions are aroused when "our home on wheels" is threatened. It also affords individuals the protective position from which one can make threatening signals in a relatively anonymous position. The territory of the car "extends beyond the simple limits of the metal body in the same way that the personal space over which we claim jurisdiction covers a larger area than that occupied by the body" (Marsh & Collett, 1986, p. 157).

When drivers view the invasion of their car-space as unwarranted, "aggression is an inevitable consequence" (Marsh & Collett, 1986, p. 158). A common, but exceedingly dangerous, response to tailgating is to dab a foot on the brake pedal. When the driver who is following sees the light flash red, he/she will often respond with panic braking-with the skidding and weaving producing a smirk of satisfaction on the face of the driver in front. However, making contact with the vehicle is a greater affront to dignity (Marsh & Collett, 1986).

Territorial defenses can have damaging consequences. There are few occasions in life where individuals can cause the death of other people with such ease and impunity as when they lose their tempers on the road (Marsh & Collett, 1986). If the overtaking driver crashes headlong into an oncoming car because someone has denied him/her space, the blame will very rarely fall on him/her. Individuals have rationalized their behavior as driving "normally," but under certain circumstances cars can quite literally be used as weapons (Marsh & Collett, 1986, p. 159).

As evidenced by the above situations, external obstacles may be responsible for triggering road rage incidents. Traffic accidents and parking spaces have been cited as sources of aggravation among drivers (Harding ct al., 1998). Accidents have the ability to make the individual late for his/her destination, cause extensive damage to the vehicle, and force the occupants to get out of the car and interact. The defining moment for many people is competition for parking spaces. If a driver feels that he/she has been unfairly denied a parking space, which he/she was waiting for, an incident may ensue (Harding et al., 1998). This is especially the case if the driver was initially anonymous. All of these are situational factors that have the potential to increase the likelihood of a road rage incident.

One of the primary situational indicators of road rage behaviors is the anonymity of the other drivers. Research has demonstrated that aggressive driving and road rage incidents have been facilitated by the anonymous nature of the other drivers and passengers (Ellison, Govern, Petri, & Figler, 1995; Ellison-Potter et al., 2001). Individuals who maintain anonymity in the driving context (e.g., their identities are shielded from others' views) are in positions in which they cannot be evaluated, criticized, judged, or punished by others (Zimbardo, 1969). Individuals in anonymous situations often lose respect for self as well as others (Zimbardo, 1969); and such anonymity may result in courtesy becoming scarce on the highways (Ellison-Potter et al., 2001).

The anonymity variable has been extensively researched by Ellison et al. (1995). Their primary hypothesis was that anonymity is positively related to aggression, which they operationalized by horn honking (Ellison et al., 1995). The sample (N=63, 38 males, 25 females) was selected from the population of drivers of convertibles and 4x4 vehicles in the Baltimore and Washington Metropolitan areas. In their study, after a female confederate identified a potential subject's vehicle, she would pull her car directly in front of the subject (e.g., driver) as the traffic light turned red. When the traffic light turned green, the confederate activated an alarm that was programmed to sound after 12 seconds. During that time the confederate appeared to look straight forward giving no indication that the light had changed nor driving through the light. She would record the frequency of honking and looked for possible reaction from the subjects that suggested aggressive behavior (profanity, obscene gestures) (Ellison et al., 1995). Then, the confederate recorded the sex and estimated age of the subject, number of people in the car, color and type of car, and whether or not the driver wore sunglasses (Ellison et al., 1995).

Ellison et al. (1995) found support for their primary hypothesis: individuals were more aggressive toward drivers who were in convertibles with the tops up (e.g., anonymous condition) as opposed to those drivers who were identifiable by the convertible top being down (e.g., identifiable condition). Therefore, subjects in the anonymous condition exhibited significantly shorter horn-honking latencies, longer horn-honking durations, and more frequent horn honks in the 12-second time period (Ellison et al., 1995).

In a follow-up study, Ellison-Potter et al. (2001) examined the effects of driving anger, aggressive stimuli, and anonymity on aggressive driving behaviors. Their present study assessed introductory psychology students (N=289, 133 males, 156 females) on the Driving Anger Scale (DAS), which was created by Deffenbacher, Oetting, & Lynch, 1994. Participants high or low on trait driving anger (as determined by the median split on the DAS) were then randomly assigned to anonymous/nonanonymous and aggressive/nonaggressive conditions with respect to the Low-Cost Driving Simulator (Ellison-Potter et al., 2001). This apparatus includes a monitor, in which different frustrating scenarios are programmed, a steering column, brake, and an accelerator. The DAS and the simulator are used in conjunction to allow for an overall assessment of the driving experience as well as information about the participant's score.

The findings of the study support an anonymity effect. Participants in the anonymous conditions (i.e., those who were told they were driving a convertible with the top up) exhibited significantly greater average speeds, ran more red lights, were involved in more collisions, and killed more pedestrians, than did participants in the identifiable conditions (i.e., those who were told that they were driving a convertible with the top down) (Ellison-Potter et al., 2001).

The research has demonstrated that the anonymity variable is important to the discussion of aggressive driving and road rage behaviors. As mentioned earlier, Meadows (2001, p. 103) contends that the "anonymity of the highway as well as the privacy of the car can be stimulants for further actions." Moreover, this study's definition of road rage recognizes that an altercation is more apt to take place between strangers. This relative anonymity, ease of escape, and mobility of the automobile offer some drivers the opportunity to victimize others on the road (see EllisonPotter et al., 2001).

According to Novaco (1991) road violence is a derivation of strained social and personal controls, which can act in concert with external situations, such as traffic congestion, work pressures, or family strain. Research (Novaco et al., 1979; Novaco et al., 1990) has demonstrated that frustration from commuting impacts mood and behavior in the work environment after commuters arrive at work as well as in the home environment after the return commute. Although the transportation environment may bring drivers' emotions to the surface, it is important to examine whether these emotions are fleeting or ingrained personality characteristics.

There has been continued emphasis on identifying factors that contribute to increased driving risk, with the goal of reducing the frequency and impact of traffic violations, accidents, and fatalities (Donovan et al., 1988). Research focusing on how emotional and personality factors influence driving behavior and accident risk has shown that general anger, aggressiveness, impulsiveness, and social unconventionality are related to increased accident risk and other accident-related variables, such as traffic violations and risky driving (Arnett, Offer, & Fine, 1997; Donovan, Marlatt, & Salzberg, 1985; Mayer & Treat, 1977). Therefore, human factors, most notably personality characteristics, attitudes, and behaviors, were found to contribute to high-risk driving (Adams, 1970; Beirness & Simpson; 1988; Donovan et al., 1983; Donovan et al., 1985; Donovan et al., 1988; Jessor, 1987; Jonah, 1986; Mayer & Treat, 1977; McFarland, 1968; McGuire, 1976; Tsuang, Boor, & Fleming, 1985).

A study conducted by Jonah (1986) reviewed the literature pertaining to accident risk and risk-taking behaviors among young drivers in the United States and Canada. The literature supported the contention that young drivers have a high propensity to take risks while driving; have a higher likelihood of being involved in an accident; and engage in higher incidences of speeding and driver conflicts (Jonah, 1986). At the same time, the research points out that younger drivers are less likely to use their safety belts while driving (Jonah, 1986). Jonah (1986, p. 262) further contends that

> The research evidence bearing on driver risk-taking supports
> the notion that young drivers are over-represented in traffic
> accidents as a result of their propensity to drive too fast, drive
> too close to vehicles in front, accept gaps that are too narrow
> and drive while impaired by alcohol.

In addition, there is evidence to suggest that the same people who engage in risky driving behavior also perform other risky behaviors and that this risk propensity is related to accident involvement (Jonah, 1986).

In research conducted by Beirness and Simpson (1988), the findings were also consistent with risk taking behaviors among young drivers. Through their longitudinal cohort study they investigated the social, psychological, and behavioral factors in accident involvement and risky driving among youth. Their research identified lifestyle correlates of risky driving behaviors, specifically assessing traditional values, self-confidence, and peer influences of high school students (N=1,986), as they relate to self-reported accident involvement and risky driving in the past year. Included in the survey instrument was the Sensation Seeking Scale (Zuckerman, 1979) which includes two subscales: Thrill and Adventure Seeking (TAS) scale and the Experience Seeking (ES) scale. High scores on the TAS reflect a "general willingness or desire to engage in exciting and high risk behaviors whereas high scores on the ES are indicative of a general willingness to experience novel activities and sensations" (Beirness & Simpson, 1988, p. 195).

The results of the above study (Beirness & Simpson, 1988) indicate that almost half (46.7%) of the 668 drivers in the sample had taken deliberate risks while driving during the last twelve months and 8.8 percent reported frequent risk-taking. Males were more likely than females to take risks while driving, the differences being most pronounced in the "frequent" risk-taking category. "Within the domain of the personality system, greater frequency of Intentional Risky Driving shows a modest association with higher scores on the TAS subscale as well as the ES subscales" (Beirness & Simpson, 1988, p. 199). This research suggests that individual lifestyle characteristics play a role in risky driving and accident involvement.

A study conducted by Donovan, Umlauf, and Salzberg (1988) also supports the contention that personality subtypes play a role in high risk driving. Donovan et al. (1988, p. 234) identified nine characteristics associated with increased driving risk with or without the influence of alcohol:

1. Emotional lability, irritability, and oversensitivity to criticism
2. Feelings of depression, sadness, and discontent
3. Feelings of helplessness and personal inadequacy (low level of self-efficacy)

4. Impulsivity and thrill- or sensation-seeking motive
5. Low frustration tolerance
6. Harboring grudges and resentment (covert hostility)
7. Expression of overt hostility and aggression
8. Easily influenced or intimidated by others (low level of assertion)
9. Perceived inability to control one's own destiny (external locus of control).

Donovan et al. (1988) investigated the validation of subtypes among high-risk drivers based upon attitudinal, personality, and hostility measures. The driving–related attitudes included "driving aggression; competitive speeding; driving-related internality, in which the individual attributes the cause of accidents to factors within personal control; driving-related externality, in which the attribution of causality is to factors such as fate or change; driving for tension reduction or increased personal efficacy; and driving inhibition, in which the individual drives more cautiously when aroused or angered" (Donovan et al., 1988, p. 236). The personality variable included measures of assertiveness, emotionality, internal and external perceptions of control, and sensation seeking. The hostility factors were measured through levels of assaultiveness; indirect hostility, irritability and impatience; verbal hostility; and resentment.

The sample for the Donovan et al. 1988 study consisted of male drivers (N=193) who had been involved in an earlier study conducted by Donovan et al. (1985) of the characteristics associated with high-risk driving behavior. These participants were volunteers who were selected after attending a two-hour traffic safety education program sponsored by the Washington State Department of Licensing. These participants were required to attend safety education classes because they acquired a combination of four traffic violation convictions and/or accidents in a one year period or five incidents within two years (Donovan et al., 1988).

The Donovan et al. (1988) research findings suggest that high-risk drivers, as a group, have a number of attitudinal, affective, and behavioral characteristics that may contribute to their driving risk. The participants in Cluster 2 tended to be individuals with "a high degree of impulsivity as evidenced by their sensation seeking and competitive speeding, acting out as evidenced by the likelihood of overt expression of anger, and alienation as evidenced by their external perception of control" (Donovan et al., 1988, p. 241). Those participants in Cluster 3 are more likely to be bad drivers who are under personal stress and are going through difficult periods in their lives.

These studies unequivocally support the contention that young drivers take greater risks by driving faster than older drivers. Younger drivers are also more likely than older drivers to place themselves in driving situations where they will come into conflict with other drivers. In each of the above studies, the findings have identified and supported the dispositional argument that personality characteristics are an important variable for assessing one's likelihood of engaging in risky driving behaviors.

Frustration, Anger and Aggressive Driving

The frustration and aggression experienced by drivers are becoming a major public health issue (Shinar, 1999), which lead some researchers to advance the concept of road rage (Fumento, 1998; Vest, Cohen, & Tharp, 1997). As early as 1976, Naatanen and Summala proposed that aggressive road user behavior is often the result of the driver's frustration at being unable to progress unimpeded by traffic, but they also implied that this kind of frustration could be provoked by any transportation situation. According to Harding et al. (1998, p. 237), the suggested explanation is that "exposure to the frustrations and stresses of driving, together with the dehumanizing anonymity of the driving situation, bring about a situation where the suppressed or formant needs for status defense or enhancement manifest themselves as road rage."

Furthermore, there is extensive research that demonstrates how emotional and personality factors influence driving behavior and accident risk (Arnett et al., 1997; Donovan et al., 1985; Mayer & Treat, 1977). Specifically, the propensity to become angry while driving has been related to psychological and health concerns of drivers, as evidenced by pre and post commute reactions (Novaco et al., 1979; Novaco, Stokols, & Milanesi, 1990). This "driving anger" is defined as more frequent and intense anger than experienced while operating a motor vehicle. Similarly, Deffenbacher et al. (1994) refer to driving anger as the extent to which anger is experienced in driving-related contexts.

In addition to driving anger, trait anger is also a concern when examining driving related situations. Trait anger is a broad predisposition to experience anger more frequently and intensely across situations (i.e., the tendency to become more easily angered by affronts, insults, injustices, and frustrations) to react with more anger, and to experience more negative physical, social, vocational, and psychological consequences (Deffenbacher, 1992 as cited in Deffenbacher et al., 1994, p. 84). Thus, both driving anger and trait anger characteristics are relevant to investigating the theoretical underpinnings of road rage behaviors.

Turner, Layton, and Simons (1975) examined the role of aggressive behavior, victim visibility, and horn honking in a naturalistic setting. Their research consisted of a three-part study in Salt Lake City. In the first study, Parry's (1968) driving survey was administered to a random sample of drivers (N=59) in the Salt Lake City area. The findings suggest that a high proportion of "frequent" drivers sometimes become angry or are irritated by the driving behaviors of others. Seventy-seven percent of males and 56 percent of females reported "swearing under their breaths" at other drivers, while 50 percent of male and 15 percent of female drivers admitted "flashing their lights in anger" at other drivers (Turner et al., 1975). A shocking example of driver hostility is that 30 percent of the drivers sampled reported "at times, I've felt that I could gladly kill another driver." The findings also suggest that if the verbal reports are accurate reflections of actual driving situations, then a large number of drivers might be frequently irritated by the behavior of other drivers.

The second part of the study used an experimental design to determine how drivers (N=83) would react to a being obstructed by a late model pick-up truck at a signal light for 12 seconds by another vehicle. The variables were manipulated in terms of aggressive stimulation and victim visibility. The aggressive stimulation variable had three levels: an empty gun rack in the pick-up; a rifle placed in the gun rack, and a bumper sticker stating "Rifle & Friend"; and a rifle placed in the gun rack with a bumper sticker stating "Rifle & Vengeance" (Turner et al., 1975, p. 1101). In addition to the physical characteristics of the pickup truck, the visibility of the victim was also manipulated (curtain could be opened or closed thus obstructing the view of the driver). The researchers contend that victim visibility and the rifle/vengeance condition increased horn honking. The present findings suggest that "dehumanization and the presence of a rifle, which is perceived as an aggressive stimuli, can increase the probability of aggressive responding in a naturalistic setting" (Turner et al., 1975, p. 1102).

The third part of the study conducted by Turner et al. (1975) used a sample of drivers, who owned their own vehicles, to examine the independent effects of the presence of a rifle and the vengeance bumper sticker on horn honking as a measure of aggression. The sample (N=200; 137 males, 63 females) was exposed to a situation in which a pickup truck displayed one variable of the following categories: rifle or no rifle; vengeance bumper sticker or no bumper sticker. Hidden observers noted the demographic characteristics of the drivers and activated a stopwatch when the traffic light turned red; the observers then recorded the latency and frequency of honks expressed by the participant (Turner et al., 1975). The results of the study demonstrate that the rate of honking in the rifle/vengeance condition with male drivers (of both new and older vehicles) was significantly higher than the average of the other three rifle/bumper sticker conditions (Turner et al., 1975). The general conclusion of their research is that the findings of the three studies support the notion that anger and aggression cues may result from obstacles and obstruction in the transportation environment.

The limitations of the above study address the validity and generalizability issues of horn honking as a measure of aggression. Horn honking can be questioned as it may be done to signal another driver (without aggressive qualities) or it could be done as an "antagonistic behavior" as opposed to being done in annoyance (Novaco, 1991). Although Turner et al. (1975) acknowledged this problem, they only addressed the criterion validity issues by focusing on variations in responding (i.e., horn honking) that pertained to the conditions of aggressive stimuli. It is also important to note that even though their research did take place in a natural setting, it does not guarantee external validity.

Although driving is a common activity among individuals, the research has suggested that in certain driving instances, anger while driving is highly correlated with trait anger (Deffenbacher et al., 2000). The literature on the influence of emotion on driving performance shows "that emotional arousal can influence perception and information processing; this influence could presumably be strong enough to disrupt driving proficiency sufficiently to increase accident risk" (Deffenbacher et al., 1994, p. 84). Furthermore, Deffenbacher et al. (1994, p. 84) found that "elevated anger may prompt aggressive and other risk-taking behavior (e.g., driving too fast, tailgating, flashing bright lights, aggressive verbal or physical behavior), behaviors that can increase accident risk, and risk of other deleterious behavior such as physical assault between drivers or arguments with passengers."

In another study by Deffenbacher et al. (2000) the role of aggression as a characteristic of high-risk drivers was supported. In this research they explored two main issues (1) characteristics of individuals who become angry while driving and (2) the feasibility of two interventions for high-anger drivers. Furthermore, the research tested five predictions from state-trait anger theory, which addresses the issue of whether the individual adapted to driving anger, an underlying personality characteristic or the situational nature of the interaction (Deffenbacher, Oetting, Thwaites, et al., 1996). Of the 1,080 students who completed the short form of the Driving Anger Scale (DAS), the client analogue consisted of 57 (23 men, 34 women) psychology students who scored in the upper quartile of the college norms with scores >53 (Deffenbacher, Oetting, & Lynch, 1994); furthermore, it also indicated a personal problem with driving anger and a desire for counseling for that problem (Deffenbacher et al., 2000, p. 6).

The participants were subject to taking the short form DAS (alpha=.80) and long form DAS (alpha=.90; see Deffenbacher et al., 1994), recording their anger levels in four driving scenarios, completing a driving log, and reporting on accident-related variables as well as aggressive and risky driving behaviors. Measures of trait anger, anger expression, and trait anxiety were included to assess other emotional characteristics that might contribute to elevated stress and risk while driving (Deffenbacher et al., 2000, p. 7).

Of the findings, anger effects were found on all DAS subscales, demonstrating that those high in driving anger report anger in response to a number of situations, not just one or two sources of frustration and provocation (Deffenbacher et al., 2000, p. 7). Driving in ordinary traffic elicited less anger than did driving in rush hour traffic and being yelled at by another driver. However, "reports in the past year of arguments with passengers and other drivers and of physical fights with drivers revealed significant multivariate effects for gender, anger, and their interaction" (Deffenbacher et al., 2000, p. 9). Physical injury to self and to others and damage to the car, resulting from the individual's anger rather than an accident, revealed significant multivariate effects for gender and anger (Deffenbacher et al., 2000, p. 9). For example, high-anger male drivers experienced more anger-related property damage to vehicles and injury to self than low-anger drivers and were more likely to argue with passengers and to argue and fight other drivers (Deffenbacher et al., 2000). Therefore, high-anger drivers reported more trait anger and anxiety; anger suppression; and outward, less controlled forms of anger expression.

Deffenbacher, Lynch, Oetting, and Swaim's (2002) comprehensive research study developed and examined the Driving Anger Expression Inventory (DAX), which serves to create a typology of the ways that individuals express their anger while driving. Participants (N=290) included undergraduate introductory psychology students at a large state university in the western United States. The respondents were given a battery of instruments: Driving Anger Expression Inventory (DAX) (Deffenbacher et al., 2002), Driving Anger Scale (DAS) (Deffenbacher et al., 1994), Driving Scenarios (Deffenbacher et al., 2000), Driving Survey (Deffenbacher et al., 2001), Driving Logs (Deffenbacher et al., 2001) and the Trait Anger Scale (TAS) (Spielberger, 1988, 1999). The DAX is a 62-item inventory (see Deffenbacher et al., 2002, p. 722-723), which was developed from interviews with students, faculty, and community members. The respondents were asked to describe how they express their anger while driving on a 4-point scale (1 almost never to 4 almost always) (Deffenbacher et al., 2002). The DAS, which is a 14-item scale, where the participants rate their level of anger on a 5-point, Likert scale (1 not at all, 5 very much). The DAS has a reliability ranging from .80 to .92, and "10 week test-retest reliability of .84" (Deffenbacher et al., 2000; Deffenbacher et al., 1994). Anger on the DAS is associated with general trait anger, impulsiveness, and trait anxiety as opposed to situational anger.

In addition to the driving scales, driving scenarios were also presented to participants. The driving scenarios encompassed three areas: ordinary traffic, stuck in heavy rush hour traffic, and being yelled at by another driver (Deffenbacher et al., 2000). The participants were asked to report their anger on seven, 5-point semantic differentials (e.g., hotheaded-coolheaded) (Deffenbacher et al., 2002). Furthermore, the respondents took the Driving Survey (Aggression alpha=.85-.89; Risky Behavior Alpha=.83-.86; Deffenbacher, Lynch, Oetting, & Yingling, 2001; Deffenbacher, Lynch, Deffenbacher, & Oetting, 2001) which assessed the frequency of (a) six accident related outcomes, (b) 13 items assessing driving related aggression and (c) 15 items assessing risky behavior (Deffenbacher et al., 2001). The participants were also asked to keep Driving Logs. These logs contain information regarding the number of times and miles driving, a daily rating of their anger on a scale of 1 to 100, and whether or not they engaged in the aggressive and risky behaviors (Deffenbacher et al., 2002). Lastly, the sample was asked to complete the trait anger scale (TAS) (Spielberger, 1988), which is a 10-item measure of general feelings of anger on a 4 point scale (1 almost never, 4 almost always). This scale has an alpha reliability of .81 to .91 (Spielberger, 1988, 1999).

Because the main focus of this study was to develop a viable DAX scale, the results of the varimax rotation and Kaiser normalization procedure concluded that the there are five factors for expressing anger while driving (Deffenbacher et al., 2002). The Verbal Aggressive Expression scale has an alpha level of .88. The eleven-item, Personal Physical Aggressive Expression scale has a reliability of .81. Using The Vehicle to Express Anger scale also had a high level of reliability (Alpha =.86), whereas the Displaced Aggression scale has a lower alpha level of .65. Lastly, the 15-item factor of Adaptive/Constructive Expression scale has a high alpha level of .90 (Deffenbacher et al., 2002). Although the Adaptive/Constructive expression was not associated with the other forms of anger expression, the "four aggressive forms correlated positively with each other, thus accounting for 9 to 23 percent of the variance in each other" (Deffenbacher et al., 2002).

In addition to these results, a significant gender effect was found. According to Deffenbacher et al., (2002, p. 723-724), "men were more likely to express their anger through direct physical aggression (i.e., an expression of anger towards others rather than the offending driver)." Because the Displaced Aggression scale had a low alpha level (.65), a new Total Aggressive Expression scale was constructed which had an alpha level of .90. Employing this, a small gender effect was found (Deffenbacher et al., 2002).

As seen in the previous literature and in this study, driving anger and general trait anger were moderately and positively correlated. Although there is some overlap in the measures, they have been treated as fairly independent anger constructs (Deffenbacher et al., 2002). These constructs were also positively correlated with the three aggressive forms of anger expression and the overall aggressive expression index, yet is negatively correlated with adaptive/constructive expression (Deffenbacher et al., 2002). This held true for the correlation between trait and driving anger with traffic situations (Scenarios); yet, with respect to the day to day driving instances (Daily Logs), only driving anger was positively correlated (Deffenbacher et al., 2002). Lastly, the reports on the Driving Survey suggest that general trait and driving anger correlated positively with aggression and risky behavior; conversely, adaptive/constructive expression correlated moderately and negatively with aggression.

It is important to note that one of the findings suggests that although the frequency of driving and the total number of miles driven were not highly correlated, they both were associated with the frequency of becoming angry while driving as well as with the frequency of aggressive and risky behaviors, yet at a lesser degree of intensity (Deffenbacher et al., 2002). Another pertinent issue is that it is possible that the increased frequency of driving may be associated with being in a hurry.

The literature has identified various ways in which individuals become frustrated, aggressive, and angry while driving. Each of these studies examined the emotional and personality factors that influence driving behaviors, specifically the differences associated with trait anger and driving anger. Much of the research included asking the participant about his/her attitudes concerning driving situations, participating in driving simulations, and assessing their driving behaviors. The literature suggests that drivers who maintain both trait and driving anger are more likely to engage in aggressive driving behaviors, yet those who have driving anger are better able to delineate the incidents that occur in the transportation environment that elicit aggressive responses. Therefore, it is important to examine the reasons why individuals discriminate between general anger and driving anger.

Stress and Road Rage

Much of the stress encountered by individuals is a product of the continuous bombardment of common daily hassles, such as time pressure, job concerns, and financial considerations; however, research has recently cited automobile driving as a salient source of everyday stress (Gulian et al., 1990; Novavo et al., 1990; Selzer & Vinokur, 1975). Therefore, the transportation environment has contributed to a source of stress for many drivers (Novaco et al., 1979; Novaco et al., 1990). Stress has been defined as a "hypothetical state of imbalance between environmental demands and the response capabilities of the person or system to cope with these demands" (McGrath, 1970 as cited in Novaco et al., 1979, p. 363). Thus, stressors are "aversive events or elements in various environmental fields that disturb the organism's equilibrium, interfere with its performance, or even threaten its survival" (Novaco et al., 1979, p. 363). Examples of stressors may include traffic congestion, aggressive drivers, inappropriate lane changes, construction sites, and obscene gestures given by drivers. Traffic congestion, in particular, has been identified not only as a behavioral constraint but also as a source of frustration for many drivers. Consequently, it has affected individual aggression levels in drivers (Novaco et al., 1979).

The Novaco et al. (1979) study examined the interplay between the transportation environment and various stress reactions as measured by self-report indices. The participants in the research (N=100) were employees from two Irvine Industrial Area companies, who volunteered and were selected to participate contingent upon having traveled their particular commuting route to work for the past six months. Novaco and his colleagues (1979) found that transportation environments with high impedances (i.e., the physical parameters of distance traveled and the amount of time for travel) have a significant influence on the stress level of the participants (e.g., tense, irritable, nervous and impatient; p<.05). The study also found that the type or size of vehicle and the resources within the vehicle that enable the commuter to control features of his/her environment (such as space, seating comfort, insulation from noise, air conditioning, and music) may also influence the degree of stress that is experienced (Novaco et al., 1979, p. 364).

In a follow-up study, Novaco et al. (1990) examined the transportation or commuting environment (with respect to both physical and perceptual impedances) and its linkage to transportation stressors. The participants in the sample (N=79) were re-contacted and recruited from the Novaco et al. (1979) study. The participants responded to questions concerning the physical impedances in their daily morning commute, answered questions pertaining to subjective impedances and constraints on movement, and reported on various health indicators, coping behaviors, moods, and attitudes regarding transportation for both their morning and evening commutes (Novaco et al., 1990). The researchers (Novaco et al., 1990, p. 248-249) found that "participants with higher degrees of subjective impedance maintained more negative moods (e.g., tense, irritable, tired, sad, burdened, and intolerant; p<.001)". Therefore, impedances in the transportation environment have an impact on individuals' moods both while driving and once they enter the home or work environment.

Rasmussen, Knapp, and Garner (2000) explored the relationship between driving induced stress among urban college students in Las Vegas, Nevada. The survey instrument assessed the frequency and distance of commuting, recorded the number of traffic accidents and citations, addressed stress from different sources, inquired about the frequency of specific incidences, and assessed driving habits (Rasmussen et al., 2000). The sample was comprised of students (N=407) who were enrolled in three sections of introductory psychology classes. The mean age of the students was 23.3 years, but the range was from age 18 to 51 years old (Rasmussen et al., 2000).

The study concluded that commuting by automobile was an identified source of stress for most participants, yet this stress was considered no greater than the stress that is associated with taking a college examination (Rasmussen et al., 2000). At the same time, the results of the study suggest some participants took precautionary measures by carrying defensive weapons for protection. Weapons mentioned in the study included firearms, baseball bats or clubs, and mace (Rasmussen et al., 2000). A 2001 study by Hennessy and Wiesenthal found that drivers with a disposition to view driving as a generally stressful activity also reported engaging in more driving aggression than do drivers who consider driving to be less stressful.

These driving stress studies demonstrate that elements in the environment have an impact on individuals' moods and attitudes while driving. In some cases, these moods take on negative attributes such as tension, irritability, and intolerance. These psychological states may be manifest in one's driving abilities; moreover, they may culminate into an altercation with another driver.

Many drivers have experienced at least a slight provocation while behind the wheel of a vehicle, and at times this provocation becomes a stressor for the individual. The transportation environment is full of obstacles and impedances that may cause undue stress to the individual. For example, traffic congestion, road construction, tailgaters, slow drivers, time constraints, and someone cutting in front of another driver have all been cited as stressors from drivers. As cited previously in the literature, these are all external concerns of the driver that have internal consequences. Thus, stressors coupled with dispositional characteristics need to be identified and analyzed separately and in conjunction with each other.

Indicators of Aggressive Driving

There is a broad spectrum of behaviors that range from the mundane to severe manifestations of aggressive driving, many of which can culminate into incidents of road rage. Some of these behaviors are antecedents to more extreme acts of driver aggression. Examples of these predictors of aggressive driving include: speeding, overtaking others on the roadway, and running red lights; conversely, seat belt usage has been inversely related to driver aggression. It is important to notes that these can also can correlates of aggressive driving.

A driver's willingness to expose him/herself to the risk of a vehicle accident usually is the result of traveling at excessive speeds (Kostyniuk, Molnar, & Eby, 2001). According to the Michigan Omnibus State Traffic Safety Survey (1995) 90 percent (N=740) of the respondents reported exceeding the 55 mile per hour speed limit. An analysis of driving records showed that drivers with the fastest driving speeds were more likely than others to have crashes or violations on their driving records (Kostynuik et al., 2001). The National Highway Traffic Safety Administration (1998 as cited in Beirness et al., 2001, p. 6) found that "speed is reported to be a factor in 30 percent of all fatal motor vehicle crashes accounting for the loss of over 13,000 lives each year." Furthermore, a study conducted by Hendricks, Fell and Freedom (2001) found that approximately 19 percent of serious injury crashes were attributable to speed.

Research (Kostyniuk et al., 2001) has demonstrated that speed and age variables have been associated in driving experiences. The Kostyniuk et al. (2001) study found a clear age effect for both men and women, with younger drivers being more likely to travel at fasters speeds than the middle aged or older drivers. Also, Wasielewski (1984) found a statistically significant decline in travel speeds with age and noted that women were less likely than men to be among the drivers at very high or very low speeds. The Wasielewski study (1984) also found that men reported driving faster than women, yet the speeds decreased with age.

Other types of risky behavior are the driver's willingness to "cut off" another driver or to "run a red light." In the Evans and Wasielewski (1983) study, vehicles were photographed on highways in Michigan and Ontario using a motor driven 35 millimeter camera. The researchers matched the vehicle's license plate number, which was captured on the film, with the driver's official record. The researchers calculated the vehicle headway (i.e., the distance from one vehicle to the vehicle ahead) and estimated the driver's age. They found that younger drivers (under age 21) took greater risks by traveling with shorter headways than did older drivers; moreover, those who traveled with shorter headways had more accidents and violations on their drivers' records (Evans & Wasielewski, 1983).

According to a 1998 study by AAA, (1998 as cited by Beirness et al., 2001) 25 percent of Americans admitted to driving aggressively at some time in the past year. Fifty percent said they have seen others engage in aggressive driving in the past couple days (AAA, 1997). In a survey conducted by Transport Canada, 29 percent of Canadians admitted that they "often pass other cars on the highway even if I'm not in a hurry" and 25 percent indicated that they "sometimes enter intersections as the light is about to turn red" (Kiar, 1998 as cited by Beirness et al., 2001). The Retting et al. (1998) study, which used automated cameras at two large urban intersections in Virginia to observe red light violations, found that on average there were three red-light violations per hour. In a subsequent study (Retting et al., 1999 as cited by Beirness et al., 2001) the number of drivers running red lights was as high as 26 per 10,000 vehicles.

Safety belt use has been negatively correlated with high risk driving behavior. "The failure to wear a seat belt does place the driver-and any other vehicle occupant for that matter—at a greater risk of an injury if they are involved in an accident" (Jonah, 1986, p. 261). Therefore, drivers who chose not to secure their safety belts appear to be greater risk takers than drivers who do buckle their safety belts.

Research by Foss, Bierness, and Sprattler (1994) demonstrated that drinking drivers tend to use safety belts less frequently than other drivers. Kostyniuk et al. (2001) found that self-reported safety belt use among women (78.1%) has been consistently higher than men (59.8%). Within each gender group, the 16 to 29 year old age group shows the lowest belt usage while the 60 year old and older age group shows the highest rates (Kostyniuk et al., 2001, p. 510). Furthermore, the men in the under age 30 category have the lowest safety belt usage rate, and the rate may be decreasing (Kostyniuk et al., 2001).

Existing Aggressive Driving Scales

In light of the precursors of aggressive driving and road rage behaviors, several driving behavior scales (Deffenbacher et al., 1994;

Deffenbacher et al., 2002; Donovan & Marlatt, 1982; Larson, 1996) have been developed to measure various dimensions of the driver and the driving experiences. Each of these scales has a slightly different focus with respect to driving attitudes and experiences, some concentrate on the role of anger and others on the extent of risky behavior, and driver's risk taking attitudes.

One survey questionnaire, which was developed by Donovan and Marlatt (1982), assessed individuals' driving related experiences, drinking-related behaviors (i.e., alcohol consumption), demographic information, driving attitudes, and personality variables. The driving-related attitudes emphasized driving aggression, competitive speeding, driving-related internality and externality, and driving inhibitions (Donovan & Marlatt; 1982). The limitation of the study is that its main focus is the role of aggression. Its items and questions weave together anger and driving related instances, making it difficult to untangle the concepts being examined in this study.

Deffenbacher et al. (1994) developed the Driving Anger Scale (DAS). The DAS has both a short (14 items) and long form (33 items), each consisting of a diverse item pool of driving contexts that might arouse anger. The short form of the DAS (Alpha=.80) provides a unidimensional measure of driving anger; the long form of the DAS (Alpha=.90) includes subscales measuring anger in six different driving-related situations: (1) hostile gestures (Alpha=.87); (2) illegal driving (Alpha=.80); (3) police presence (Alpha=.79); (4) slow driving (Alpha=.82); (5) discourtesy (Alpha=.81); (6) traffic obstructions (Alpha=.78). Participants were asked to rate each of these situations on a five-point, Likert format (1=not at all, 2=a little, 3=some, 4=much, 5=very much) scale, according to the amount of anger elicited by each item. The short form correlates with the long form (r=.95); moreover, both forms provide an internally consistent measure of the general trait of driving anger.

Individuals who score high in driving anger would be expected to become angry more frequently because more of these situations arouse anger and to experience a greater intensity of anger in these situations (Deffenbacher et al., 1994, p. 84). Therefore, the DAS identifies trait-driving anger, which refers to the likelihood that an individual will become angry while driving (Deffenbacher et al., 1994); but at the same time, anger on the DAS has also been associated with higher general anger, impulsiveness, and trait anxiety (Deffenbacher et al., 2001; Deffenbacher et al., 2002).

Although this instrument has respectable reliability and validity, the main focus of these particular questionnaire items surrounds driving anger. The items are designed to elicit responses that characterize the individuals' levels of anger for each of the individual questions. However, the purpose of the present study is to elicit responses that capture how the participant drives, responds to traffic incidents, and responds to other drivers. Furthermore, the theoretical framework for this study includes anger as a mediating variable, such that the role of anger will need to be teased out from the driving related questions.

Another measure of aggressive driving is the Larson Driver's Stress Profile (Larson, 1996). This is a self-report measure used to assess the frequency of driving anger and impatience as well as the frequency with which drivers engage in behaviors designed to compete with and "punish" other drivers (Larson, 1996). The Driver Stress Profile contains 40 items, and 4 subscales. The four subscales comprise items tapping into anger (Alpha=.78), impatience (Alpha=.82), competition (Alpha=.89), and punishment (Alpha=.85). The Cronbach's alpha level for the full scale has a reliability of .93 (Blanchard et al., 2000). The items were arranged in a rational hierarchical fashion from least aggressive and dangerous to most aggressive and potentially dangerous (Larson, 1996).

According to the Blanchard et al. study (2000), it appears that the Larson Stress Profile (1996) and the Deffenbacher et al. Driving Anger Survey (DAS) (1994) correlate fairly well. There is considerable overlap in these two measures, yet they appear to be measuring different characteristics. The DAS specifically pertains to driving related anger while the Driver Stress Profile pertains to the frequency of driving related anger, impatience, competitive, and punishing behaviors (Blanchard et al., 2000).

The most recent scale was developed by Deffenbacher, Lynch, Oetting, and Swaim (2002). Deffenbacher and his colleagues created the Driving Anger Expression Inventory (DAX), which serves as a measure of expressing anger while driving. The DAX is a 62 item inventory (see Deffenbacher et al., 2002, p. 722-723), which was developed from interviews with students, faculty, and community members. The respondents were asked to describe how they express their anger while driving on a 4-point scale (1 almost never to 4 almost always) (Deffenbacher et al., 2002).

This inventory includes five factors of expressing anger while driving: Verbal Aggressive, Personal Physical Aggressive, Vehicle to

Express Anger, Displaced Aggression, and Adaptive/Constructive Expression scales (Deffenbacher et al., 2002). The Verbal Aggressive Expression scale has an alpha level of .88. The eleven-item, Personal Physical Aggressive Expression scale has a reliability of .81. Using The Vehicle to Express Anger scale also had a high level of reliability (Alpha =.86), whereas the Displaced Aggression scale has a lower alpha level of .65. Lastly, the 15 item factor of Adaptive/Constructive Expression scale has a high alpha level of .90 (Deffenbacher et al., 2002). Because the Displaced Aggression scale had a low alpha level (.65), a new Total Aggressive Expression (TAE) scale was constructed (i.e., all of the above scales minus the Displaced Aggression and the Adaptive/Constructive scales) and it had an alpha level of .90. The Total Aggressive Expression (TAE) scale is employed in this study.

The second scale to be utilized in this study is a shortened version of the Driving Survey (Deffenbacher et al., 2001). The Driving Survey (DS) is a compilation of measures of aggression, risky behavior, and crash-related events. There are three core subscales in the survey: driving related aggression, risky behavior, and crash-related outcomes. There are 13 items in the driving-related aggression subscale (e.g., having an argument with or making an angry gesture at another driver) (Deffenbacher et al., 2001). The risky behavior subscale is comprised of 15 items that pertain to breaking the norms of the road (e.g., running a red light or speeding 20+ miles an hour over the limit). The third subscale consists of six crash-related outcomes (i.e., losing concentration while driving, a minor loss of vehicular control, a close call, a moving (non-parking) ticket, a minor accident, and a major accident). However, since the crash-related items do not form a reliable scale (current Alpha = .55, reported Alpha = .41 to .45) (Deffenbacher, Deffenbacher et al., 2003; Deffenbacher, Lynch, et al., 2003) the present study will not use these items. The participants will be asked to report the frequency (0 to 5+ with 5+ being treated as a 5 in analyses) of each of the subscales over the last three months (Deffenbacher, Deffenbacher et al., 2003). It is expected that high anger drivers will report more aggressive, risky behavior than low anger drivers (Deffenbacher et al., 2000, 2002; Deffenbacher, Deffenbacher, et al., 2003).

Although most of these scales contain important constructs and have demonstrated acceptable reliability and validity, the present study uses survey questions from the Deffenbacher et al. (2002) Driving Anger Expression Inventory, specifically the Total Aggressive

Expression (TAE) subscale and the Driving Survey (Deffenbacher et al., 2001). All of the above scales do not conform to the present research questions, in that, these scales ask the respondent about his/her participation in acts of aggressive driving and road rage behaviors. The present study is more concerned with the actual behaviors that the respondents have engaged in the past; thus, the survey questionnaire must address the behaviors in which the participants engaged, not their attitudes toward road rage situations.

There are three justifications for using the TAE subscale of the DAX (Deffenbacher et al., 2002) and the Driving Survey (Deffenbacher et al., 2001). The justifications for using the road rage items are: (1) they ask questions concerning behaviors that are specific to the research questions, (2) they do not entangle the role of anger in the driving experience questions (therefore, the role of anger can be extrapolated and anger items will be measured through other means) and, (3) both the TAE and Driving Survey (DS) have demonstrated validity and reliability. Given these reasons, these scales are used to measure the dependent variable of road rage behaviors.

From the literature, it is apparent that individuals who engage in road rage behaviors are a public safety concern. Although there has been debate concerning the delineation between aggressive driving and road rage behaviors, for this study the definition of road rage encompasses incidents in which a motorist commits various infringements on the road that act to annoy, endanger, or threaten to injure or damage property of another motorist or passenger, in response to a traffic dispute. This definition was further qualified to include violence or property damage between strangers that erupted as a result of a spontaneous traffic altercation. Thus, the definition is all encompassing with respect to precipitators of road rage (e.g., tailgating, weaving in traffic, speeding) as well as assaultive behaviors resulting from traffic grievances.

The current psychological literature has demonstrated the importance of situational and dispositional characteristics associated with aggressive driving behaviors and instances of road rage (Beirness et al., 2001; Deffenbacher et al., 1994; Deffenbacher et al., 2000; Deffenbacher et al., 2001; Deffenbacher et al., 2002; Donovan et al., 1988; Ellison et al., 1995; Ellison-Potter et al., 2001; Harding et al., 1998; Joint, 1995; Jonah, 1986; Mizell, 1997; Novaco et al., 1979; Novaco et al., 1990; Shinar, 1997; Turner et al., 1975). The research also has indicated that aversive or unpleasant situations increase the likelihood of aggression, especially when individuals cannot escape from the unpleasant stimuli (Bandura, 1973; Mueller, 1983). Specifically, these situational triggers of road rage behaviors may include: "encounters with slow drivers; other drivers cutting in or overtaking; stereotyped sex role-attributions of driving incompetence by males in relation to females; accidents between vehicles; and competition for parking spaces" (Harding et al., 1998, p. 231). The coupling of these situational attributes with the anonymous nature of the drivers suggests a potential increase in aggression between drivers. The dispositional traits attributed to risky driving behaviors are aggressiveness, impulsiveness, frustration, and general anger (Arnett et al., 1997; Donovan et al., 1985; Mayer & Treat, 1977). The research further suggests that younger individuals are more likely to take deliberate driving risks (Beirness & Simpson, 1988).

     In sum, the driving experience has psychological undertones in which the driving experience may elicit certain responses to the driving environment. Hodgdon et al. (1981; as cited by Jonah, 1986) have suggested the following reasons for risk-taking among youth: outlet for stress, aggression, expression of independence, means of increasing arousal, impressing others, and/or means to another end (i.e., speeding to avoid being late). Jessor (1984; as cited by Jonah, 1986, p. 266) perceives youth who engage in risky behaviors, (e.g., driving-related and others), as serving the following functions:

> to take control over their lives by acting independently, to express opposition to adult authority and conventional society, to cope with anxiety, frustration, fear of failure at school, to gain acceptance into a peer group or to maintain one's position within a peer group, to show that one is 'cool,' or to demonstrate to others that one has matured and can now engage in adult behaviors (e.g., driving after drinking).

     Although the psychological and stress literature provides a foundation for reasons why individuals may engage in road rage behaviors, there is still a need for further inquiry. The psychological literature has focused on the roles of anger, aggression, and frustration as well as other dispositional characteristics of risky drivers. The stress research has not only emphasized the role of dispositional and situational factors but also the role of impediments in the transportation environment that may contribute to the individual's stress level and ultimately to their level of aggression on the road. In addition to the stress literature, the concepts of justice and equity have been intertwined with why individuals have engaged in aggressive driving behaviors. From the equity/justice literature, violence has been viewed as a necessary and justified response to what is perceived to be an injustice.

Given these main concepts being examined (i.e., disposition, situational context, anger, stress, and injustice) it appears to be a natural progression to investigate if a criminological underpinning may be operating. Specifically, since Agnew's general strain theory encompasses many of the above concepts, this theory is examined in relation to its ability to explain why individuals engage in aggressive driving and road rage behaviors.

CHAPTER 3

General Strain Theory

Both the stress and psychological literature have emphasized the presentation of negative stimuli; however, with the exception of Agnew (1985) this relationship has been largely overlooked in the criminological literature. Given the nature of the driving experience, especially the interplay between situational and dispositional factors, Agnew's general strain theory (GST) (1992) may facilitate an understanding of why individuals engage in aggressive driving behaviors as well as road rage incidents. As noted previously in the literature, individual differences in predispositions to be aggressive drivers are important to the driving experience. Furthermore, driving represents a situation in which people are forced to take a high degree of interest in the movements and behaviors of strangers; yet how individuals react to certain driving situations varies dramatically (Connell & Joint, 1996).

The driving experience and transportation environment are filled with opportunities for independence, freedom, and excitement. The fundamental symbolism of driving is that it is suggestive of images of speed, excitement, and vitality (Marsh & Collett, 1986). Although the precise nature of the thrill of driving is difficult to define, it encompasses feelings of invulnerability as well as providing drivers with a shelter for many activities (Marsh & Collett, 1986). However, when these attributes are compromised by other drivers as well as confronted with negative circumstances, an opportunity exists for drivers to aggressively defend their positions and engage in road rage incidents.

Evolution of Agnew's General Strain Theory (GST)

Subscribing to the idea that the transportation and home environments as well as individual differences play an integral role in whether an individual engages in road rage behavior, it is important that a theory address these components in a general sense. Agnew's strain theory (1992) has evolved over the years to include three major sources of strain: (1) strain as the actual or anticipated failure to achieve positively valued goals, (2) strain as the actual or anticipated removal of positively valued stimuli, and (3) strain as the actual or anticipated presentation of negatively valued stimuli. According to Agnew's general strain theory (GST) (1992), the interplay between one's environment (especially if it is aversive in nature) and the individual's emotional response to that environment (specifically an anger response) may help to explain why individuals engage in road rage behaviors. This section traces the evolution of strain theory, examines the propositions of the GST, and reviews the support and criticisms of the theory as well as its limitations in terms of this study.

Agnew's (1992) general strain theory draws upon the previous works of Merton (1938), Cohen (1955), and Cloward and Ohlin (1960), and expands on Agnew's (1984) earlier works on goal achievement and revisions of strain theory (Agnew, 1985; 1989). Merton's (1938) theory of anomie emphasized the disjuncture between culturally recognized goals and legitimate means to attain these goals. Cohen's (1955) research highlights the goals of middle class adolescents. Cloward and Ohlin's (1960) study contended that adolescents who participate in delinquent subcultures were more likely to experience goal-blockage that leads to delinquency. Agnew (1984) suggested that adolescents pursue multiple goals, yet immediate goals rather than long-range goals are emphasized. Moreover, it should be noted that Merton, and Cloward and Ohlin, emphasized the adolescent's inability to achieve a goal of monetary success.

Although these early strain theories differ from one another, they revolve around the same premise that "delinquency results when adolescents are unable to achieve their goals through legitimate channels" (Agnew, 1984, p. 435). As a result, adolescents may resort to illegitimate modes of goal achievement or may retaliate against the source of their frustration with anger (Agnew, 1984). However, the early research failed to support strain theory (Elliot & Voss, 1974; Gold, 1963; Hirschi, 1969).

Early Criticisms of Strain Theory
According to Kornhauser (1978) the primary criticism of the early strain theories revolved around the research on the disjunction between

aspirations and expectations. Although studies have attempted to test this idea in relation to occupational and educational goals, research suggests that delinquency is more likely to occur when both aspirations and expectations are low, and delinquency is less likely to occur when both aspirations and expectations are high (Gold, 1963; Hirschi, 1969; Johnson, 1979; Liska, 1971). According to Agnew (1984), another criticism of early strain theories deals with the relationship between social class and delinquency. However, this concept was challenged through research (see Hindelang, Hirschi, & Weiss, 1981; Johnson, 1979; Tittle, Villemez, & Smith, 1978) as middle class adolescents have also engaged in delinquent activity (Braithwaite, 1981; Elliot & Ageton, 1980). Lastly, these theories have been questioned because they cannot explain the fact that most delinquents refrain from crime in late adolescence (Hirschi, 1969) as well as why delinquents abstain from committing delinquent acts over a long period of time (Hirschi, 1969).

Given these criticisms, revisions to strain theory have occurred. The majority of the revisions suggest that adolescents may pursue a variety of goals and that goal commitment should be considered a variable in the research rather than an absolute rule, (Elliott & Voss; 1974; Elliot, Ageton, & Cantor, 1979; Greenberg, 1977); thus arguing that middle-class delinquency may be explained by strain theory. Furthermore, it has been suggested that adolescents are more compelled to achieve immediate goals rather than long-term goals (Coleman, 1961; Elliott & Voss, 1974).

Agnew's reconceptualization of strain theory broadens the source of strain as well as its application in explaining various forms of offending behaviors. According to Agnew's revised strain theory (1984), the main reason that adolescents turn to delinquency is to vent their frustration. He further notes that "delinquency may lower levels of frustration, but it will not reduce the disjunction between goals and goal achievement" (Agnew, 1984, p. 443). Therefore, a striking similarity exists between the premise of strain theory and the frustration-aggression theorists. The frustration-aggressive model (See Zillman, 1979) emphasizes that individuals not only seek certain goals, but also attempt to avoid painful and aversive situations. The blockage of pain-avoidance behavior constitutes another major source of strain. Agnew (1984, p. 447) contends that "adolescents are often placed in aversive situations from which they cannot legally escape. This blockage of pain-avoidance behavior frustrates the adolescent and may lead to illegal escape attempts or anger-based delinquency." Although Agnew (1984) built on the existing premise of strain theory, his early research did not support this premise.

In a follow-up study, Agnew (1985, p. 154) reintroduced the concept of blockage of "goal-seeking behavior" and "blockage of pain-avoidance behaviors."

> In the blockage of goal-seeking behavior, the individual is walking *toward a valued goal* and his or her path is blocked. In the blockage of pain-avoidance behavior the individual is walking away from an *aversive situation* and his or her path is blocked (Agnew, 1985, p. 154).

Although these concepts are different, it is possible for the same situation to be associated with both types of strain. At the same time, adolescents may encounter situations that are aversive; however, these situations do not interfere with goal attainment (Agnew, 1985). It is important to note that the blockage of pain-avoidance behavior may lead to frustration and aggression, especially when the individual believes that the exposure is undeserved (Zillman, 1979 as cited by Agnew, 1985).

Agnew (1985) also introduced the concepts of the aversive environment and the role of anger. The aversive environment is a situation in which adolescents "lack power and are often compelled to remain in situations which they find aversive" (Agnew, 1985, p. 156). Adolescents in aversive environments may engage in delinquent behaviors as a means to escape from the aversive environment or to remove the source of the aversion (Agnew, 1985). "When the escape or removal of the aversive source is not possible, the adolescent may become angry and strike out in rage at the source of aversion or a related target" (Agnew, 1985, p. 156). Thus, the aversive environment has a direct impact on delinquency and an indirect effect on delinquency through anger (Agnew, 1985).

In order to assess the causal relationship between environmental adversity and delinquency, Agnew (1989) conducted a longitudinal study using data from the Youth in Transition study with a nationally representative sample of adolescent boys. The first data collection took place in the fall of the 1966 (N=2,213) and the second data collection commenced in the spring of 1968 (N=1,886).

Agnew's (1989, p. 377) contention that the environmental adversity may lead to delinquency is based on three reasons:

> (1) the environment may cause the adolescent to attempt an illegal escape or to attack the source of aversion, (2) the environmental adversity may anger the adolescent, and in turn, that anger may be taken out on others, and (3) the environmental adversity may reduce the adolescent's level of social control.

The data indicate that "adversity has an instantaneous effect on delinquency, but delinquency does not have an instantaneous effect on adversity" (Agnew, 1989, p. 383). According to this test of the revised strain theory, the "inability to escape from aversive stimuli is frustrating and this is what motivates or causes delinquent behavior (i.e., leads to illegal escape attempts or anger-based delinquency)" (Agnew, 1989, p. 384).

General Strain Theory (GST)

Agnew's previous works (1984; 1985; 1989) culminated in the foundation for the general strain theory (GST) (Agnew, 1992) of crime and delinquency. Agnew's GST has its roots in social psychology; however, it emphasizes both the individual and his/her immediate social environment. Overall, GST cites sources of strain as being more pervasive and extensive than previous theorists have articulated. The three major types of strain include a full range of stressful events: "preventing one from achieving positively valued goals; removing or threatening to remove positively valued stimuli that one possesses, and presenting or threatening to present one with noxious or negatively valued stimuli" (Agnew, 1992, p. 50). Although each of these is presented as being theoretically distinctive, they may sometimes overlap in practice.

<u>Strain: Actual or Anticipated Failure to Achieve Positively Valued Goals</u>

The first type of strain refers to the failure to achieve positively valued goals. This type encompasses three subcategories: (1) the disjunction between aspirations and expectations/actual achievements; (2) the disjunction between expectations and actual achievements; and (3) the disjunction between just/fair outcomes and actual outcomes (Agnew, 1992). The first subcategory incorporates elements of classic strain theory (i.e., the gap between aspirations and expectations); therefore, arguing that "strain stems from the inability to achieve certain ideal goals emphasized by the (sub)cultural system" (Agnew, 1992, p. 51). Accordingly, strain is measured in terms of the "disjunction between aspirations and actual achievements, which reflects immediate rather than future goals and actual achievements rather than expected achievements" (Agnew, 1992, p. 52). However, this subcategory of strain has received weak empirical support (see Agnew 1991, for a summary).

The second subcategory suggests that strain occurs when there is a disjuncture between expectations and actual achievements (rewards) (Agnew, 1992). It is argued that adolescents formulate their expectations based on their past experiences as well as from comparing themselves with others who are similar to them (Agnew, 1992). When the expectations are not reflected in the adolescent's actual achievement, the adolescent will experience strain. According to Agnew (1992), the justice literature further purports that the inability to attain such expectations may lead to an emotional response, such as anger, resentment, rage, dissatisfaction, disappointment, and unhappiness. Those who experience this gap coupled with an emotional response are more likely to view delinquent acts as a possible option to reduce the disjunction (Agnew, 1992). Although the literature has not focused on this subcategory, there are limited data to suggest that the expectations-achievement gap is related to anger/hostility (Ross et al., 1971).

The third subcategory discusses strain as the disjunction between just/fair outcomes and actual outcomes. This disjuncture "claims that individuals do not necessarily enter interactions with specific outcomes in mind, but rather they enter interactions expecting that certain distributive justice rules will be followed, rules specifying how resources should be allocated" (Agnew, 1992, p. 53). Therefore, they expect an equitable relationship in terms of the inputs and outputs that are contributed and received in a given situation. However, if the input/output ratios are unequal, individuals are likely to feel the outcome is unjust and feel distressed. In other words, strain results when people perceive they are being treated unfairly or not equitably (Tyler, 1990). One of the reactions to this perceived inequity involves deviance, usually to restore the equity of the situation (Agnew, 1992). Although there has not been extensive empirical research on this relationship between equity and delinquency, the data suggest that inequity is likely to result in anger and frustration (Agnew, 1992). Thus, anger is an important consideration in the theory. A few studies (Cook & Hegtvedt, 1991; Donnerstein & Hatfield, 1982; Hegtvedt, 1990) suggest that insulting and vengeful behaviors may result from this inequity.

Each of these subcategories contributes to the strain caused by the failure to achieve positively valued goals. Most of the criminological research has focused on this type of strain as being responsible for delinquency in society. However, the literature on aggression ascertains that the blockage of goal-seeking behavior is not a strong predictor of aggression, especially when the goal has been experienced before (Bandura, 1973; Zillman, 1979). According to Agnew (1992, p. 56), "no study has examined all of these types of goals, but taken as a whole, the data do suggest that there are often differences among aspirations (ideal outcomes), expectations (expected outcomes), 'satisfying' outcomes, 'deserved' outcomes, fair or just outcomes, and tolerance levels." These multiple sources of strain are important in the definitional sense and are relevant in terms of possible sources of frustration.

Strain: Actual or Anticipated Removal of Positively Valued Stimuli
The second and third types of strain are derived from the stress literature (Pearlin, 1983), which focused on events that involved the loss of a positively valued stimuli or the addition of a negative or noxious stimuli. Therefore, the second type of strain refers to the negative relationship involving the actual or anticipated removal of positively valued stimuli from the individual (Agnew, 1992). Agnew (1992) refers to stress inducing events that predominantly affect individuals when something of value is lost, such as the loss of a boyfriend/girlfriend, or death of a close relative or friend. This is an

important concern given that this loss or impending loss "may lead to delinquency as the individual tries to prevent the loss of the positive stimuli, retrieve the lost stimuli or obtain substitute stimuli, seek revenge against those responsible for the loss, or manage the negative affect caused by the loss by taking illicit drugs (Agnew, 1992, p. 58). It is important to note that there is little research on this type of strain.

Strain: Actual or Anticipated Presentation of Noxious Stimuli

The third type of strain refers to strain as the presentation of negative or noxious stimuli. It is further noted that the inability to legally escape from the negative stimuli may lead to a variety of deviant responses. According to Agnew (1992), these responses may include: (1) escaping or avoiding the negative stimuli; (2) terminating the negative stimuli; (3) exacting revenge against the source of the negative stimuli; and/or (4) managing the negative situation by taking illicit drugs. Although a negative or noxious stimuli encompasses a broad range of activities, research has demonstrated that noxious stimuli such as physical punishment (Straus, 1991), negative relationships with peers (Short & Strodtbeck, 1965), stressful life events (Gersten et al., 1974; Linsky & Straus, 1986), and verbal threats and insults, physical pain, personal space violations (Anderson & Anderson, 1984; Berkowitz, 1986) are linked to delinquency and aggression. Furthermore, in his study, Agnew (1989) concluded that anger was a mediating variable with delinquency, when social control and deviant beliefs were controlled.

Strain and the Role of Anger

Although these types of strain are theoretically distinct, they may overlap in practice. Each type of strain (individually and collectively) increases the likelihood that individuals will experience a range of negative emotions, such as anger, fear, depression, and disappointment (Agnew, 1992). Of these emotional states, anger is the most critical emotional reaction for general strain theory (Agnew, 1992). Anger results when,

> individuals blame their adversity on others, and anger is a key emotion because it increases the individual's level of felt injury, creates a desire for retaliation/revenge, energizes the individual for action, and lowers inhibitions, in part because

individuals believe that others will feel their aggression is justified (Averill, 1982; Berkowitz, 1982; Ch 10; Zillman, 1979 as cited by Agnew, 1992, p. 60).

Agnew and White (1992) further purport that adolescents are pressured into delinquency by these negative affective states, most notably anger and related emotions that result from negative relationships.

Anger may serve as a "corrective" response (Agnew, 1992, p. 60) to the adversity, and at the same time, alleviate the strain the individual is experiencing. The emotional reactions of anger and frustration may increase the likelihood of a criminal response. Therefore, a possible response to an undesirable affective state of anger, is that delinquency can be instrumental (trying to regain what one has lost or was prevented from obtaining), retaliatory (striking back at the source of strain), and escapist (seeking solace from disagreeable states of anger and strain) (Paternoster & Mazerolle, 1994). According to Berkowitz (1982), data suggest that vengeful behavior may result when there is no possibility of eliminating the adversity that stimulated it. Therefore, anger (which is discussed further in this chapter) is a central component of the general strain theory and delinquency linkage.

Coping Mechanisms/Adaptations to Strain

In concert with the stress literature, Agnew proposes various management strategies such as personal and social support mechanisms that may attenuate the effects of stress on adolescents (Compas, 1987; Compas, Orosan, & Grant, 1993). These adaptations take the form of cognitive, emotional, and behavioral responses (Agnew, 1992). The cognitive coping strategies emphasize the individual's subjective interpretation of the initial adversity; therefore, individuals are attempting to minimize the importance of adversity or any negative outcomes that may result (Agnew, 1992). Some of the ways that individuals adapt are by claiming that the adverse condition is not very important to their goals, values and/or identity. For example, individuals may minimize adversity by "convincing themselves that they deserve the adversity they have experienced" (Agnew, 1992, p. 68).

The behavioral and emotional coping strategies also seek to minimize the amount of strain. The behavioral responses attempt to "maximize positive outcomes and minimize negative outcomes" which in some cases may culminate with the individual taking revenge on the aggressor (Agnew, 1992, p. 69). Both of these adaptations allow the individuals to employ conventional or deviant methods to minimize their strain. Individuals may try to attain "positively valued goals, protect or retrieve positively valued stimuli, or terminate or escape from negative stimuli" (Agnew, 1992, p. 67). To examine the vengeful behavior coping mechanism, the individual blames the adverse situation on others and he/she creates a "desire for revenge that is distinct from the desire to end the adversity" (Agnew, 1992, p. 69). Thus, the individual is more likely to engage in deviant behavior to spite the person, not necessarily to end the situation. Lastly, the emotional coping mechanisms are the impetus for when the individual acts on the negative emotions resulting from the adversity, which could include using drugs, starting an exercise regime, taking meditation, and using relaxation techniques (Agnew, 1992).

<u>Constraints of Coping Strategies</u>
According to the above adaptations, individuals may resort to either a conventional or delinquent adaptation to the strain they experience. Agnew (1992) discusses the constraints to both delinquent and nondelinquent coping strategies. It is important to note that individuals do not experience these constraints equally, some may be more constraining than others (Agnew, 1992). Individuals are constrained in their chosen adaptation by a variety of internal and external factors. One constraint may involve "whether or not the strain affects the person's goals, values/identities and/or if the person has alternative goals/values/identities in which to seek refuge" (Agnew, 1992, p. 71). Therefore, if strain affects a person's goals/values/identities and the person does not have recourse, the resulting strain is more likely to lead to a delinquent adaptation (Agnew, 1992). A second constraint depends upon the individual's own coping resources, such as temperament, problem-solving skills, self-esteem, and other dispositional characteristics (Agnew, 1992). The traits that persons have affect the adaptation strategy they chose to employ. For example, data suggest that individuals with high self-esteem and self-efficacy are more resistant to stress and strain (Averill, 1982; Compas, 1987; Rosenberg, 1990).

Third, conventional social support may be a possible constraint for the individual. In research conducted by Thoits (1984), it was found that social support facilitates the coping strategy to be employed by the individual. Individuals who have social supports are more likely to respond to strain with conventional responses. Fourth, individuals can be constrained by the cost/benefit ratio of engaging in delinquency, the individual's level of self-control, and the access to "illegitimate means" that are necessary to commit a delinquent act (Agnew, 1992, p. 72). Each of these constraints moderate whether the delinquent coping strategy is a viable alternative for the individual to minimize strain.

Fifth, the larger social environment may impact the probability of delinquent or nondelinquent coping (Agnew, 1992). The social environment may influence the importance one attaches to the selected goals/values/identities that one holds. The environment may affect the individual's sensitivity to particular strains by influencing his/her beliefs regarding what constitutes an adverse situation (Agnew, 1992). The larger social context may influence the way in which the individual cognitively reduces the severity of strain. Last, the environment may "make it difficult to engage in behavioral coping of a nondelinquent nature" (Agnew, 1992, p. 72). Each of these environmental concerns may influence the individual's decision as to how to cope with the strain, whether the coping mechanism follows a delinquent or nondelinquent response.

Strain and Disposition

In addition to the larger social context, the individual's disposition or is an important determinant to whether the individual will choose a delinquent or nondelinquent coping strategy. Disposition takes into account the temperament of the individual, the previous learning history of the delinquent, the belief system of the adolescent, and the person's attributions regarding the cause of the adversity (Agnew, 1992, p. 73). As previously stated in the psychological literature and by Agnew (1992, p. 73), "adolescents who attribute their adversity to others are much more likely to become angry...[and] that anger creates a strong predisposition to delinquency." Another key variable is if the individual has delinquent peers. It has been suggested that individuals who associate with delinquent peers are more likely to be exposed to delinquent models and beliefs, and to receive reinforcement for delinquency (see Akers, 1985). Furthermore, the constraints to coping strategies and adolescent dispositions have not been empirically researched in criminology (Agnew, 1992).

Research by both Cloward and Ohlin (1960) and Hoffmann and Ireland (1995) contend that when anger becomes the response to strain and it is coupled with an individual externalizing blame, the probability of deviant adaptations increase. Agnew's theory (1992) suggests that the magnitude of strain (extent), the duration of the strain (length of time one experiences strain), the recency of the strain (timing of the strain), and the clustering of stressful events function to increase the likelihood of a delinquent adaptation.

Summary of Agnew's GST

Agnew's general strain theory (1992) presents a refined version of the traditional strain theories (Cloward & Ohlin, 1960; Cohen, 1955; Merton, 1938) that expands to include all types of negative reactions between the individual and others. Specifically, strain theory focuses on the negative relationships that adolescents have with others that pressure them toward delinquent adaptations. This theory highlights three main categories of strain or negative relationships with others: "(1) the actual or anticipated failure to achieve positively valued goals, (2) the actual or anticipated removal of positively valued stimuli, and (3) the actual or anticipated presentation of negative stimuli" (Agnew, 1992, p. 74). Not only are the types of strain identified, but strain theory also specifies the relationship between strain and delinquency. This relationship was further delineated to suggest that strain is likely to have a cumulative effect on delinquency after a certain threshold is attained. Lastly, GST (Agnew, 1992) identifies the various adaptations (e.g., cognitive, behavioral, and emotional) that adolescents can employ to mediate the types of strain and describes the factors that account for a delinquent or nondelinquent adaptation (Agnew, 1992).

Empirical Research on Agnew's GST

Agnew and White's research (1992) provided the first comprehensive empirical test of Agnew's general strain theory (1992) and they found qualified support for the theory. Their research (Agnew & White, 1992) used the Rutgers Health and Human Development (RHHD) data set to conduct a partial test of GST. It was a partial test given the lack of certain items in the RHHD. Its primary focus was to examine whether (1) composite measures of strain will have an effect on delinquency and drug use, while measures of social control and differential association are held constant; and (2) the effect of strain on delinquency and drug use will be conditioned by several variables (i.e., delinquent friends and self-efficacy) (Agnew & White, 1992, p. 478). According to the theory delinquent friends should increase the impact of strain, while self-efficacy should reduce it (Agnew & White, 1992).

The data analyses are based on the first wave of the Rutgers Health and Human Development Project (RHHDP) prospective longitudinal study that focused on alcohol and drug use (Agnew & White, 1992). The respondents were responsible for completing a full day of questionnaires, a home interview, and an examination at the project site. The sample was drawn from New Jersey adolescents aged 12, 15, and 18 between 1979 and 1981. Although 1,380 adolescents were interviewed during that time, eligible respondents were initially identified through a series of randomly generated telephone calls (N=1,076). "Ninety-five percent of the first wave respondents were re-interviewed three years later (1982-1984) using essentially the same battery of instruments" (p. 479). It is important to note that the participants were slightly more likely to have better educated parents and higher family incomes; furthermore, 90 percent of the sample was white. Also, the longitudinal analysis was limited to those respondents who were 12 and 15 years of age at wave one.

Items from the HHDP instrument reflected strain theory, social control, and differential association. Due to the nature of the questions, one type of strain could not be measured: failure to achieve positively valued goals (Agnew & White, 1992). The researchers admit that it was sometimes difficult to classify a variable as strain or a social control measure. However, they partially resolved the dilemma by classifying variables dealing with negative relations with others as strain items (see discussion in Agnew & White, 1992, p. 480-482).

The results of their analyses suggest that for the first hypothesis, five of the strain variables (Negative Life Events, Life Hassles, Negative Relations with Adults, Parental Fighting, and Neighborhood Problems) have a significant effect on delinquency and/or drug use (Agnew & White, 1992, p. 485). In addition to the strain predictors, other social control and differential association variables were significant (parental attachment, school attachment, peer attachment, time spent on homework, grades, and friend's delinquency). Results of the second hypothesis demonstrate that the effects of strain on delinquency/drug use are conditioned by delinquent friends and self-efficacy (Agnew & White, 1992). Therefore, the delinquent friend variable strongly conditions the impact of strain on delinquency and drug use, and self-efficacy has a significant impact on delinquency but not on drug use (Agnew & White, 1992).

The above data support GST, but this support must be viewed as tentative since the analyses are cross sectional in nature. The respondents were asked to report the extent of their delinquency over a three-year period and their drug use over a one-year period. However, the theory purports that strain should have a contemporaneous rather than lagged effect on delinquency and drug use (Agnew & White, 1992). The data "indicate that strain has a casual effect on delinquency, but delinquency does not have a causal effect on strain" (Agnew & White, 1992, p. 491).

Paternoster and Mazerolle (1994) attempted to replicate and extend the Agnew and White (1992) study. Their longitudinal research used several different types or sources of general strain, items to measure the magnitude and duration of strain, and items that may be considered as coping mechanisms. Furthermore, their research was designed to determine if:

> the effect of strain on delinquency is greater for those youths with a large proportion of delinquent peers, with low self-control, with weak self-efficacy, who have weak conventional social support, and with weak moral inhibitions against offending (Paternoster & Mazerolle, 1994, p. 240).

Data were collected in two waves (Wave 1, N=1,725; Wave 2, N=1,525) from the National Youth Survey (NYS), and participants were interviewed in 1997 and re-interviewed in 1998 (Paternoster & Mazerolle, 1994).

Paternoster and Mazerolle's (1994), operationalization of strain was similar to Agnew and White's (1992) study, in which strain was measured by Neighborhood Problems (Alpha=.74), Negative Life Events (Alpha=.50), Negative Relations with Adults (Alpha=.86), School/Peer Hassles (Alpha=.70), and Traditional Strain measures. It is important to note that the authors acknowledge the interrelatedness of these concepts with other theories, yet Agnew (see Agnew 1992, Agnew 1994; Agnew & White, 1992) devoted considerable attention to these issues. Moreover, this research also measured social control items. The measures include: Moral Beliefs (Alpha=.84), Delinquent Peers (Alpha=.82), Delinquent Disposition (Alpha=.76), Grades, and Family Attachment (Alpha=.67) (Paternoster & Mazerolle, 1994). Lastly, delinquency was measured through an extensive list of delinquent behaviors.

The findings of their study (Paternoster & Mazerolle, 1994) suggest that strain is significantly related to delinquency. Of the five strain measures, four were significant (i.e., Neighborhood Problems, Negative Life Events, School/Peer Hassles, and Negative Relations with Adults). Therefore, adolescents who live in neighborhoods with various social problems, who have experienced stressful events, who have problems with peers and with school, as well these having had bad relationships with their parents and teachers commit significantly more delinquent acts than those experiencing less strain (Paternoster & Mazerolle, 1994). At the same time, they "found that having conventional moral beliefs and earning good grades effectively inhibits delinquent involvement whereas having delinquent peers significantly contributes to delinquency" (Paternoster & Mazerolle, 1994, p. 245).

When discussing the findings for the interaction effects of strain with delinquent and nondelinquent responses, only one of the interaction effects was statistically significant: the interaction between strain and self-efficacy, but in the opposite direction than predicted (Paternoster & Mazerolle, 1994). Consistent with Agnew and White's (1992) research, they found that "negative relationships with adults, feelings of dissatisfaction with friends and school life, and the experience of stressful events (family break up, unemployment, moving) were positively related to delinquency" (Paternoster & Mazerolle, 1994, p. 252).

Lastly, the authors (Paternoster & Mazerolle, 1994) devised a causal model linking GST social control and delinquent peers with delinquency and hypothesized that GST affects social control and delinquent peers. Consistent with Agnew's position, general strain is negatively related to social control and positively related to delinquent peers. Strain leads to "involvement in delinquency, then, because it in part weakens adolescents' ties to conventional sources of social control and strengthens their ties to delinquent others" (Paternoster & Mazerolle, 1994, p. 251).

Although comprehensive in nature, this study is not without its limitations. The main limitation is that the authors failed to take into account the role of anger as a mediating variable. As Agnew (1992) developed his theory, he emphasized that anger is an important theoretical construct. Furthermore, given that the data were taken from NYS (which was not designed as a test of GST), the issue of experiencing negative stimuli through day to day events was not able to be included in the study (Paternoster & Mazerolle, 1994).

Brezina's (1996) research found some support for the adaptive nature of delinquent responses to aversive stimuli. The purpose of his study was to determine if delinquency can act as an effective problem-solving response to aversive environments. Brezina (1996) specifically examined the escape-avoidance, compensation, and retaliation forms of delinquent adaptations. He hypothesized that strain generates negative affect, including feelings of anger, resentment, fear, and despair; and secondly, that delinquent behaviors reduce the effects of strain on negative affect (Brezina, 1996).

To test these hypotheses, he used cross-sectional and longitudinal data from the second and third waves of the Youth in Transition (YIT) survey. The second wave of data yielded responses from 11th grade males in the spring of 1968 (N=1,886) and the third wave of data was collected from 12th grade males in the spring of 1969 (N=1,799). The cross-sectional analysis was based on the second wave of data while the longitudinal analyses were based on the data from waves 2 and 3 (Brezina, 1996). The cross-sectional analysis found that strain is positively associated with the experience of anger, resentment, anxiety, and depression while controlling for other variables. Through longitudinal analysis of national survey data, he found support for the hypothesis that exposure to strain has a causal impact on negative affect (Brezina, 1996). He found that involvement in delinquent behavior reduced the impact of aversive stimuli on the level of negative affect (Brezina, 1996).

Aseltine, Gore, and Gordon's (2000) study examined the generality of GST through multiple measures of life stresses, relationship difficulties, and delinquency (i.e., nonviolent delinquency, aggressive/violent delinquency, and marijuana use). The researchers also analyzed the role of anger and hostility as well as the impact strain has on personal and social resources (Aseltine et al., 2000). They found through the covariance structure models that anger and hostility play a causal role in facilitating more aggressive forms of delinquency (Aseltine et al., 2000).

Aseltine et al. (2000) collected data from ninth, tenth, and eleventh grade students living in the greater Boston metropolitan area. The initial sample was selected in 1988 (N=1,208) and then the same participants were subsequently interviewed in 1989 (N=1,036) and 1990 (N=939) (Aseltine et al., 2000). The students were considered a representative sample of the public high school population, with a wide range of socioeconomic status and life situations. In terms of the descriptive characteristics of the sample, this sample was mostly Caucasian (94%) and Catholic (68%), and it did not include individuals who were from extremely disadvantaged circumstances (Aseltine et al., 2000).

The life stresses variable was measured through a 61-item questionnaire adapted from instruments detailing life events experienced by the participant in the past year. Some of the items included stressors such as school and money problems, job difficulties, health problems, parental separation or remarriage, and changes in household composition (Aseltine et al., 2000; Coddington, 1972; Compas, Davis, & Forsythe, 1985; Johnson & McCutcheon, 1980; Newcomb, Huba, & Bentler, 1981). The family conflict variable was measured through three items that asked about the frequency of arguments with mother and father (independently) and the degree to which family members fight, argue, or disagree with each other (Aseltine et al., 2000, p. 260). The peer conflict variable measured how often peers criticize the respondent, make demands on him/her, and create tensions or arguments while the respondent is around them.

The anger variable was measured by the hostility subscale of the Symptom Checklist-90 (Alpha=.85). Participants recorded, in a Likert scale format, how distressed they were over the past month given the following: "frequent arguments; uncontrollable outbursts of temper; urges to beat or harm someone; urges to break things; or shouting or throwing things" (Aseltine et al., 2000, p. 260). The anxiety variable was also derived from the Symptom Checklist-90 (Alpha=.84). This variable was measured by the frequency of a "feeling of annoyance and irritation, nervousness, or tension experienced during the past month" (Aseltine et al., 2000, p. 260). In addition to these variables, personal resources and social context measures are used to test for conditional associations between strain and delinquency. These measures include variables such as: mastery, family attachment, self-esteem, and exposure to delinquent peers (Aseltine et al., 2000). The exposure to delinquent peers measure consisted of the peers' own self-reports of aggressive behavior, nonviolent delinquency, and marijuana use over the past year. The respondents had to list names of their friends in school and then the names were matched to other respondents' surveys in the sample.

The delinquency and drug use measures used in this study were adapted from "Monitoring the Future" studies of Bachman, Johnston, and O'Malley (1987). Their measure of nonaggressive delinquency included items such as: "stealing or trying to steal things, including shoplifting; running away; driving while impaired; and joyriding or taking a car without permission" (Aseltine et al., 2000, p. 260). Aggressive delinquency was measured through self-reporting of the following items: "purposely damaging property, carrying a hidden weapon, and getting into physical fights" (Aseltine et al., 2000, p. 260). For each delinquency measure a summary index was created of the number of times each type of offense was committed during the past year. Lastly, the drug use indicator was represented by the frequency of marijuana use in the past year.

Support was found for the first hypothesis, which asked the question, is exposure to stresses and relationship strains positively associated with deviant conduct. The total effects of stressful life events on all three measures of deviance were positive and statistically significant (Aseltine et al., 2000). Qualified support was found for the second hypothesis; there was a significant relationship between family conflict and aggression that was mediated by anger. Of the conditional effects of strain on delinquency, one of the findings suggests that the occurrence of stressful life events in the context of high levels of peer delinquency does not predict delinquency (b=.010, SE=.036) while such stresses are strongly associated with delinquency among those with more conventional peers (b=.072, SE=.018) (Aseltine et al., 2000). Although contradictory to what Agnew's GST would predict, this finding is similar to that reported by Paternoster and Mazerolle (1994).

Mazerolle et al. (2000) examined whether strain has direct or indirect effects on three types of delinquent outcomes: violence, drug use, and school-related deviance. Moreover, their study included an anger scale to determine the extent to which anger mediates the effect of strain on delinquent involvement. Their study incorporates GST measures stemming only from exposure to noxious stimuli and the loss of positively valued stimuli types of strain. These measures were then combined into an overall strain index (Mazerolle et al., 2000). Anger was operationalized by asking respondents to answer five items (see Brezina, 1996) which comprised the anger scale (Alpha=.73). The delinquency scales were taken from the National Youth Survey (Elliot, Huizinga, & Ageton, 1985; Elliot, Huizinga, & Menard, 1989), which delineated violent delinquent behaviors, drug-using behaviors, and school related deviance. Finally, this study also controlled for elements of social control theory (Hirschi, 1969) and measures from differential association (Akers et al., 1979; Burkett & Jensen, 1975).

The researchers gave the self-administered Youth Lifestyle Survey to high school students (N= 263) in the spring of 1991 in a large, metropolitan area in the Midwestern United States. The demographic composition of the sample indicated that 85 percent were from middle to upper class households, the average age of the participants was 16.4 years, 52% percent were female and 86 percent of the students were White.

Mazerolle et al. (2000) found that strain has direct (i.e., independent) effects on violence while controlling for other variables. However, exposure to strain was not related to illicit drug use or school-related deviance independently (Mazerolle et al., 2000). GST has a significant effect on self-reported violent behavior among adolescents (b=.230, p< .001). Anger was also significantly related to violent delinquency among adolescents (b=.132, p <.05). The last model included predictors for all theoretical and demographic variables including anger; violence was significantly related to exposure to strain (b=1.63, p < .05), deviant affiliations (b=.173, p <.05), and being male (b=.195, p < .05) (Mazerolle et al., 2000). These results are consistent with the research that youth with high levels of anger disproportionately experience and/or perceive strainful circumstances that can lead to violence.

The limitations associated with this study concern the cross-sectional design of the survey, the sample of adolescents, and the measures used in the analysis. Due to the cross-sectional design of the study, the relationships between strain and delinquency may have been unclear (Mazerolle & Piquero, 1998). The sample selected for this study was comprised of individuals who were predominantly from higher socio-economic backgrounds, which may reflect lower levels of strain and anger, thus a low-risk sample. The measures themselves were limited. The measure of GST did not include all the experiences of strain that adolescents are exposed to; it did not include the failure to achieve positively valued goals. Although the debate still exists concerning the measurement of anger in relation to strain theory (i.e., situational versus trait anger), this study only used trait anger as its measure of the negative emotion (see Mazerolle & Piquero, 1998).

A study conducted by Baron (2004) suggested that strain was a significant indicator of criminal behavior, especially it interacted with conditioning variables. Baron (2004, p. 457) examined the role of strain (e.g., as evidenced by emotional abuse, physical abuse, sexual abuse, homelessness, relative deprivation, monetary dissatisfaction, unemployment and victimization) as it lead to crime and drug use among homeless street youth. He also investigated the role of anger and conditioning variables (e.g., deviant peers, deviant attitudes, external attributions, self-esteem, and self-efficacy). Six (emotional abuse, physical abuse, sexual abuse, violent victimization, relative deprivation, and monetary dissatisfaction) of the ten types of strain had a significant relationship with anger. It is important to note that Baron (2004) used a trait measure of anger as opposed to a situational measure of anger. Baron (2004) also tested the above model while controlling for gage and gender; this revealed that violent victimization and emotional abuse to be the only significant predictors of anger. The conditioning variables of deviant peers and deviant attitudes were also related to the total crime dependent variable (Baron, 2004).

Role of Anger Expanded

Mazerolle and Piquero (1998) conducted a partial empirical test of GST that examined the mediating effects of anger as well as the possible instrumental, escapist, and violent adaptations to strain. They found partial support for GST, but only for models predicting intentions to fight. Although the results from their analysis did not provide support for the deviant outcomes that stem from the presentation of negative stimuli and the removal of positively valued stimuli, some support was garnered for the effects of anger on deviant outcomes (Mazerolle & Piquero, 1998). More specifically, measures of anger (b=.290, p< .05) and feelings of injustice (b=.540, p< .05) were significantly related to intentions to engage in violent behavior (i.e., fighting) while controlling for other variables (Mazerolle & Piquero, 1998).

Their study was unlike previous tests of GST, in that a measure for anger was included. Furthermore, each type of strain was used in this study: the failure to achieve positively valued goals, the removal of positively valued stimuli, and the presentation of negative stimuli. The remaining items consisted of measures for anger, offense-specific questions, moral beliefs, deviant peer exposure, and scenario based questions (Mazerolle & Piquero, 1998). The measure for anger was represented by the temper component of the Grasmick et al. scale (1993). A scenario methodology also was used to elicit responses from all participants about drinking and driving behaviors (N=429), from females about shoplifting behaviors (N=186), and from males about fighting behaviors (N=249). These finding are based on a sample of undergraduate students in introductory criminology courses at a major mid-Atlantic university in the fall of 1994 who completed a questionnaire. The students enrolled in the courses represented a "fairly broad sample of students across the entire university" (Mazerolle & Piquero, 1998, p. 198).

In regard to the gender variable, they found that gender had a significant and positive effect on anger, revealing that females had a higher likelihood than males to report anger while controlling for various types of strain (Mazerolle & Piquero, 1998). Although this finding contradicts expectations about the gendered nature of anger, it is consistent with the research (Mirowsky & Ross, 1995; Thomas, 1993) on the gender and anger relationship.

The Mazerolle and Piquero (1998) study is not without its limitations, which include measurement and sampling issues. The measurement issue concerns the conceptual and empirical overlap of the sources of strain, most notably the removal of positive stimuli and the presentation of negative stimuli as independent categories for GST (Mazerolle & Piquero, 1998). Although Agnew (1992) discusses the difficulty in separating these sources of strain, Mazerolle and Piquero (1998) constructed a composite score to account for this and then used factor analysis on the scale. Another limitation surrounds the measure for anger. This study measured anger as a "static indicator," which may only be partially related to "the more dynamic focus of GST" (Mazerolle & Piquero, 1998, p. 208). There is a debate as to whether the anger variable represented disposition or situation induced anger. The sampling issue lies with the use of college students. Although social science research has traditionally used college students, college students may not reflect a strained group of individuals.

Similar to the Mazerolle and Piquero study (1998), Capowich, Mazerolle, and Piquero (2001) assessed general strain theory in the context of situational anger and social influences. Specifically, this study has expanded the role of anger to examine anger arising from given situations, as opposed to trait anger (Capowich et al., 2001). Situational anger refers to anger derived from certain circumstances, whereas trait anger refers to a dispositional or general state of anger. This study has also addressed an important, yet virtually ignored component to Agnew's strain theory, which investigates the role of social support networks and its potential influence on criminal adaptations to strain. Social support systems include individuals' personal relationships as well as other mechanisms that provide support to the individuals.

In order to test GST, the roles of anger and social support networks, Capowich et al. (2001) collected data from undergraduate students (N=315) at a large Western university in April and May 1997. The dependent variable focused on the intentions to commit crime. Specifically, the respondents were asked to react to three scenarios (i.e., fighting/assault, theft, and driving under the influence of alcohol) in which they estimated the likelihood that they would react the same way as the protagonist in the scenario (Capowich et al., 2001, see p. 457). The independent variables included a composite measure of Agnew's strain, negative emotions, anger, social support, perception of social support, and immediate social support. The strain subscale included the three sources of strain (i.e., failure to achieve positively valued goals, presentation of negative stimuli, and removal of positive stimuli). It is important to note that the items concerning strain were purposely geared to common events experienced by college students (Capowich et al., 2001). Because the strain questions were dichotomous in nature (e.g., yes/no, response format), the reliability analysis was somewhat low (.58).

In addition to the strain items, the role of anger was also delineated into situational anger and trait anger. Although dispositional anger (e.g., Brezina, 1996, p. 42-44) is an important concept to the theory, the theory is more consistent with situational (or state) anger (Agnew,

1992, p. 58-59). The role of anger was measured through the use of scenarios (see Capowich et al., 2001, p. 457), where the respondent had to note his/her level of anger associated with the situation. The role of support was also measured in this study. Support was measured in terms of social support, perception of support, and immediate support (Capowich et al., 2001). Lastly, the control variables consisted of the respondent's prior behavior, moral beliefs, peer criminal activities, and gender.

In relation to the dependent variable (i.e., fighting), the results of their analysis suggest that individuals reporting a greater number of strainful events in the past year (b=.088) were more likely to report a higher intention to fight, which is consistent with GST (Capowich et al., 2001). Furthermore, their analysis found that negative emotions produced a significant and positive effect on intentions to fight. At the same time, situational anger arising from the fighting scenario had a significant and positive effect on intentions to fight; therefore, demonstrating the importance of situational anger (R^2=.267) in relation to the GST framework (Capowich et al., 2001). With their last model, they added control variables thought to be related to predicting criminal behavior. Specifically, they found that males with previous fighting experience, and individuals who had knowledge of their peers' involvement in fighting were significantly more likely to report intentions to fight (Capowich et al., 2001). Consistent with model 3 and GST, situational anger retained its positive and significant effect on intentions to fight.

Although this research included integral components of GST that have been otherwise ignored in the empirical literature, this study has limitations. One of the main limitations is that the survey was used with a college sample. Although there are advantages and disadvantages to using college samples, for this particular study the researchers (Capowich et al., 2001, p. 449) noted that the sample "…was not representative of the larger population, [as] college students might have relatively low levels of stress and strain compared to other segments in society, and they enjoyed a relatively high level of support." The researchers follow up this argument contending that:

> College is a stressful time in a person's development because it is a time when young people begin spending extended periods of time away from home, making new friends,

experimenting with their independence, and experiencing the highs and lows of adult personal relationships (Capowich et al., 2001, p. 449).

In this context, an undergraduate college sample may be an acceptable sample due to the types of strain that they may experience.

Because the role of anger is an important theoretical component to GST, Mazerolle, Piquero, and Capowich (2003) expanded on the earlier studies to examine the links between strain, situational and dispositional anger, and delinquent outcomes. Situational anger, also referred to as state anger, refers to anger that is evoked due to a specific circumstance. Dispositional anger, also known as trait anger, reflects a relatively stable characteristic of an individual. According to GST, when anger occurs in response to strain, the possibility of a delinquent adaptation increases. Therefore, with structural equation modeling, they examined "whether individuals with high levels of trait anger have an increased likelihood of experiencing strain, becoming angry due to strain, and responding with deviance, net of controls" (Mazerolle et al., 2003, p. 5).

Mazerolle et al. (2003) examined GST in relation to both situational and dispositional anger in their study. GST was measured through two strain indicators: one consisted of a composite score of negative life events while the other indicator included questions concerning inequitable experiences at school (i.e., disjunction between just and fair outcomes versus actual outcomes). Anger was measured with respect to both situational and trait anger measures. The dependent variables for this study include scenarios geared to illicit behavioral intentions related to intentions to commit crime, namely, assault and shoplifting (Mazerolle et al., 2003). The control variables included respondent's prior behavior, moral beliefs, gender, and peer criminal activities. Questionnaires were distributed to a random sample (N=338) of undergraduate students at a large university in the United States during the spring semester of 1997.

Results from the models predicting intentions to assault suggest that strain (e.g., experiencing inequitable situations) and situational anger were predictive of intentions to assault independent of controls (Mazerolle et al., 2003). Specifically, males and individuals experiencing inequitable experiences at school have an increased probability of intentions to assault. Furthermore, situational anger had the strongest impact on the model; the explained variance in the model increased from .10 to .32 (Mazerolle et al., 2003). In predicting intentions to assault, Mazerolle et al. (2003, p. 24) found that "situational anger, strain arising from experiencing inequitable events, dispositional anger, sex, prior assault, weak moral beliefs against assault, and being exposed to peers who assault exhibit significant effects. Among the significant relationships, the largest effect was observed for situational anger."

Although trait anger was a salient influence predicting intentions to assault, it did not appear to mediate the effects of strain. Conversely, situational anger did mediate, at least partially, the effect of strain on intentions to assault (Mazerolle et al., 2003). Consistent with GST, the findings show that some measures of strain are associated with situational anger; however, the results also suggest that dispositional anger is predictive of situational anger.

GST is explicit in discussing the role of anger for the theory: negative emotional states, namely anger, are expected to increase as a response to strain (i.e., in the absence of coping mechanisms) and is expected to increase the likelihood of a delinquent outcome (Agnew, 1992). However, as illustrated in the literature, many studies used a trait measure of anger in the GST model. Although some studies identified the state-trait anger debate, a study conducted by Broidy (2001) represents the first attempt to examine whether trait and situational anger behave in similar or different ways in the strain, anger, deviant outcome relationship (Mazerolle et al., 2003).

Role of Anger Coupled with Coping Mechanisms

Broidy (2001) was one of the first researchers to address the roles of anger and coping mechanisms in the strain model. Broidy (2001) conducted a test of GST with a nonrandom sample (N=896) of undergraduate students at a Northwestern University. Using a self-report survey, three hypotheses addressed the following: each of the three types of strain are associated with anger and other negative emotions, anger and other negative emotional responses to strain are each associated with the use of legitimate coping strategies, and controlling for the use of legitimate coping, strain-induced anger will increase the likelihood of illegitimate outcomes (Broidy, 2001).

In order to measure strain, items were designed to tap into the failure to achieve positively valued goals (i.e., success and fairness of goals, goal blockage), and the loss of positively valued stimuli, and presentation of negative stimuli were measured by a list of 21 stressful life events. Negative emotions were assessed through questions asking the respondent how he/she feels when he/she cannot reach his/her goals and in response to negative life events (Broidy, 2001). The legitimate and illegitimate coping strategies were also measured. The legitimate coping mechanism was measured through responses to a checklist of ways that respondents behave when confronted with goal blockage and stressful life events (Broidy, 2001). The illegitimate or criminal outcomes were derived from questions concerning the respondent's involvement in deviant behavior (e.g., stealing something worth $10 or less, selling marijuana or other illegal drugs) over the past five years. Lastly, the control variables included questions related to demographic variables, personality, and social influences. Some controls consisted of self-esteem, peer involvement in delinquency, deviant opportunities, and membership in clubs (Broidy, 2001).

The results of the study offer some support for GST (see Broidy, 2001 for a summary of results). Consistent with strain theory, these results indicate that strain is associated with anger and other negative emotions. However, the results differ by type of strain and by type of negative emotion (Broidy, 2001). "Lack of fairness in goal outcomes and stressful life events increase the likelihood that individuals respond to strain with anger, whereas blocked goals reduce the likelihood of anger in response to strain" (Broidy, 2001, p. 29). The results also suggest that unfair outcomes and stress have significant positive effects on anger, and blocked goals have a significant negative effect on anger (Broidy, 2001). Furthermore, the findings suggest that anger has a significant positive effect on crime. The results also suggest that strain-induced anger significantly increases the likelihood of criminal outcomes. On the other hand, it was found that anger is unrelated to the likelihood of legitimate coping, which is not consistent with GST (Broidy, 2001).

The limitations of this study focus on the cross-sectional design with a homogeneous college sample. This does not allow for firm conclusions concerning the causal relationships among the variables examined. Furthermore, the data fail to provide measures of the success or availability of legitimate coping mechanisms (Broidy, 2001).

Sharp, Terling-Watt, Atkins, and Gilliam (2001) pilot tested GST with a sample of college students. Their research examines GST's role in explaining the purging behavior (i.e., eating disorder) of female college students as mediated by anger and depression (Sharp et al., 2001). The sample (N=96) included college women who were recruited via flyers requesting participation; researchers describing the study in general education classes and requesting participation; and through recruiting respondents from two sororities and two dormitories. It was argued that college students, as a result of frustration due to new environments, social uncertainty, and reduced external social control, may face increased strain, leading to negative affective states (Sharp et al., 2001). Of the sample, 86 percent were white, 88 percent were single, and the mean age of the participant was 21.02 years.

The GST measure consisted of a number of potential sources of strain including negative life events (see Turner, Wheaton, & Lloyd, 1995 and Agnew & White, 1992 for sources of the questions). The dependent variable of purging behavior was measured by two questions in which the response categories elicited ordinal level data (Sharp et al., 2001). Two mediating variables were included in the model: Anger and Depression. Anger was measured by the sum of the participant's responses on two items, and depression was measured by the participant's additive score on the CESD-11. They found that of the strain variables (negative life events, goals, parental hostility, unattractiveness, and fairness) only one variable (the goals) had a significant direct relationship with the strain and purging behavior (Sharp et al., 2001).

In terms of the mediating variables (Anger and Depression), if taken separately, both were positively associated with purging behavior. However, when the variables are taken collectively, only depression (high levels of depression) remained significant (Sharp et al., 2001). This is the opposite of the relationship between anger and delinquency that Agnew and White (1992) found. According to Agnew and White (1992), anger would be associated with delinquency only when depression was low. These findings must be noted with further caution as the sample size was small, excluded men, and was mostly comprised of white college students.

GST and Gender

Because strain theory is an extension of the stress and psychological literature, it is important to grasp an understanding of the role of gender in terms of how adolescents react to stressful situations. As noted in the stress literature (Aneshensel, 1992; Kessler & McLeod, 1984), males and female react to stress in diverse ways. Females tend to internalize reactions to stress and males tend to externalize. For example, females who experience stress are more likely to become depressed or withdrawn, yet males tend to become more aggressive, get involved in delinquency, and/or use drugs (Hoffmann & Su, 1997).

Leadbeater, Blatt, and Quinlan (1995) proposed two theoretical models to explain the relationship between stressful events and adolescent behavior. The interpersonal model (Leadbeater et al., 1995) examines adolescents with acute sensitivity to interpersonal relations (i.e., concerned with affection from others, fear of abandonment, desire for attachment, difficulty expressing anger) and their ability to react to stress through destructive behavior. On the other hand, the individualistic model focuses on adolescents who are sensitive to negative reaction from others and tend to use anger to avert criticism (Leadbeater et al., 1995). These adolescents are more likely to engage in delinquency and aggressive behaviors toward others. Leadbeater et al. (1995) contend that the interpersonal model is more likely to apply to female adolescents and the individualistic model is more likely to apply to male adolescents. Support has been found for the Leadbeater et al. contention (Archer, 1989; Chodorow, 1989), yet other studies have found that male and female adolescents react similarly to stressful events in terms of externalizing and internalizing behaviors (Attar, Guerra, & Tolan, 1994).

Upon outlining the sex-distinct patterns of stress reactions, Hoffmann and Su (1997) examined the role of gender in relation to Agnew's general strain theory (Agnew, 1992). Using data from the High Risk Youth Study (1992-1994), they conducted a longitudinal study to evaluate how parental factors (i.e., substance abuse and affective disorder) impact adolescent substance use, deviant behavior, and mental health (Hoffmann & Su, 1997). Their prospective cohort design identified parents who had the above factors as well as parents who were not diagnosed with the above factors. They recruited parents from mental health clinics in the Midwest United States, who had at least one child between the ages of 10-13, and who lived in the same home (Hoffmann & Su, 1997). The control group was comprised of families recruited from outpatient clinics at the same medical center, community advertisements, and sites where adolescents are likely to be found (e.g., YMCA). A total of 601 families with 861 children and adolescents agreed to participate.

The researchers administered the Structured Clinical Interview from the DSM-IIIR (Spitzer, Williams, Gibbon, & First, 1990a, 1990b as cited by Hoffman & Su, 1997) and the Family History Questionnaires to the participants. Using these assessment tools, there were 321 psychiatrically impaired families (representing 452 adolescents) and 280 nonpsychiatrically impaired families. Due to some cases that were excluded for various reasons, the final sample size (N=803) was 393 females and 410 males (Hoffmann & Su, 1997). The participants were then assessed in terms of school behavior, grades, and delinquency measures. The delinquency outcome variable was measured by two scales; one scale measured violent offenses and the other measured property offenses. The second outcome variable measures drug use (i.e., drug and alcohol use).

The results of a structural equation model suggested "that there are few important sex differences; stressful life events have a similar, short-term impact on delinquency and drug use among females and males" (Hoffmann & Su, 1997, p. 46). Using LISEREL, the authors tested the null hypothesis that there were no differences between males and females in the stress delinquency model. Contrary to the hypotheses that there will be sex differences in delinquency, there were no differences in the model (Hoffmann & Su, 1997). With regard to gender, the same held true for the stressful events and drug use model. In other words, stressful life events among males and females were similarly associated with delinquency and drug use (Hoffmann & Su, 1997).

Although there are limitations associated with this study, it offers alternative explanations as to why these results occurred. First, although the data on delinquency and drug use fail to support the interpersonal and individualistic models, these models have been useful in predicting depression and affective disturbances. Second, sex-distinct patterns may not fully be developed until late adolescence, yet the study did not run an analysis on only older adolescents. At the same time, socialization processes of both males and females are becoming more "sex-neutral"; therefore, adolescent behavior patterns are becoming more similar (Hoffmann & Su, 1997, p. 70). Third, defining the stressful events may not have been as precise as needed. Lastly, Agnew (1992) discusses anger as a mediating variable in the general strain model; as such, if anger is generalized among both males and females who experience similar levels of stress, then there should be little differentiation in levels of delinquency (Hoffmann & Su, 1997).

Although the above authors found no support for gender differences in Agnew's strain theory in relation to delinquency and drug use, Broidy and Agnew (1997, p. 276) contend that "GST is in a good position to exploit the observation that females suffer from a range of oppressive conditions and that this oppression is at the root of their crime." GST considers different types of strain, such as goal blockage, the loss of positive stimuli (e.g., loss of friends and romantic partners), and the presentation of negative stimuli (e.g., excessive demands, and verbal/sexual/physical abuse). Certain data (Compas, 1987) suggest that females subjectively rate these strainful events as more stressful or undesirable than do males. Some stressors that have special relevance to women may include a wide variety of abuses (sexual, verbal, and physical) or aversive home and work environments.

Although differences in the amount of strain cannot explain gender differences in crime, differences in the type of strain may be helpful in explaining differences in offending patterns. In terms of the failure to achieve positively valued goals, men and women appear to have different conceptions of goals. Several strain and feminist theorists have argued that "males are most concerned with material success and extrinsic achievements, whereas females are more concerned with the establishment and maintenance of close relationships and with meaning/purpose in life" (Cohen, 1955; Lyons & Hammer, 1989 as cited by Broidy & Agnew, 1997). These arguments are also substantiated in the stress literature. Therefore, males and females may have distinctive goals. In terms of perceptions of fairness and equity, men and women may also differ. Men are more likely to emphasize distributive justice (fairness of the outcomes) while women are more concerned with procedural justice (fairness in the procedure used to derive the outcome) (Broidy & Agnew, 1997).

With respect to the loss of positive stimuli and the presentation of negative stimuli, gender differences may also exist. For example, "females are more likely to report gender-based discrimination, low prestige in work and family roles, excessive demands from family members, and restrictions on their behavior...which confines them to the 'private sphere'" (Campbell, 1984; Gove, 1978; Mirowsky & Ross, 1989; Thoits, 1991 as cited by Broidy & Agnew, 1997). Males are more likely to experience financial stress and strain with peers by means of competition and jealousy (Broidy & Agnew, 1997). Gender differences also occur with respect to interpersonal conflicts and victimizations. Data suggest that interpersonal conflicts/victimizations are especially upsetting and that they play a central role in violent crime (Luckenbill, 1977). It may be difficult for a woman "to engage in serious violent crime if she spends little time in public, feels responsible for children and others, or is under pressure to avoid behaving in an aggressive manner" (Broidy & Agnew, 1997, p. 280).

Broidy and Agnew's (1997) research attempts to explain the gender differences in types of strain. Their study applied GST to the fundamental questions (1) how to explain the higher rate of crime among males and (2) how to explain why females engage in crime (Broidy & Agnew, 1997). They contend then GST cannot explain the higher rate of male crime by arguing that males experience more strain than do females. At the same time, they argue that GST might explain gender differences in crime. Their argument focuses on the different types of strain experienced, the emotional responses to strain, and the differences in coping strategies (Broidy & Agnew, 1997).

First, males experience strain that is more conducive to serious violent and property crimes, whereas females experience strain that is conducive to family violence or more self-directed forms of crime (e.g., drug use) (Broidy & Agnew, 1997). Second, although both men and women may experience anger in response to strain, women are more likely to experience depression, guilt and anxiety coupled with their anger, which reduces the likelihood of aggressive or confrontational crimes yet increases the likelihood of self-destructive and escapist offenses. Last, "males may be more likely to respond to a given level of strain or anger with serious property and violent crime because of differences in coping, social support, opportunities, social control, and the disposition to engage in crime" (Broidy & Agnew, 1997, p. 287).

Broidy and Agnew (1997) further purport that GST is well suited to explain female crime. Drawing from feminist literature, GST contends that oppressed individuals will attempt to reduce their strain or manage the negative emotions associated with it by resorting to crime. Females tend to have goals that emphasize close interpersonal ties with others, and more recently, are encouraged to strive for similar educational and occupational goals as males (Broidy & Agnew, 1997). Yet at the same time, these goals may be problematic for women, given high divorce rates, abusive relationships, and structural impediments. Furthermore, women have been increasingly confronted with financial strain, and for some women the disjunction between their actual and expected financial situation plays a central role in their crime (Box, 1993; Box & Hale, 1983; Chesney-Lind & Sheldon, 1992 as cited by Broidy & Agnew, 1997).

The last two types of strain also have special relevance to females. Data indicate that females are more likely to be affected by loss of positively valued stimuli (e.g., loss of family member and friend through death or divorce) than males (Kessler & McLeod, 1984). Females often are prevented or discouraged from engaging in a wide range of behaviors they may value (Broidy & Agnew, 1997). Lastly, data suggest that "females are often subject to varying types of abuse by family members and others, including emotional, physical, and sexual abuse; thus females are subject to many types of negative treatment" (Broidy & Agnew, 1997). Several researchers have commented on the association between female victimization and female crime (Chesney-Lind & Sheldon, 1992; Daly, 1992). However, it is important to note that these strains do not affect all women equally, and it is suggested that those women who experience the most strain would also be highest in crime (Broidy & Agnew, 1997).

Given the above arguments and their foundations in the psychological and stress literature, Agnew's GST has been applied to female crime as well as taken gender into consideration with respect to coping mechanisms. Although the above comments and research have rendered some support, it is necessary to continue to empirically test GST in relation to gender differences. This study will take gender into consideration when assessing the strain and road rage relationship.

Coping Mechanisms: Peer Influences and Self-Control

According to GST, a relationship exists between strain and crime/delinquency, yet there are certain conditioning influences that exist which may mediate these effects. Agnew (1992) suggests that both internal and external factors affect the emotional impact of strain as well as shape individuals' coping mechanisms. These mechanisms include both personal resources and social resources. Examples of personal resources are temperament, intelligence, and self-esteem, whereas examples of social support include peers and neighborhood resources (Broidy, 2001). However, the repertoire of coping mechanisms at individuals' disposal may include both delinquent and nondelinquent adaptations (Agnew, 1992).

Agnew (1992) has suggested that delinquent adaptations to strain are more likely to be acted upon for those with predispositions to engage in delinquency because of "certain temperamental variables" (perhaps self-control; see Gottfredson & Hirschi 1990) and those with delinquent peers. Agnew (1992), Agnew and White (1992), and Capowich et al. (2001) further contend that only some strained individuals turn to delinquent adaptations, citing that individuals may also be affected by factors such as: the availability of delinquent peers, the strength of moral inhibitions, their level of self-control (delinquent disposition), coping resources, and conventional social support. There is some evidence to suggest that strain may increase the social bond with delinquent peers as well as facilitate flight to delinquent peers (Paternoster & Mazerolle, 1994). Agnew (1992) argues that the relationship between strain and deviant behavior is conditioned by a youth's personal and social resources as well as peer contexts; therefore, the role of delinquent peers may be a conditional factor in the youth's delinquent adaptation to strain.

Peers as a Coping Mechanism

According to Sutherland's theory of differential association, the source of crime and delinquency lies in the intimate social networks of individuals (Warr, 1993). A proposition central to differential association theory is that being in the company of delinquent peers facilitates delinquency directly, without necessarily affecting one's definitions or values relative to delinquency (Johnson et al., 1987). As such, it is argued that individuals who are "selectively or differentially exposed to delinquent associates are likely to acquire that trait as well" (Warr, 1993, p. 18). Tests of differential association theory have examined the correlation between self-reported delinquency and the number of delinquent friends reported by adolescents. There is extant evidence to substantiate that participation in a deviant peer group increases an individual's likelihood of committing delinquent acts (Akers, Krohn, Lanza-Kanduce, & Radosevich, 1979; Elliott, Huizinga & Ageton, 1985; Jessor & Jessor, 1977; Mears, Ploeger, & Warr, 1998; Warr, 1993). Therefore, research suggests that deviant associates and engaging in deviant behavior are linked.

Generally research has demonstrated that peer groups can either control or encourage criminal behavior; at the same time, this is dependent upon the group's characteristics as well as the individual's relationship with the group (Agnew & Brezina, 1997; Giordano et al., 1986). According to research by Agnew and White (1992), the cross-sectional effect of stress on delinquency and drug use is most acute for adolescents with a greater number of delinquent peers, and its effect on delinquency is accentuated when self-efficacy is low. Agnew and White (1992, p. 489) further suggest that "social support may encourage delinquency when an individual is part of a delinquent/deviant network of peers." Conversely, others (Cullen & Wright, 1997) contend that individuals have the power in insulate themselves from deviant adaptations even if they are part of a delinquent peer group. Thus, differential associations with peers may be associated with producing deviant behavior (Johnson, Marcos, & Bahr, 1987).

Given that peers may influence an individual's behavior in either a positive or negative fashion, it is important to examine the role that peers play in mediating strain. Consistent with Agnew and White's (1992) approach to measuring differential associations with peers and family members, the present study requires respondents to identify their closest friend and report the aggressive driving behaviors that they have engaged in. Not only is the relationship among peers an important dynamic to identify but also the quality and strength of the relationship among these peers should be examined.

Self-Control as a Coping Mechanism
GST predicts that many factors condition the effects of strain on deviant outcomes, some of which include the importance attached to

goals, values, or identities that are threatened; coping skills and coping resources (e.g., money, self-esteem, self-efficacy); conventional social supports; level of social control; and association with delinquent peers (Agnew et al., 2002). GST also maintains that certain factors affect one's disposition toward deviant responses. As such, Agnew's GST (1992) specifically holds that an individual's temperament (e.g., level of self-control) may act as a coping mechanism for whether an individual would be able to cope with his/her strain effectively. For example, individuals low in self-control may not possess the social skills necessary for effective interaction with others, since they may not be as well socialized as others (Agnew & Brezina, 1997). Furthermore, individuals with low levels of self-control have fewer restraints on their behavior, allowing for the likelihood of their acting in ways that antagonize others (Angew & Brezina, 1997).

Agnew, Brezina, Wright, and Cullen (2002) further argue that low self-control may condition the impact of strain on delinquency for many reasons; one of which is because it may reduce the ability of individuals to restrain themselves from acting on their immediate impulses and desires, including those of a delinquent nature. Agnew et al. (2002, p. 48) contend that the traits that comprise low self-control "increase the likelihood that individuals will react to strain with strong negative emotions, will have trouble coping with such strain through legitimate channels, and will find crime an attractive option." As a result, one's level of self-control is integral to the likelihood of the person committing a deviant act.

According to Gottfredson and Hirschi (1990, p. 87) self-control is conceptualized as "the differential tendency of people to avoid criminal acts whatever the circumstances in which they find themselves." Gottfredson and Hirschi (1990, p. 90) describe individuals who have low self-control as "impulsive, insensitive, physical (as opposed to mental), risk-taking, short-sighted, and nonverbal." In sum, individuals exhibiting low levels of self-control tend to engage in activities that provide excitement and provide simple and immediate gratification of desires. These characteristics are congruent with underlying attributes of criminal and deviant behaviors. Gottfredson and Hirschi maintain that crime does not require "planning or skill" and that most crimes are "mundane, simple, trivial, easy acts aimed at satisfying desires of the moment" (1990, p. xv). Thus, people who have low self-control have personalities predisposing them toward committing criminal acts.

Those with low levels of self-control are more likely to commit crime and are more likely to be unsuccessful in school, the labor force, and marriage (Grasmick et al., 1993).

Because it is believed that individuals have little control over their actions, external controls are put in place to restrain individuals' levels of self-control. When these desires conflict with long-term interests, those lacking self-control opt for the desires of the moment, whereas those with greater self-control are governed by the restraints imposed by the consequences of acts displeasing to family, friends, and the law (Gottfredson & Hirschi, 1990, p. xv).

Consequently, the characteristics associated with high levels of self-control are related to delayed gratification, tenacity, cautiousness, long-term goals, and planning (Gottfredson & Hirschi, 1990). These attributes are related to individuals' levels of self-restraint and available external controls, and are not thought to be associated with criminal or deviant behaviors. Lastly, Gottfredson and Hirschi (1990, pp. 89, 96) acknowledge that "situational conditions" and "other properties of the individuals can counteract the causal effects of low self-control," but also they claim "high self-control effectively reduces the possibility of crime."

The research on self-control has suggested that individuals who exhibit low levels of self-control are more likely to engage in "analogous behaviors" or crime equivalents. On the other hand, individuals who have high levels of self-control are less likely to engage in analogous behaviors or crime equivalents. Analogous behaviors refer to behaviors that may be viewed as "deviant" conduct (e.g., accidents, smoking, excessive drinking, driving fast, gambling, unprotected sexual relationships). There are "analogous" to crime because these activities are also gratifying (Pratt & Cullen, 2000). Gottfredson and Hirschi (1990) contend that individuals who commit crimes also tend to commit analogous behavior, engage in deviant conduct, and participate in activities that provide easy and immediate gratification.

In relation to an individual's level of self-control, numerous empirical assessments of the theory have found that those with low self-control are comparatively more likely to commit criminal or imprudent acts (Arneklev, Grasmick, Tittle, & Bursik, 1993; Bartusch, Lynam, Moffitt, & Silva, 1997; Benson & Moore, 1992; Brownfield & Sorenson, 1993; Burton, Cullen, Evans, Alaird, & Dunaway, 1998;

Burton et al., 1994; Cernkovich & Giordano, 2001; Cochran, Wood, Sellers, Wilkerson, & Chamlin, 1998; Gibbs & Giever, 1995; Gibbs, Giever, & Martin, 1998; Grasmick et al., 1993; Keane, Maxim & Teevan, 1993; LaGrange & Silverman, 1999; Longshore, Turner, & Stein, 1996; Longshore, 1998; Longshore & Turner, 1998; Nagin & Paternoster, 1993; Polakowski, 1994; Paternoster & Brame, 1997; Paternoster & Brame, 1998; Piquero & Rosay, 1998; Piquero & Tibbetts, 1996; Pratt & Cullen, 2000; Sorenson & Brownfield, 1995; Tibbetts & Myers, 1999; Wood, Pfefferbaum, & Arneklev, 1993; Wright, Caspi, Moffitt, & Silva, 1999; Wright et al., 2001). Given the above studies, the empirical literature indicates that low self-control is a predictor of crime and deviance of at least moderate strength (for a meta-analysis, see Pratt & Cullen, 2000). Moreover, other studies suggest that self-control is consistent over time contending that the relationship between self-control and crime persists throughout the life span (Wright et al., 1999; 2001; Cernkovich & Giordano, 2001). Lastly, studies that have controlled for competing criminological theories, such as, strain, social bond, and differential association-social learning theories (Brownfield & Sorenson, 1993; Burton et al., 1994; Burton et al., 1998; Nagin & Paternoster, 1993; Piquero & Tibbetts, 1996; Polakowski, 1994) found that measures of low self-control have had statistically significant effects on crime and deviance.

Gottfredson and Hirschi's concept of self-control is not without its criticisms. One of the primary criticisms alleges that the theory is tautological. It has been noted that because crime is easy to commit, involves little planning, requires minimal physical skills, and provides immediate gratification, it is not surprising that offenders tend to be impulsive, nonverbal, and short-sighted (Akers, 1991). Furthermore, Gottfredson and Hirschi recommend that self-control theory should be measured preferably with behavioral scales comprising items measuring participation in analogous behaviors. Again, a tautology exists: "if analogous behaviors are caused by low self-control, how can they then be used to measure self-control" (Pratt & Cullen, 2000, p. 933).

In defense of the contention that Gottfredson and Hirschi's theory is a tautology, Pratt and Cullen (2000, p. 932) suggest that "as long as self-control and crime are measured independently and with valid measures, tautology in empirical tests will be avoided." Another rebuttal to the tautology argument is that "criminologists have made the opposite mistake: that of divorcing their understanding of criminals from their understanding of crime" (Pratt & Cullen, 2000, p. 932).

In sum, the strain research has suggested that an individual's level of strain may be mediated by the type of coping mechanism he/she has at his/her disposal, therefore, it is important to identify how an individual's level of self-control factors into one's strain threshold. As previously stated, Agnew (1992) noted that one's temperament or disposition is key to mediating effects of strain. As such, an individual's temperament (e.g., level of self-control) may act as a coping mechanism for whether an individual would be able to cope with his/her strain effectively. Because few studies have included the role of self-control as a coping mechanism in the strain model, this study will analyze the respondent's level of self-control and assess its viability in mediating strain. Consistent with past research on self-control, the present study will ask respondents questions concerning their level of self-control as per the Grasmick et al. (1993) scale.

As GST stipulates, individuals who experience strain are likely to also experience negative affective states, namely anger, which is the most critical emotional reaction (Agnew, 1992). Although many of the earlier studies included the role of anger (Aseltine et al., 2000; Brezina, 1996; Broidy, 2001; Capowich et al., 2001; Mazerolle & Piquero, 1997; Mazerolle & Piquero, 1998; Mazerolle et al., 2000), anger was measured as a trait characteristic. Upon further scrutiny of GST and its relationship with anger, it was thought that situational anger may be a better fit with the strain-anger relationship. Mazerolle and Piquero (1998) addressed this debate between trait and situational anger; however, it was not incorporated into their initial analysis. Although Broidy (2001) included a measure of anger contextualized to exposure to strain, Mazerolle, Piquero, and Capowich (2003) have delineated and analyzed anger (i.e., situational and dispositional) as well as coping mechanisms in their study.

GST acknowledges that only some strained individuals turn to delinquency and it also predicts that several factors condition the impact of strain on delinquency. Thus, if GST is to better explain delinquency, it must identify the factors that influence the reaction to strain (Agnew et al., 2002). For this reason both delinquent peers and an individual's level of self-control will be examined in this study. It is expected that individuals with many delinquent peers will be more likely to engage in road rage behaviors than those who do not have many delinquent peers. With respect to self-control, individuals with low levels of self-control are more likely to engage in road rage behavior than those with high levels of self-control.

Last, GST (Agnew, 1992) has garnered a fair amount of empirical support since its introduction (Agnew & Brezina, 1997; Agnew & White, 1992; Agnew et al., 2002; Aseltine et al., 2000; Brezina, 1998; Broidy, 2001; Cernovich et al., 2000; Hoffmann & Cerbone, 1999; Hoffmann & Su, 1997; Mazerolle & Piquero, 1997; Mazerolle et al., 2000; Mazerolle et al., 2003; Paternoster & Mazerolle, 1994). The present study aims to expand on these previous studies, yet this study is unique in that it incorporates the three sources of strain, examines the role of situational anger as a mediating variable, assesses dispositional anger as a control variable, and includes both peer relationships and self-control as coping mechanisms into the strain model for predicting road rage behaviors. Expanding on the recent strain studies, this study explores the role of anger, specifically, to assess the viability of situational anger measures as well as the dispositional measures of anger in the strain model. In addition to analyzing anger as a mediating variable, this research includes the role of coping mechanisms as mediators of strain and anger. Furthermore, this study uses an adult population as opposed to an adolescent population that the earlier studies have employed.

CHAPTER 4

An Analysis of Method

This study employed a quantitative approach, specifically a cross-sectional survey design was used. According to Babbie (1998), survey research is one of the best methods available for the goal of collecting original data for describing a population too large to observe directly. He further stated that the purpose of a survey is to generalize from a sample to a population so that inferences can be made about the attitudes, behaviors, or characteristics of the population (Babbie, 1990). Survey methods also act as a "search device" when studying a new topic, such as road rage (Babbie, 1990).

The reasons for using the survey method were four fold. First, the survey method allowed for the economy of the design. The ability to administer the questionnaire to groups of 30-45 students provided the opportunity for efficient administration. Using college students for long self-administered instruments, such as the questionnaire used in this study, was advantageous because they are literate and experienced in completing self-administered, self-report instruments. Therefore, it was reasonable to assume that this would improve the completion rate and reduce measurement error. Second, there was a rapid turn-around in the data collection process; this allowed the researcher to process large amounts of data in a relatively short period of time.

Third, surveys have proven to be useful in describing the characteristics of a large population (Babbie, 1998). In this study, the population consisted of college students in Western Pennsylvania. Fourth, standardized questionnaires allowed for strength in measurement and comparability of the data. The survey instrument consisted of closed ended questions, which allowed the researcher to compare answers given by students and examine answers between schools.

The survey instrument consisted of questions from various existing surveys as well as newly developed items. The questions adapted from the existing surveys included the strain measures (Capowich et al., 2001), road rage items from both the Driving Survey (Deffenbacher et al., 2001) and Total Aggression Expression (TAE) subscale of the Driving Anger Expression Inventory (DAX) (Deffenbacher et al., 2002), the self-control items (Grasmick et al., 1993) and the trait anger items (Spielberger, 1999). Once the questions were compiled, the resulting survey instrument was pre-tested with a group of students at the mid-sized university.

Given the results of the pretest, the survey was then self-administered to the undergraduate populations at both a mid-sized public university and small independent college. This was done to ensure that the survey was measuring the intended constructs. According to Babbie (1990), pre-testing is done as an initial check on one or more aspects of the research design, specifically, for this study, the survey questionnaire. The methodological purpose of pre-testing the instrument was to ascertain the applicability of particular (or all) questions contained within the instrument (Babbie, 1990); furthermore, the survey was pre-tested in the manner intended for the study. Based on the information obtained from the pre-test, the survey instrument was deemed appropriate for expanded use with the sample. Therefore, the primary mode of data collection involved the use of a questionnaire.

Research Questions and Hypotheses

Several research questions were designed to determine the extent of and variation in road rage behaviors as well as to assess the relationships among strain, anger, and coping mechanisms. The specific research questions follow:

(1) To what extent do college students participate in road rage?

(2) Is there a correlation between the Total Aggression Expression (TAE) subscale of the Driving Anger Expression Inventory and the Driving Survey?

(3) To what extent does a person's level of strain influence road rage?

(4) To what extent does strain have an effect on situational anger?

(5) Is anger a mediating variable in the strain model?

(6) To what extent is situational anger associated with coping mechanisms?

(7) To what extent do coping mechanisms (self-control and peer behaviors) mediate the effects of strain on road rage?

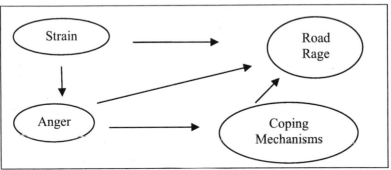

Figure 1. Research model.

Research Hypotheses

Once the research questions were delineated, corresponding hypotheses were devised. These hypotheses were used as steps toward answering the questions of the study. The first two hypotheses examined the extent of road rage among college students as well as examined the association between the two measures of the dependent variable (i.e., road rage). The remainder of the hypotheses focused on the relationships among the theoretical variables in the study (strain, anger, coping mechanisms, and road rage).

The first research question posited the hypothesis, "How much of a problem is road rage among college students?" Previous literature has noted that aggressive driving and road rage have been on the rise in recent years. The literature also noted that individuals between the ages of 18 and 26 were more likely to engage in road rage; therefore, a sample which include these ages may provide an inside look into road rage among students. However, it is not assumed that college students are more likely than other segments of society to engage in this type of behavior, but rather this population was chosen because it fits the age category in which prior research indicates a higher occurrence of acts. Furthermore, since there is no comparison group available, this hypothesis only attempted to ascertain the level of participation in aggressive driving and road rage among college students in Pennsylvania.

The second research question asked: "Is there a correlation between the Total Aggression Expression (TAE) subscale of the Driving Anger Expression Inventory and the Driving Survey? In the literature acts of aggressive driving and road rage have been reported to be on the increase; therefore, for this study it was necessary to determine the extent and nature of offending. In order to properly determine the extent, reliable data collection methods were needed. After researching the existing surveys, two scales were deemed appropriate and used. Given the domain of aggressive driving and road rage, these surveys provided similar yet somewhat diverse questions concerning the dependent variable. A high correlation between the two measures was expected due to the nature of the questions in the survey. The next five research questions have corresponding hypotheses, all of which were devised based on the review of the literature. These hypotheses focused on the role of strain, anger, coping mechanisms (self-control and peer behavior) and their potential effects. The literature suggests that strain increases the likelihood that individuals will experience a range of negative emotions, namely anger, yet this may be mediated by the coping mechanisms that the individual has at his/her disposal (Agnew, 1992). Therefore, in order to test the theoretical model (See Figure 1), each of these components was examined.

Given the third research question, the corresponding hypothesis included: "Individuals who experience higher levels of strain are more likely to experience higher levels of road rage." This hypothesis was necessary to determine if there is a direct effect from strain to road rage. As purported in past research Mazerolle and Piquero (1997), used data from a college-aged sample and found that their composite measure of strain was related to an increase in the participant's intention to engage in assaultive behaviors, while controlling for other predictors.

The fourth research question concerned the relationship between strain and situational anger. It posited this hypothesis, "Individuals who experience higher levels of strain are more likely to experience higher levels of situational anger." Past research (Capowich et al., 2001), which examined the role of strain and anger, noted that a link did exist between anger and crime. Therefore, this hypothesis notes if a connection or link exists between strain and situational anger. This hypothesis addressed the second path in the theoretical model put forth in the study.

The corresponding hypothesis for the fifth research question was: "Individuals who experience higher levels of situational anger are more likely to engage in road rage." As noted in the research (Agnew, 1992), individuals who experienced strain were likely to experience a negative affect, namely, anger. The earlier hypotheses were designed to determine the potential linkage between strain and the dependent variable as well as strain and situational anger. In order to test the theoretical model, the role of situational anger needed to be addressed in relation to the dependent variable, while accounting for strain and other control variables.

The sixth research question concerned the association between situational anger and the coping mechanisms. There were two corresponding hypotheses with this research question. The first hypothesis stated: "Individuals with high levels of situational anger are more likely to have low levels of self-control." The second hypothesis stated: "Individuals with high levels of situational anger are more likely to have close peers who have engaged in past road rage behaviors." These hypotheses were necessary to determine the linkage between the negative affect and the coping mechanisms. Agnew (1992) purported that even though a person may experience strain, which may give rise to a negative affect, people still may not succumb to a deviant adaptation. These hypotheses were devised to determine the association between situational anger and one's temperament (as evidenced by one's level of self-control) and also an external source (as evidenced by one's association with deviant peers). These hypotheses allow for the association to materialize if the associations are present in the model with this sample.

The corresponding hypothesis for the final research question was: "Individuals with higher levels of strain, higher levels of anger, low levels of self-control, and high levels of peer deviant behavior are more likely to engage in road rage." This hypothesis allowed for the final piece of evidence to test the theoretical model. It then provided a detailed interpretation of the full theoretical model with respect to road rage.

With regard to the last five research questions and their corresponding hypotheses, the full theoretical model materialized. Furthermore, the hypotheses used in building the model contained important control variables that further added to the analysis of the theory. In addition to these hypotheses testing the theoretical model, the literature suggests that demographic characteristics have been found to be significant indicators of driver aggression (AAA Foundation for Traffic Safety, 1997a; Beirness et al., 2001; Kostyniuk et al., 2001; Larson, 1996; Puente & Castaneda, 1997; Wasielewski, 1984). The demographic and control variables used in the study allowed for further analysis of the roles of: age, gender, race, commuter status, number of miles driven daily, driver's education course, number of times stopped by police for a traffic violation, number of traffic citations, number of speeding tickets, number of accidents, and trait anger.

These control variables were chosen based on prior research. The Kostyniuk et al. research (2001) suggested that there was an age effect for both men and women, with younger drivers being more likely to travel at faster speeds than middle-aged drivers or older drivers. Hauber (1980) found that age is a greater predictor of driver aggression than sex, where young females were found to report greater driver aggression than older males. The Wasielewski study (1984) found that men were more likely to drive faster than women. Conversely, a study by Deffenbacher et al. (1995) found that young men and young women exhibited equal driving anger. With regard to the driving variables, Wilson and Greensmith (1983) found that subjects who had an accident record drove more quickly on clear roads, moved about more, and overtook others in traffic more than those without an accident record. Furthermore, Furnham, and Saipe (1993) suggest that the dangers of driver aggression were associated with increased accident involvement.

Sampling Strategy

Existing data have demonstrated that the majority of aggressive drivers are between the ages of 18-26 (AAA Foundation for Traffic Safety, 1997b; Larson, 1996; Puente & Castaneda, 1997). Other studies suggested that the profile of an aggressive driver involves "a young (under age 30), male, with a high school education, who enjoys thrill seeking and risk-taking, who engages in behaviors that compromise health and safety, who exhibits aggressive and hostile tendencies, and has a record of previous driving violations and accidents" (Beirness & Simpson, 2001, p. 5). Researchers (Cameron, 1982; Jonah, 1986; Mayhew, Donelson, Beirness, & Simpson, 1986) have suggested that the combination of risk-enhancing personal characteristics and alcohol appear to be common among young males, the group most prominently involved in alcohol-related accidents and fatalities. Lastly, research had demonstrated that age is the most important factor in aggressive driving incidents (Arnett, 1994; Beirness & Simpson, 1988; Jonah, 1986).

For these reasons, a sample of college students was surveyed through the use of a self-administered questionnaire. The sample comprised undergraduate college students from two institutions located in Pennsylvania. The two institutions of higher education that were selected were a mid-sized public university and a small independent college. The unit of analysis was the students in randomly selected classes at both of these locations.

The undergraduate population of the mid-sized university was 11,834 (Institutional Research, 2002). Of this population, 44.1 percent (or 5,218) was male. Class standing also was delineated; 38.3 percent was freshmen (4,528), 19.8 percent was sophomores (2,339), 21.1 percent was juniors (2,500) and 20.8 percent was seniors (2,467). In terms of the undergraduate racial and ethnic composition, there were African-American (6.2%), American Indian or Alaskan Native (.24%), Asian or Pacific Islander (.93%), Hispanic (.95%), and Caucasian students (89.48%). The population also was broken down into residential and commuter status. Residential students, students who live in college-owned, operated, or affiliated housing, comprised 32 percent of the undergraduate population; therefore, commuter students, which are those who live off campus or commute, comprised 68 percent of the population.

The undergraduate population of the small independent college contained both similarities and differences in terms of the size, composition, and residence status of students. The total undergraduate population was 2,739 (Admissions, 2002). Of the population, 36.8 percent (or 1,008) was male. The class standing break-down was as follows: freshmen 40.6% (1,112), sophomores 22.3% (612), juniors 19.1% (525), seniors 17.6% (483), and post baccalaureate .2% (7) of the population. The racial and ethnic composition was American Indian and Alaskan (.3%), Asian/Pacific Islander (.5%), African-American (2.0%), Caucasian (87.9%), Hispanic (1.0%), Multi-ethnic (.5%), Other (.2%), and Unknown (7.6%). Residential and commuter status also were delineated. Residential students made up 67.3 percent

(1,843) of the population, while 32.7 percent (896) were commuter students.

The targeted sample size was 500 students. Because two institutions were used and they had enrollment differences (11,834 versus 2,739 students), the samples were drawn proportionately to ensure that the smaller institution had enough cases for the independent variables to be sufficiently analyzed. The targeted subsample size for the university was 380 students, and for the college, it was 120 students. This was based on supporting the method of analysis and generalizability to the undergraduate population at both of the listed schools. Given a general rule of 30 cases per independent variable, 500 total cases exceeded the minimum sample size needed for most regression purposes. The larger sample size also resulted in more stable estimates (Weisburd, 1998).

The sample was drawn from two institutions for two reasons. The first reason was that the schools are located in different types of settings. The small college is located in a more urban setting whereas the mid-sized university is located in a more rural setting. Given the differences in the types of roadways and traffic situations, the students' driving experiences may be different. The second reason for selecting the two institutions was that the university has a larger population (68%) of students who are commuters while 32.7 percent of students at the independent college are commuters. It is important to note that there are more commuter students in the rural setting than commuter students in the urban setting, which posits interesting questions concerning location and driving habits.

For the present study, a single-stage, stratified, proportionate, cluster sample was drawn. The classes were randomly selected from each of the strata from the course lists at both the mid-sized university and small college. The table below represents the stratified listing of undergraduate courses.

Table 2: Sample Construction: Public and Independent Schools

Class Standing	Proportion of the Population Public University: (N=11,834)	Proportion of the Population Independent College: (N=2,739)
Freshman	38% of 11,834 38% of 380 (N)=144 Clusters: ENGL 101 HIST 195	41% of 2,739 41% of 120 (N)=49 Clusters: ENGL 103 MATH 108
Sophomore	20% of 11,834 20% of 380 (N)=77 Clusters: ENGL 121, 202	22% of 2,739 22% of 120 (N)=26 Clusters: RLST 205, 206
Upperclassmen	42% of 11,834 42% of 380 (N)=159 Clusters: LBST 499	37% of 2,739 37% of 120 (N)=45 Cluster: PHIL 401, RLST 405

The goal of this sampling strategy was to obtain a representative sample from both college and university sites. As a result, the sample was stratified by class standing and sections were randomly selected from the noted course listed above. According to Babbie (1990, p. 86), the goal of stratification is "to organize the population into homogeneous subsets and to select the appropriate number of elements from each subset." This allowed for a more accurate representation of the populations. Lastly, the individual courses were selected by using a random numbers table.

Public University Sample Construction
In order to draw a representative sample of the public university, the researcher obtained demographic statistics of the undergraduate population. To organize this population, the sampling strategy required stratification by class standing (i.e., freshmen, sophomore, and upperclassmen). The freshman class made up 38 percent of the undergraduate population (as mentioned earlier the target sample size from this university is 380 participants); therefore, 144 participants were needed to satisfy this class level. The sophomore class comprised 20 percent of the population; thus 77 respondents were needed. The

upperclassmen strata comprised 42 percent of the undergraduate population, thus required 159 participants for this stratum to be satisfied. In order to assure these strata were represented, required courses from the liberal studies curriculum were used as the sampling frame.

The researcher then obtained information from the directory of the Advising Center in the Department of Criminology concerning courses that students were likely to take given their class standing (i.e., freshman, sophomore, junior, senior) (personal communication, Jamie Martin). The freshman sub-sample was randomly selected with a random number table using the English 101 and History 195 courses. Since the average class size of these courses was 30 students, 6 classes were randomly selected from these two clusters. The sophomore subsample was randomly selected from the English 121 and English 202 classes. Thus, 4 classes were selected from these two clusters. The upperclassmen subsample was selected from the Liberal Studies 499 course, and 7 classes were selected from this cluster.

Table 3: Sample Course Selection by School

Class Standing	Public University	Independent College	
Freshman	Eng. 101 Hist. 195	Math Problem Solving Western Classics	MATH 108 ENGL 103
Sophomore	Eng. 121 Eng. 202	Marriage & Family Catholic Vision	RLST 255 RLST 260
Upperclass	Liberal Studies 499	Applied Ethics Social Ethics	PHIL 401 RLST 405

Independent College Sample Construction

The same process was used to draw the sample from the independent college. The population was stratified by class standing (i.e., freshmen, sophomore, and upperclassmen). See Table 2. The freshman class represented 41 percent of the undergraduate population (as mentioned earlier the target sample size from this university is 120 participants); therefore, 49 participants were needed to satisfy this class level. The sophomore class comprised 22 percent of the population; thus 26 respondents were needed. The upperclassmen strata comprised 37 percent of the undergraduate population, thus requiring 45 participants for this stratum to be satisfied. In order to assure these strata were represented, required courses from the core curriculum were used as the sampling frame.

Information on the core curriculum, specifically the common core and the distribution core courses, was obtained. This information was used to assess which classes were likely to be taken by each of the class levels (Academic Schedule, 2003). The freshman subsample was randomly selected from the English 103 and Math 108. Since the average class size of these classes was 20 students, 4 classes were randomly selected from these three clusters to obtain the 49 participants. The sophomore subsample was randomly selected from the Religious Studies classes. In order to obtain 26 participants, 3 classes were selected from this cluster. The upperclassmen subsample (N=45) was selected from the Philosophy 401 and Religious Studies 405 courses; and 4 classes were selected from this cluster.

Sampling Limitations

While there were concerns with using availability samples (Babbie, 1998), these samples have been the accepted mode for much of the cited research. Furthermore, the use of college aged youth as respondents for empirical research has been widely exercised in criminology and other social sciences (Nagin & Paternoster, 1993; Piquero & Tibetts, 1996; Tibbetts & Herz, 1996). Nagin and Paternoster (1993) purported that a sample of university students is likely to contain a number of marginal deviants. As pointed out in the literature and previously, road rage behaviors are not uncommon to university-aged respondents. Gottfredson and Hirschi (1990) also contend that research should be concentrated on the point of life when the crime rate is maximally variable; in this case, younger individuals with little driving experience would meet this criterion.

However, since an individual's level of self-control was being taken into account, the utilization of university students posed another possible problem. In order for students to excel in academia, students must demonstrate a certain amount of diligence and tenacity. It has been noted in the literature that students who are in college may have reached a certain threshold of self-control, especially with respect to task persistence and future time orientation. This was contrary to the characterization of one who has a low level of self-control. As a result, Gottfredson and Hirschi (1990) purported that university students were most likely to be characterized by high levels of self-control, therefore, were relatively restricted in deviance involvement. Although these concerns were relevant, based on previous research, it was expected that variation in offending would not be a problem. In terms of rates of offending among students, Gibbs et al. (1998) and Gibbs and Giever (1995) found sufficient variation in deviance, and reported a substantial level of deviant involvement among university students. This finding suggested that there is sufficient variation in deviance among university students.

With respect to the utilization of an undergraduate student sample, a sample of university students should be relatively articulate. Block (1969) found that persons who are generally more competent and verbal are more accurate in their recall (Block, 1969 as cited by Halverson, 1988, p. 442). Based on this reasoning, college students should be able to effectively recall their driving experiences and offending behaviors. Lastly, a sample of college-aged youth appeared to offer an acceptable method for assessing the relationships between theoretically informed predictors and intentions to engage in various deviant behaviors (Mazerolle & Piquero, 1998).

In addition to the above concerns, another potential problem concerned the independent college sample, in that it may not be entirely representative of the college. It may be problematic, in that the classes chosen to represent the class standings, specifically the sophomore standing, may not elicit a representative number of sophomores. The courses were selected based on the core curriculum requirements, which are further separated into the common core and the distribution core courses. The common core is comprised of required classes that are geared for students to take in their first year or in their first year after completing another section or course of the common core courses. For example, all students have to take religious traditions course (e.g., religious persons and traditions or understanding scripture) in their first year. After fulfilling their requirements, students are advised to take another religious studies course, which may not be available until their sophomore year.

As a result there may be freshmen, sophomores, and upperclassmen in the required course. It may be difficult to find a homogeneous group among the distribution core courses. However, since one of the focuses of this study is to look at differences in age, the delineation between lower and upperclassmen will suffice. Also, once the data were retrieved, the researcher made a comparison between the study population and the college population to approximate the representativeness of the sample.

With respect to the composition of the sample gender and age representation may be a limitation. In terms of gender, the population of females at the mid-sized public university and independent college is 55.9 percent and 63.2 percent, respectively. According to the research, males are more likely to engage in road rage behaviors, thus, the rates of offending may be offset by the underrepresentation of males in the sample. However, there is research to suggest that females are becoming more aggressive on the roadways. In terms of using a college sample, there may not be as much variability in age. The typical age of college students ranges from 18 to 23 years of age; however, there may be nontraditional students in the selected classes, thus there will be some age variation in the data. Nevertheless, the sample should capture that age range which has been characterized as being most likely to engage in aggressive driving behaviors.

Lastly, a limitation of this study relates to external generalizability. Since the college undergraduates may not be typical of all undergraduate students or the public at large, the results of the study cannot be generalized beyond the population of the particular institutions being studied.

Questionnaire Construction

A self-report survey questionnaire, which included measures of road rage, strain, anger, coping mechanisms, and demographic information, was administered to the individuals in the sample. The road rage measures included selected items from the Total Aggression Expression (TAE) subscale of the Driving Anger Expression Inventory (DAX) (Deffenbacher et al., 2002) and the Driving Survey (Deffenbacher et al., 2001). Agnew's general strain theory was measured by items adapted from the 1997 Capowich et al. survey instrument which assessed strain (Capowich et al., 2001). The role of anger, with both dispositional and situational aspects, was measured. Trait (dispositional) anger was used as a control variable and was measured with items taken from the State-Trait Anger Expression Inventory (STAXI-2) (Spielberger et al., 1999). Situational (state) anger consisted of questions pertaining to the respondent's rating the degree of anger felt given a specific situation tailored to the dependent variable (road rage).

Because the coping mechanisms being studied addressed the role of self-control and peer relationships, both of these constructs were assessed separately. Self-control was measured by the Grasmick et al. (1993) scale. The role of peers was measured through the use of items asking the respondents about the behaviors of their closest peer relationship. The demographic questions included items pertaining to age, gender, race, commuter status, number of miles driven daily, driver's education course, number of times stopped by police for a traffic violation, number of traffic citations, number of speeding tickets, number of accidents, and trait anger.

Strain Scale

The strain measures were taken (with permission) from a 1997 survey instrument developed by Capowich et al. (2001). Strain was measured with a composite measure that captures the three sources of strain noted by Agnew (1992): failure to achieve positively valued goals, the presentation of negative stimuli, and the removal of positive stimuli. Respondents were asked if any of the following events occurred in their homes or to members of their family in the previous year. Some of the events included: divorce, family move, significant other broke up with respondent, failed an important exam, family had serious money problems, mother/father remarried, and/or the death of a close friend (Capowich et al., 2001). The responses were coded as no-yes (0,1); therefore, the scale was coded so that higher values reflect greater strain.

The Capowich et al. (2001) scale was used with undergraduate students; therefore, the items were geared toward strainful events that are common to the lives of college students. Capowich et al. (2001) used factor analysis to assess if the strain items indicated unidimensionality; furthermore, a reliability analysis yielded an alpha coefficient of .58. Although this was a somewhat low alpha level, it may be due to the dichotomous nature (0-no, 1-yes) of the individual items (Capowich et al., 2001). It is important to note that even though Nunnally (1978) suggests that a value of .70 is an acceptable level for an alpha, it is not unusual to see published scales with lower alphas (DeVellis, 1991). According to DeVillis (1991, p. 85) comfort ranges for research scales are as follows: an alpha level below .60 is considered an unacceptable level; between .60 and .65 is undesirable; between .65 and .70 is minimally acceptable; between .70 and .80 is respectable; .80 to .90 is very good; and much above .90 one should consider shortening the scale. However, Hoffmann and Miller (1998) contend that a low alpha level for a strain scale is not surprising, in that, stressful life events often reflect discrete and independent episodes in individuals' lives.

Although the alpha level was below acceptable standards, the primary justification for using this strain scale is for theoretical purposes. Because this study examined the role of strain in explaining road rage behaviors, a strain scale is necessary. Many of the strain studies have used such scales pertaining to stress, negative life events, neighborhood problems, school and peer hassles, and life hassles as measures of strain (Agnew & White, 1992; Aseltine et al., 2000; Paternoster & Mazerolle, 1994). As mentioned previously, the psychological research has also used stress models to explain aggressive driving incidents. Given the above justifications, the Capowich et al. (2001) strain scale will be used.

Role of Anger

In past empirical studies, the role of anger with respect to GST had been measured through the use of trait anger measures; however, this study used both situational and trait anger measures. Situational anger is a type of anger that "fluctuates over time as a function of frustration, perceived affronts, injustice, or being verbally or physically attacked" (Spielberger, Reheiser, & Sydeman, 1995). The trait anger (also referred to as dispositional anger) construct measured how often angry feelings were experienced over time; thus, it may be considered a stable indicator of anger.

This study included a measure of situational (state) anger. According to GST situational anger appeared to be more consistent with the anger that emerges from particular incidents (Agnew, 1992; Agnew, 1995). Therefore, the measures of situational anger were designed to link anger to the specific situation involving strain. The respondents were asked to rate their level of anger given a particular situation. Some situations included: being cut in front of on the highway; being tailgated by another vehicle for more than 1 mile; being given an obscene gesture due to your driving; being verbally confronted due to your driving; being behind a vehicle driving slowly in the left land, obstructing you from passing. The response format asked the respondent to rate his/her level of anger on a four-point continuum (i.e., Not at All (1), Somewhat (2), Moderately (3), Very Much (4)). These items were coded so that higher values reflect greater situational anger.

In order to measure the control variable of trait anger the STAXI-2 Trait Anger scale was used (Spielberger et al., 1999). The STAXI-2 Trait Anger scale consisted of 10 items measuring individual differences in anger proneness as a personality trait. This scale had two, 4-item subscales (i.e., Angry Reaction and Angry Temperament scales) and two independent questions. These subscales measured how frequently a person experienced anger with or without provocation (Spielberger et al., 1999). The response format for each of these scales consisted of a four point Likert scale (i.e., 1-Almost Never, 2-Sometimes, 3 Often, 4-Almost Always).

Table 4: Trait Anger Items

STAXI-2 Trait Anger Scale	Items (survey questionnaire)	Example Question
Angry Reaction	113, 114, 115, 118, 119, 121	I am quick tempered.
Angry Temperament	116, 117, 119, 120, 121, 122	I get angry when I'm slowed down by others' mistakes.

Note. Trait Anger Scale--Alpha levels, females=.85; males=.86. (Spielberger et al., 1999)

Self-Control Scale
Because individuals have coping mechanisms that may mediate the effects of strain and anger, it was important to identify which mechanisms may influence whether or not an individual engages in road rage behaviors. One of the coping mechanisms identified in the present study was an individual's level of self-control. Self-control is defined as the level of control an individual yields over his/her propensity to commit crime and analogous acts (Gottfredson & Hirschi, 1990). Individuals who have low self-control have personalities predisposing them to criminal acts; thus crimes committed in the

pursuit of their self-interests. Conversely, individuals with high levels of self-control are more likely to refrain from criminal activities.

In order to assess the role of self-control as a coping mechanism, the Grasmick et al. (1993) scale was used to measure the control variable of self-control. The Grasmick et al. (1993) scale is one of the most widely used measures for assessing an individual's level of self-control and had been used with juveniles, university students, and adults (Arneklev, Cochran, & Gainey, 1998; Arneklev et al., 1993; Cochran et al., 1998; Gibbs & Giever, 1995; Gibbs, Giever, & Martin, 1998; Longshore et al., 1996; Longshore, 1998; Longshore & Turner, 1998; Nagin & Paternoster, 1993; Piquero & Rosay. 1998; Piquero & Tibbetts, 1996). The Grasmick et al. (1993) scale included the identification and measurement of the six components of the personality trait of low self-control. These components comprised: (1) impulsivity, (2) preference for simple rather than complex tasks, (3) risk seeking, (4) preference for physical rather than mental activities, (5) self-centered orientation, and (6) a temper linked to a low tolerance for frustration (Grasmick et al., 1993). This scale was a 24-item scale, which included four items for each of the six components. The response format was a four point Likert scale, ranging from strongly disagree (1) to strongly agree (4). Higher scores suggested lower levels of self-control. Self-control was found to be a unidimensional measure, the most obvious break in eigenvalues was the difference of 2.32 between the first and second factors, compared to .27 between the second and third factors, thus, suggesting a one-factor model. The scale also has demonstrated reliability (Alpha =.80) (Grasmick et al., 1993).

Other studies using the Grasmick et al. (1993) scale yielded similar results. The Arneklev et al. (1998) study administered the Grasmick et al. (1993) self-control scale to undergraduate student populations (N=127) at two time intervals, which yielded Cronbach's alpha levels of .8633 and .8945 respectively. Research conducted by Wood et al. (1993) used the Grasmick et al. (1993) scale with high school students (N=975) and found good reliability of the self-control scale (Cronbach's Alpha= .88).

Table 5: Self-Control Items

Component of Self-Control	Items (survey questionnaire)	Example Question
Impulsivity	130-133	I often act on the spur of the moment without stopping to think.
Simple Tasks	134-137	I frequently try to avoid projects that I know will be difficult
Risk Taking	138-141	I sometimes find it exciting to do things for which I might get in trouble.
Physical Activities	142-145	I almost always feel better when I am on the move than when I am sitting and thinking.
Self-Centered	146-149	I try to look out for myself first, even if it means making things difficult for other people.
Temper	150-153	When I'm really angry, other people better stay away from me.

Note. The response format for each of these items is a four point Likert scale (1) Strongly Disagree, (2) Agree Somewhat, (3) Disagree Somewhat, (4) Strongly Agree

Peer Behavior Items
There was ample evidence to substantiate that participation in a deviant peer group increased an individual's likelihood of committing delinquent acts (Akers, Krohn, Lanza-Kanduce, & Radosevich, 1979; Elliott, Huizinga, & Ageton, 1985; Jessor & Jessor, 1977; Johnson et al., 1987; Matsueda, 1982; Mears, Ploeger, & Warr, 1998; Simons & Robertson, 1989; Warr, 1993). Therefore, questions concerning the respondent's peer relationships were elicited. Following the approach taken by Agnew & White (1992), the role of peers as a coping mechanism was measured by asking the respondent to identify the respondent's closest friend and his/her behaviors. For example, one

question asked was: During the last year, has your closest friend engaged in [act]? Some of the acts include: speeding, obscene gestures, verbal confrontations on the road, and physical confrontations on the road. In addition, questions addressing the type of relationship were asked (e.g., How long have you been friends with your closest friend identified in the above question; On average, how much time per week do you spent with your closest friend?). The response format for each of these questions was open ended, in which the respondent supplied his/her answer. Lastly, the respondent was asked if his/her relationship with his/her closest friend had influenced his/her behavior (i.e., commit an offense). This question allowed the researcher to note if the peer relationship has a negative/positive influence on actual past offending.

Aggressive Driving Scale and Road Rage Items

In order to assess the extent of road rage among college students, the dependent variable was measured in two ways. The first type of measurement was in the form of the Total Aggression Expression (TAE) subscale of the Driving Anger Expression Inventory (DAX) (Deffenbacher et al., 2002). The second road rage assessment was in the form of items adapted from the Driving Survey (Deffenbacher et al., 2001). Both measures were analyzed independently as dependent variables.

The Driving Anger Expression Inventory (Deffenbacher et al., 2002) consisted of items designed to measure if the participant had engaged in aggressive driving and road rage behaviors in the last three months. This inventory included five factors of expressing anger while driving: Verbal Aggressive, Personal Physical Aggressive, Vehicle to Express Anger, Displaced Aggression, and Adaptive/Constructive Expression scales. However, due to the nature of this study and the low reliability level of the Adaptive/Constructive Expression and Displaced Aggression scales, they were not used in this study. They were not selected because the questions in these subscales combined both attitudes and behaviors concerning driving while angry.

More specifically, the questions focused on how the individual deals with being upset or angry while driving and the other subscale focused on how and on what to release their anger while driving. The distinction was made between behaviors that individuals participated versus attitudes that individuals held when confronted with driving situations.

Thus the Total Aggression Expression (TAE) subscale was used as the dependent variable for this study. This subscale is a composite of the Verbal Aggressive Expression, Physical Aggressive Expression, and the Use of Vehicle to Express Anger scales. The respondents were asked to describe how they express their anger while driving on a 4-point Likert scale (1 almost never, 2 sometimes, 3 often, 4 almost always) (Deffenbacher et al., 2002). The individual's score on each scale was the sum of ratings on the items in that scale; furthermore, the individual's scores on each of the scales were be summed for a composite score of aggressive driving.

Table 6: Total Aggression Expression Scale (TAE) Items

Total Aggressive Expression Subscales	Alpha level for subscale	Items	Example Question
Verbal Aggressive Expression	.88	22, 23, 26, 28, 31, 41, 42, 45, 46, 47, 48, 50	I swear at the other driver aloud.
Personal Physical Aggressive Expression	.81	18, 25, 27, 29, 30, 34, 35, 37, 38, 49	I try to get out of the car and have a physical fight with the other driver.
Use of The Vehicle to Express Anger	.86	19, 20, 21, 24, 32, 33, 36, 39, 40 43, 51	I try to cut in front of the other driver.

Note. The response format for each of these items is a four point Likert scale (1) Almost Never, (2) Sometimes, (3) Often, (4) Almost Always.

The Verbal Aggressive Expression, Personal Physical Aggressive Expression and Use of the Vehicle to Express Anger subscales are combined as a Total Aggressive Expression index, which has demonstrated reliability (Alpha = .90) and validity.

The second dependent measure that was utilized in this study was the Driving Survey (Deffenbacher et al., 2001). The Driving Survey was a compilation of measures of aggression, risky behavior, and crash-related events. Although there are three core subscales in the survey, only the driving related aggression and risky behavior scales were used in this study. The crash-related events scale was not used because it is not relevant to the dependent variable of road rage. There were 13 items in the driving-related aggression subscale (e.g., having an argument with or making an angry gesture at another driver) (Deffenbacher et al., 2001). The risky behavior subscale was comprised of 15 items that pertain to breaking the norms of the road (e.g., running a red light or speeding 20+ miles an hour over the limit). The participants were asked to report the frequency (0 to 5+ with 5+ being treated as a 5 in analyses) of each of the subscales over the last three months (Deffenbacher et al., in press). The Driving Survey also has demonstrated reliability (risky behavior subscale, current alpha= .85, reported alphas= .83-.86; aggression subscale, current alpha=.87, reported alphas =.85-.89) when administered to undergraduate students (Deffenbacher, Deffenbacher et al., 2001; Deffenbacher, Lynch, Filette et al., 2001).

Other Variables
In addition to the above, several other variables were included. The literature suggests that males are more likely to engage in road rage behaviors than females (AAA Foundation for Traffic Safety, 1997b; Beirness, et al., 2001; Puente & Castaneda, 1997; Wasielewski, 1984). However, Deffenbacher et al. (1996) found that males and females exhibited equal levels of driving anger. Therefore, in order to answer one of the hypotheses pertaining to gender and road rage behaviors, gender was included as an independent variable.

Age was included as a variable of inquiry. Kostyniuk et al. (2001) and Hauber's (1980) research suggested that there is an age effect in terms of driver aggression. Other pertinent driving related questions were asked. These questions related to whether the individual was a residential or commuter student, if the student had taken a driver's education class, and the number of traffic tickets received. Each of these variables added to the predictive value of a road rage incident.

Pre-Testing the Instrument

As mentioned previously, the survey instrument was pre-tested with a group of undergraduate students at the public university. Pre-testing the questionnaire with a sample allowed for a critique of the instrument, and it gave the researcher a better estimate of the amount of time it took the respondents to complete the instrument (Babbie, 1998). Babbie (1998) further stated that it is not essential that the individuals who are pre-testing the questionnaire comprise a representative sample, yet the researcher would be in a better position using individuals for whom the questionnaire is at least relevant. Therefore, two undergraduate criminology classes and one sociology class were selected to participate in the pretesting of the survey instrument. These classes were selected because of their accessibility, knowledge of survey method, and their familiarity with driving experiences. Participants were asked to review the survey instrument, comment on the types and readability of the questions, give any feedback concerning the format of the survey instrument, and complete the instrument.

Administration of the Survey

After obtaining approval from the Institutional Review Boards at both locations, the survey was distributed to both the university and college students during the spring semester of the 2002-2003 the academic school year. Once the sample was drawn, the professors of the selected classes were contacted (see appendix) via letter. Professors who declined the offer to participate were eliminated from the sampling frame. For those professors who granted the researcher access to their classes, the researcher coordinated the dates and times (during the data collection period) with the professors so that the researcher could distribute the surveys to the students. Given that the researcher had to collect data at both locations, a second year doctoral student was enlisted as an associate data collector.

The researcher (or doctoral student) administered the survey instrument to all the students in the selected classrooms. The researcher (or doctoral student) was present for the administration of the survey instruments. The researcher (or doctoral student) invited all of the students to participate, supplied them with the informed consent protocol, gave a brief description of the project, reviewed the voluntariness of the student's participation in the project, explained that responses were anonymous, and distributed the survey. The surveys were collected by the researcher (or research assistant) in a sealed envelope and returned to the researcher. All surveys were locked in a file cabinet, to which only the researcher and the advisor had access.

Human Subject Protections

Because human participants were used in the data collection process, it was paramount to address all human subject issues that may arise during the research process. For the present study, the human subject issues included anonymity, voluntary participation, informed consent, and no harm to participants (Babbie, 1998). Each of these issues was addressed.

In order to ensure anonymity, respondents were instructed not to place any identifying information on the survey questionnaire. The data were ultimately presented in the aggregate form and no responses were identifiable to a particular respondent in the finished product. This was communicated to participants in the informed consent letter. Therefore, participants were informed that the researcher is unable to link responses with the identity of any specific respondent. Furthermore, since the researcher (or doctoral student) was administering the survey, the instructor of record for the class was not permitted to remain in the classroom nor was the instructor able to determine students in the class who participated and who did not. Lastly, the surveys were collected by the researcher, placed in a box, and stored in a locked cabinet in the researcher's or the advisor's office.

Voluntary participation and informed consent were also concerns. All participants were asked to voluntarily complete the survey instrument. The researcher informed the students that those individuals under age eighteen were excused from participation, and they were asked to return the survey. Furthermore, the researcher advised the participants of the purpose of the study, informed them of any risks/harms associated with the survey, apprised them of the voluntariness of their responses, and assured them that they could withdraw from the study at any time. Students were also informed that they would receive no reward or benefit for their participation. In an attempt to prevent students from feeling alienated if they chose not to participate, they were asked to write "withdraw" on their survey, sit quietly until others are finished, and then place the uncompleted survey into the box. A copy of the informed consent letter was given to all of the respondents, upon participating in the survey. However, the return of the questionnaire, by students who were age eighteen and older, provided evidence of implied consent.

The safeguard requiring little or no harm to participant was addressed. Because this research topic asks the participant to reveal if he/she had committed an act of road rage, he/she may be uncomfortable answering certain questions. As mentioned before, participants were made aware of the nature of the research in the informed consent letter and by the researcher in the introduction to the survey. Students were also advised that their participation was completely voluntary and that they were able to withdraw from participating at any time during the research process.

Analysis Plan

The data generated from the survey was subject to statistical analyses. The survey questions were designed to yield nominal, ordinal, and interval level data, and both descriptive and inferential statistics were utilized. Descriptive statistics were used to observe the incidents of road rage behaviors among college students as well as the distribution of variables and any patterns or relationships in the data that warrant further investigation. Furthermore, the descriptive statistics were examined to determine the representativeness of the samples.

A correlation matrix was generated to identify bivariate relationships between the independent and dependent variables to be used subsequently in a regression equation model. The correlation matrix also determined if mulitcollinearity was a problem among any of the above variables. The absence of mulitcollinearity is an assumption that must be met when using multiple regression and path analysis (Lewis-Beck, 1980).

Using path analysis, the individual's likelihood of engaging in road rage behaviors may be partly explained or more clearly understood by taking the individual's level of strain into consideration. The goal of the multiple regression models, in terms of building the path models, was to find the line of "best fit" between the independent and dependent variables (Bachman & Paternoster, 1997). Therefore, the multiple regression runs used in the path analysis models illustrated the effect of the independent variables (strain, anger, peers, self-control) on the dependent variable (road rage behaviors). Because there was more than one independent variable and a continuously measured dependent variable (road rage), a multivariate regression equation was needed. This model helped to estimate the effect that the independent variables have on the dependent variable, according to the following equation:

$$\hat{y} = a_0 + b_1 x_1 + b_2 x_2 + b_3 x_3 + ...b_k x_k$$

Figure 2. Regression equation.

$\hat{y}$ = predicted road rage behavior
a_0 = constant
x_1 = strain
x_2 = anger
x_3 = peers
x_4 = self-control

Table 7: Analytical Plan

Nature of Analysis	Research Question and Hypotheses to be Tested	Procedure(s)
Demographics	Representativeness of the sample compared to the population	Compare the samples (university, college) to the respective populations based on the most recent university and college data.
Item analysis of individual scales and index items.		
Reliability analysis of Strain, Situational Anger, Self-Control, Peer Behavior, Trait Anger, TAE, Driving Survey scales	Internal consistency (inter-item correlation) variance and standard deviation of measures; stability of estimates.	Cronbach's alpha Inspection of the inter-item total correlations

Table 7: Analytical Plan (continued)

Nature of Analysis	Research Question and Hypotheses to be Tested	Procedure(s)
Content Validity of Strain, Situational Anger, Self-Control, Peer Behavior, Trait Anger, TAE, Driving Survey scales	Comparison of items with domain measures of behaviors as defined in the literature as representative of the construct	Inspection of item-total correlations and content of items
Guttman Scaling	Creation of a psychometric scale for further validation of validity	Coefficient of reproducibility
Correlation matrix	Correlations between the variables, check for multicollinearity, check correlation between the TAE and DS	Pearson's r
Frequencies/Descriptives	Is road rage a problem among college students?	Descriptive statistics and Frequencies
Correlation	Is there a correlation between the TAE and the DS?	Pearson's r;
Association between strain and road rage (TAE and DS)	To what extent does a person's level of strain influence road rage?	Path Analysis: OLS regression to test the magnitude of the independent effects of strain on road rage behaviors while accounting for the control variables: Path models 1a/1b
Association between strain and situational anger	To what extent does strain have an effect on situational anger?	Path Analysis: Path Model 2

Table 7: Analytical Plan (continued)

Nature of Analysis	Research Question and Hypotheses to be Tested	Procedure(s)
Association between situational anger and road rage	Is anger a mediating variable in the strain model?	Path Analysis: Path model 3a/3b
Association between situational anger and coping mechanisms (self-control and peer behavior)	To what extent is situational anger associated with coping mechanisms?	Path Analysis: Path Models 4a/4b
Association between all independent variables, control variables and dependent variables	To what extent do coping mechanisms (self-control/ peer behaviors) mediate the effects of strain on road rage?	Path Analysis, Path Models 5a/5b

Although each of the scales used in this study has been used before with demonstrated reliability and validity, this study also evaluated the performance of the scales. The items in the scales were scrutinized to determine if the items were highly correlated; therefore, the correlation matrix was analyzed. Another important indicator of a scale's performance is the reliability coefficient, alpha (DeVellis, 1991). Alpha is an indication of the "proportion of variance in the scale scores that is attributable to the true score" (DeVellis, 1991, p. 83). Therefore, the internal-consistency reliability or alpha level is an indicator of how well the individual items of a scale reflect a common underlying construct (Spector, 1992, p. 65). Cronbach's alpha was used to assess the internal consistency of the scales. Lastly, path analysis was used.

CHAPTER 5

Strain and Road Rage

In this chapter, the descriptive data first are presented and demonstrate that the current sample is very similar to the combined university/college population on several important variables. The descriptive data are delineated into the independent college and public university samples. Furthermore, the descriptive data of the independent, control, and dependent variables are summarized. Second, the reliability measures of the Strain Scale, Situational Anger Scale, Self-Control Scale, Peer Behavior Scale, Trait Anger Scale, Total Aggressive Expression Scale (TAE) of the Driving Anger Expression Scale (DAX), and the Driving Survey are examined and discussed. In addition, each of the subscales of the above scales are examined. Third, a Guttman scale is devised from the two measures of the dependent variables; this scale essentially orders aggressive driving and road rage behaviors from a less serious to more serious progression of acts.

Next, the validity of each of the scales is assessed. Fifth, bivariate correlations among the independent variables as well as correlations between the dependent variables are investigated. The information that is provided in the correlation matrix is important to investigate; however, it is not appropriate to make causal assumptions using this information. Sixth, the research questions and hypotheses are tested. Last, the path model is examined through path analysis for the purposes of examining the relationships among the variables.

As stated previously in Chapter Four, this study was conducted at both a mid-sized, public university and a small, independent college in Pennsylvania. The sampling methodology consisted of a single-stage, stratified, proportionate, cluster sample, which was devised using random selection. The overall sample was comprised of two sub-samples: students from a public university and students from an independent college.

During the weeks of April 14, 2003 through May 9, 2003, a total of 660 surveys were distributed, and 638 were completed. Of the original 660, 22 survey respondents noted that they did not drive; therefore, the surveys were incomplete and were not used for analysis purposes.

Hence, the final sample size for the study is 638. Of the 638 surveys completed, 389 respondents were from the public university students, and 249 were from the independent college students.

It is important to note that the target sample size was 500 responses; however, the researcher initially encountered a problem of non-response from professors whose classes were selected for the initial sample at both institutions. Given this dilemma, the researcher comprised a replacement list of the same courses (i.e., English, History, Math, Liberal Studies, Religious Studies). Using the random numbers table, different sections of these classes were selected as part of the replacement list. As the researcher contacted the professors of the replacement courses, a few professors from the initial sample subsequently granted permission to their courses. Consequently, the researcher collected data from all of the professors who were contacted and granted permission to survey their courses. These additional classes resulted in the actual sample size (N=638) being larger than the initial target sample size (N=500).

Descriptive Statistics

There are five important demographic items that the participants were asked to complete on the survey questionnaire: gender, age, class standing, race, and commuter/resident status. In order to assess the representativeness of the sample, these items from the survey respondents are compared to the statistics provided by the university and college. See Table 8.

Table 8: Descriptive Statistics for Sample (N=638)

Variable	Valid N	Valid %
Gender		
Male	258	40.4%
Female	380	59.6%
Age*		
18	77	12.1%
19	158	24.8%
20	96	15.0%
21	103	16.1%
22	107	16.8%

Table 8: Descriptive Statistics (continued)

Variable	Valid N	Valid %
Age		
23	42	6:6%
24	14	2.2%
25-55	41	9.0%
Class Standing		
Freshman	192	30.1%
Sophomore	131	20.5%
Junior	107	16.8%
Senior	208	32.6%
Race		
Caucasian	580	90.9%
Black	28	4.4%
Latino	8	1.3%
Asian	12	1.9%
Native American	2	.3%
Other	8	1.3%
Student Status		
Commuter	148	23.2%
Residential	490	76.8%

Note. * Age: The range of ages is 18 to 55. Those aged 24 to 55 represent 9.0% of the remaining respondents. Although the age variable in this sample demonstrated a positive skew, the age variable used in the path models does include all ages. It is important to note that the age variable was recoded into two categories (i.e., ages 18 to 23, and 24 and older). The recoded variable was entered into the path model and the results were similar to the results found with all of the ages included. Thus, the results with all ages are included in the path models.

Given the above statistics, the sample was representative of the population for both the gender and age variable. The overall sample consisted of 258 (40.4%) males and 380 (59.6%) females. According to the most recent 2002-2003 university and college data combined, there are 6,226 (42.7%) men and 8,347 (57.3%) women undergraduate students that attend both institutions. In terms of the age variable, the ages ranged from 18 to 55, with the majority (93.6%) representing the traditional undergraduate student ages (i.e., ages 18-23).

With respect to class standing, the sample yielded freshman (30.1%), sophomores (20.5%), juniors (16.8%), and seniors (32.6%). The overall population characteristics are similar for the sophomores (20.2%) and juniors (20.8%). However, there is a slight difference in the numbers between the sample and the population characteristics with respect to freshman and seniors. The current sample had more seniors (32.6%) than the overall population (20.3%) and fewer freshman (30.1%) than the overall population (38.7%). Although these numbers were dissimilar to the population characteristics, the class standing variable was only used for purposes of determining the representativeness of the sample as per the sampling strategy used. Because class standing is highly correlated with the age variable, the class standing variable was not used in the path model for analysis purposes. To be consistent with past research, the age variable was chosen for analysis purposes in the path model in this study.

In terms of the race variable, the results are similar. The sample mirrored the population characteristics, as the sample yielded Caucasian (90.9%), Black (4.4%), Latino (1.3%), Asian (1.9%), Native American (.3%) and Other (1.3%). The population characteristics include Caucasian (88.7%), Black (4.1%), Latino (.96%), Asian (.72%), Native American (.62%), and Other (4.3%) students.

Lastly, the commuter student status was examined. The sample yielded 148 commuter students (23.2%) and 490 residential students (76.8%). Given the population characteristics: commuter (61.4%) and residential (38.6%), it appears as though this sample did not represent the overall population. A possible explanation for this was that students who lived off campus, but walked to class, did not consider themselves commuter students. However, the university defined residential students as only those who live in university owned, operated or affiliated housing. Therefore, those who lived within walking distance to campus, but lived in non-university owned housing were considered commuters by the university statistics. Although this variable did not mirror the population characteristics, it played an important role with respect to students' driving experiences.

Public University and Independent College Samples

In addition to the overall sample characteristics, the sub-sample characteristics are also delineated. These characteristics include five demographic items that the participants were asked to complete on the survey questionnaire: gender, age, class standing, race, and residential/commuter status. Upon inspection of the subsample, they appear to be very similar.

Table 9: Descriptives : Public University and Independent College

Variable	Public University (N=389) Valid N	Valid %	Independent College (N=249) Valid N	Valid %
Gender				
Male	168	43.2%	90	36.1%
Female	221	56.8%	159	63.9%
Age*				
18	56	14.4%	21	8.4%
19	112	28.8%	46	18.5%
20	55	14.1%	41	16.5%
21	44	11.3%	59	23.7%
22	53	13.6%	54	21.7%
23	33	8.5%	9	3.6%
24	6	1.5%	8	3.2%
25-55	30	7.7%	11	4.0%
Class Standing				
Freshman	137	35.2%	55	22.1%
Sophomore	91	23.4%	40	16.1%
Junior	49	12.6%	58	23.3%
Senior	112	28.8%	96	38.6%
Race				
Caucasian	340	87.4%	240	96.4%
Black	22	5.7%	6	2.4%
Latino	7	1.8%	1	.4%
Asian	12	3.1%	0	0 %
Native Am.	2	.5%	0	0 %
Other	6	1.5%	2	.8%
Student Status				
Commuter	87	22.4%	61	24.5%
Residential	302	77.6%	188	75.5%

Note. *Age: The range of ages for the Public University is 18 to 50. The range of ages for the Independent College is 18 to 55.

The sample was chosen from two different institutions; this was based on the assumption that their driving experiences may be different. However, as shown in Table 9, the students at both institutions are very similar in their composition. Due to this factor as well as time expedience, this study did not compare the students on the different campuses.

Descriptive Statistics: Independent Variables

According to the theoretical framework outlined in Chapter Four, the independent variables for the study included: strain, situational anger, self-control, and peer behavior. A summary of the descriptive statistics were provided in Table 10. Table 10 presented the mean, standard deviation, low and high scores, and valid N of the independent variables. It is important to note that the N reflects only data that were complete for the entire scale. Thus, the mean was representative of completed responses for that particular scale.

Table 10: Descriptives for the Independent Variables

Variable	Mean	Std. Dev.	Minimum Score	Maximum Score	N*
Strain	5.46	3.07	0	16	637
Situational Anger	18.90	4.41	7	28	629
Self-Control	51.53	10.26	24	84	619
Peer Behavior	6.69	1.84	4	12	635

Note. * The N for the study is 638.

The Strain scale measured stressful events that are common to the lives of college students (Capowich et al., 2001). As illustrated in Table 10 above, range of scores varied from zero to 16. Seventy-three percent of the respondents reported experiencing between one and seven strainful events in the past year. The mean score for the strain scale was 5.46, indicating that the average respondent reported slightly over 5 strainful events in the past year. This mean is slightly below the mean score of the Capowich et al. (2001) study and slightly above the mean score of the Mazerolle et al. (2003) study. The mean score for the strain scale in the Capowich et al. (2001) study, which examined GST, situational anger and social networks in relation to assault, shoplifting, and driving under the influence, was 6.05. The mean score for the Strain scale in the Mazerolle et al. (2003) study investigating the link between strain, situational and dispositional anger, and crime was 5.01. Therefore, the mean in the current study was between the mean scores of the prior studies, which also used this same scale. The high score for this scale reached 16, while the low score was 0 out of a possible score of 26. This scale was expected to vary with the TAE and the Driving Survey. It also was expected that those with higher levels of strain also have higher levels of anger.

The Situational Anger scale was a newly created scale to assess the respondent's level of anger given a specific driving situation. The respondents were asked to report their level of anger on a four-point scale (1=Not at All, 2=Somewhat, 3=Moderately, 4=Very Angry) for seven driving situations. The scores ranged from 7 to 28, with 28 being the highest possible score. The mean score was 18.90, indicating that most respondents felt that the specified driving scenarios caused them to become moderately angry. There was only one individual who scored a seven, essentially reporting that none of the driving scenarios caused him/her to become angry. At the same time 98.4% of the respondents reported at least being somewhat angry given the driving scenario. Because the scale was created by the researcher, there are no comparable data at this time.

The Self-Control scale, which included 24 items, asked respondents to assess their level of control over their propensity to commit crime and analogous acts. The 4 point scale (1=Strongly Disagree, 2=Disagree Somewhat, 3=Agree Somewhat, 4=Strongly Agree) elicited scores ranging from 24 to 84, with the highest score being 84. The scale was devised so that the higher the score, the lower the level of self-control. The Grasmick et al. (1993) scale used in the current study yielded a mean score of 51.53. The mean was indicative of individuals who exhibit a moderate to low level of self-control. Furthermore, this score was higher than the mean score (X=39.9) reported by Longshore (1998); however, he used 23 items from the Grasmick et al. (1993) scale in his study. Many of the prior studies, which have used the Grasmick et al. (1993) scale, have adapted the scale with different questions or used only 23 of the 24 original items.

The Peer Behavior scale was a newly created scale that is comprised of four questions, which asked respondents to assess their closest friend's aggressive driving behaviors. The questions were devised to elicit responses to how often their closest friend speeds, gives obscene gestures, has verbal confrontations on the road, and physical confrontations on the road. The response format for these questions was a three point scale (Never=1, Sometimes=2, Always=3). The scores ranged from 4 to 12, with 12 being the total possible score. The mean score for these questions was 6.69. Because this was a newly created scale, there were no comparison data for this variable.

Descriptive Statistics: Control Variables

As both the strain literature and the aggressive driving and road rage studies had suggested, there are variables that may influence an individual's level of strain as well as their potential participation in deviant adaptations, in this case road rage. A summary of the descriptive statistics is provided in Table 11. Table 11 reported the mean, standard deviation, minimum and maximum scores, and valid $\underline{N}$ of the independent variables. It is important to note that the $\underline{N}$ reflects only data that were complete for the entire scale. Thus, the mean was representative of completed responses for that particular scale.

Table 11: Descriptives for the Control Variables

Variable	Mean	Std. Dev.	Minimum Score	Maximum Score	$\underline{N}$*
Age	21.04	3.737	18	55	638
Gender	.60	.491	0	1	638
Race/Ethnicity	.09	.288	0	1	638
Commuter Status	.23	.422	0	1	638
Miles Daily	28.24	25.141	0	150	594
Driver's Education Class	.73	.444	0	1	638
Police Stops	.47	.499	0	1	638
Traffic Citations	.28	.450	0	1	638

Table 11: Control Variables (continued)

Variable	Mean	Std. Dev.	Minimum Score	Maximum Score	N*
Speeding Tickets	.26	.438	0	1	638
Prior Accidents	.32	.466	0	1	638
Trait Anger	19.27	5.782	10	40	633

Note. * The N for the overall study is 638.

In terms of age, coded as a continuous variable, the average age of the participants was 21.04 years. Given the minimum and maximum ages (i.e., 18 to 55), it is important to note that 93.6 percent of the ages represented the traditional undergraduate student ages (i.e., 18-23). Prior research on aggressive driving and road rage behaviors demonstrated similar age ranges with respect to the traditional undergraduate student population.

The next three variables were coded as dichotomous variables. The gender variable indicated that 60% of those sampled were female. The data were coded such that male is equal to zero, and female is equal to one. The race variable shows the mean as .09, which indicates that that over 90% of participants were Caucasian. The variable was initially coded as Caucasian equals 1, Black equals 2, Latino equals 3, Asian equals 4, Native American equals 5, and Other equals 6. For analysis purposes this variable was recoded to indicate Caucasian equals 0, and nonwhite equals 1. For the commuter status variable, the majority (77%) of the students replied that they were not commuter students (no=0, yes=1).

Miles daily, a continuous variable, represents the number of miles that the participant (on average) drives per day. The average number of miles driven on a daily basis is 28.24 miles, with a range of 0 to 150 miles (std. deviation=25.141). There were forty cases with missing data concerning the number of miles driven daily. Although it is not assumed that these respondents' driving behaviors were different from the remainder of the sample, the missing data were eliminated for analysis purposes.

In relation to driver's education, the majority (73.0%) of participants had taken a driver's education class. Of those who had taken a driver's education class (N=466), 76.0 percent (354) took the course from school, 22.1 percent (103) took that course through a private agency, and 1.9 percent (9) took the course either through a court-mandated program or through a combination of the above. With respect to the style of learning used in the courses, 21.7 percent were enrolled in a course that was lecture based, 10.1 percent had hands-on experience, and 68.0 percent had both lecture and hands-on experience. One participant (.2%) noted a driving simulator as the type of learning employed in the course.

In addition to these general driving characteristics, the survey posed questions concerning the participant's driving record. These questions captured the number of times, within the past year, that the driver was stopped, cited, speeding tickets received, and/or had an accident. Approximately half of the respondents (N=337, 52.8%) reported that they were never stopped by a police officer while driving; however, 288 (47.2%) of the respondents reported that they had been stopped by a police officer at least one time. The number of stops by an officer ranged from zero to twenty-five, with the mean number of stops being 1.01. However, the data were recoded into a dichotomous format (0=never stopped, 1=stopped), the data revealed that 47% of the respondents had been stopped at least once by an officer.

In terms of the number of traffic citations reported, the majority of the respondents (71.8%) noted that they were never given a traffic citation. Yet the remaining 28.2 percent reported having at least one traffic citation within the past year. The number of traffic citations ranged from 0 to 12 citations in the past 12 months, with the mean being .51. This variable also was recoded into a dichotomous variable (0=no, 1=yes), which demonstrated that 28.2% of the individuals had reported receiving a traffic violation.

The number of respondents who received traffic citations was similar to the number that received speeding tickets in the past year. Although 74.1% of the respondents did not report receiving a speed ticket in the 12 months, 25.9 % reported having had at least one speeding ticket. At the same time, the number of speeding tickets ranged from 0 to 6. Lastly, there were 31.8% of the participants who reported that while being the driver of the vehicle they had at least one accident in the past year. The number of accidents ranged from 0 to 9 accidents in the past 12 months.

The Trait Anger scale of the STAXI-2 (Spielberger et al., 1985) evaluated an individual's dispositional anger or how often angry feelings were experienced over time. The mean score for the sample was 19.27. The scores ranged from 10 to 40, with 40 being the highest possible score. This mean score was slightly above the mean scores from past research. The research compiled by Spielberger and colleagues delineated the mean scores of the Trait Anger scale into females and males. The mean score for females was 17.78 and the mean score for males was 18.50.

Descriptive Statistics: Dependent Variables

In addition to the independent and control variables, the descriptive statistics for the outcome variables for aggressive driving and road rage surveys were presented. Table 12 displays selected frequencies and descriptive statistics for scores on the Total Aggressive Expression Scale (TAE) and the Driving Survey (DS). As previous literature suggested, there are many types and degrees of aggressive driving and road rage variables. Table 12 reported the mean, standard deviation, minimum and maximum scores, and valid $\underline{N}$ of the dependent variables. It is important to note that the $\underline{N}$ reflected only data that were complete for the entire scale. Thus, the mean was representative of completed responses for that particular scale.

Table 12: Descriptives for the Dependent Variables

Variable	Mean	Std. Dev.	Minimum Score	Maximum Score	N*
Total Aggression Expression	57.29	14.931	34	126	633
Driving Survey	33.67	23.511	0	140	622

Note. * The $\underline{N}$ for the study is 638.

The Total Aggressive Expression (TAE) scale was one of two dependent variables that assess aggressive driving and road rage behaviors among individuals. The TAE scale was a composite scale, which measured anger expressed through verbal, physical, and use of a vehicle while driving. The scale mean for the sample was 57.29. The range of scores for the respondents was 34 to 126, with 126 being the total possible score. While the Deffenbacher et al. (2002) research did not give the mean for the overall scale, it did delineate the mean for the scale into male and female. The mean score for males was 60.15, and the mean score for females was 55.90.

The Driving Survey involved the second measure of the dependent variable. The Driving Survey measured an individual's participation in aggressive driving incidents. As mentioned previously, the Driving Survey used in this study does not include the accident or the crash related subscales. This 29-item scale used in this study required the participant to report the number of times he/she had participated in the driving acts. The response format allowed the individual to mark from 0 to 5+ times, with 5+ being treated as 5 times for purposes of analyses. The scores for this sample ranged from 0 to 140, with 140 being the highest score possible. The mean score was 33.67. Although the Driving Survey (DS), in its original version, had been used in studies, this study only used 3 of the 5 subscales for analysis purposes. Therefore, there were no comparison data at this time.

Descriptive Statistics: Select Items of the TAE and DS

One impressive finding to note was that most respondents (99.5%) reported that they had engaged in some form of aggressive driving as evidenced by the TAE scores. Similar results hold true for the DS, in which 98.2% of the respondents reported that they had engaged in some form of aggressive driving. Although these statistics seemed alarming, the results were based on the frequencies of the individual items contained in the scales. The item that most individuals reported participating in was speeding. Thus, these above results demonstrate that the majority of respondents had engaged in speeding on the roadways as a form of aggressive driving.

According to the frequencies on specific acts that constitute serious forms of road rage, 18.3 percent had participated in damage to property/vehicle due to an incident stemming from a traffic altercation, 13.3 percent reported ever being involved in a verbal confrontation with another driver, and 4.7 percent were involved in a physical confrontation with another driver. It was also noteworthy to report the number of respondents who answered in the affirmative to these questions: "I bump the other driver's bumper with mine" (6.0%); "I try to force the other drivers to the side of the road" (4.4%); "I try to get out of the car and have a physical fight with the other driver" (8.4%).

The last two answers were separated out from the above physical confrontation questions because the incident may or may not have taken place (i.e., I *try*...).

Scale Reliability

Multiple item scales are often used to assess the characteristics of a single phenomenon. According to measurement theory, relationships among the scale items are logically connected to the latent variable (DeVellis, 1991). There are a number of methods to determine the reliability of a scale. For purposes of this study, the item total correlation for the scale items and the Cronbach's alpha level for the scale were reported.

Each coefficient for the scale items should range between 0 and 1, where one is a perfect correlation (DeVellis, 1991). Collectively, the items in a scale should be highly correlated with one another (e.g., with coefficients close to 1) if the scale is reliable. Items that have higher correlations illustrate that the scale is internally consistent, or reliable. The high reliability of a scale suggests that it is measuring the intended construct (DeVellis, 1991). At the same time, the square root of coefficient alpha is the correlation between a scale of N items and the construct or the domain (Nunnally, 1978).

In addition, item-total correlations were noted. Each item should correlate substantially with the other items to arrive at a set of highly inter-correlated items. The "corrected" item-total correlations represent the association between the item being evaluated and all scale items, excluding itself (DeVellis, 1991). Items with high values of correlation are more desirable than items with low values. Items should have a value at or above .30 to demonstrate appropriate shared variance among the items.

Thus, the internal consistency of the scale as determined by the coefficient alpha level was examined for each scale. Coefficient alpha or Cronbach's alpha represents the amount of variance in scale score that is shared by the items (DeVellis, 1991). This common variance, then, is assumed to be attributable to the common construct the items are intended to measure. According to DeVellis (1991, p. 85) comfort ranges for research scales are as follows: an alpha level below .60 is considered an unacceptable level; between .60 and .65 is undesirable; between .65 and .70 is minimally acceptable; between .70 and .80 is respectable; .80 to .90 is very good; and much above .90 one should consider shortening the scale.

Reliability Analysis for Strain Scale

A reliability analysis was conducted for the Capowich et al. (2001) Strain Scale. This scale asks questions regarding stressful and negative life events that undergraduate students may have encountered during the past year. The scale was intended to measure the three sources of strain noted by Agnew (1992): failure to achieve positively valued goals, the presentation of negative stimuli, and the removal of positive stimuli.

This scale consisted of twenty-six items, in which the respondent had to answer yes or no that the event had happened to him/her or to someone in his/her immediate family in the past year. The responses were coded as no =0 and yes=1. Due to the dichotomous nature of the individual items, the variation in items may be small. Because of an incomplete survey, the N for this scale was 637 students. The mean for the Strain Scale was 5.46, with a standard deviation of 3.07.

Table 13: Item Total Correlations for Strain Scale* (N=637)

Item	Item-Total Correlations
1. My family had serious money problems.	.255
2. My mother or father remarried.	.120
3. An immediate family member died.	.155
4. I, or a member of my immediate family, had a serious illness.	.256
5. A close friend died.	.184
6. I started attending a new school.	.267
7. In the past year, have you or someone in your family divorced.	.140
8. In the past year, was there a separation in your family.	.168
9. Have you or someone in your family have a serious accident	.158
10. You or someone in your family in trouble with the law.	.260
11. Father/mother, or both, unemployed.	.182
12. Did your family move.	.095
13. Has a significant other (boyfriend/girlfriend) broken up with you.	.279
14. Have you had any school problems (kicked out, caught cheating).	.190
15. Have you been dismissed from a job.	.221

Table 13: Strain Scale (continued)

Item	Item-Total Correlations
16. Has a friend broken off a friendship with you	.283
17. Have you begun a new school experience at a higher academic level. than before.	.300
18. Have you transferred to a new school at the same academic level as before.	.059
19. Have you been dismissed from a dormitory or other residence.	.055
20. Have you failed an important exam.	.285
21. Have you failed a course.	.219
22. Have you dropped a course.	.200
23. Have you changed your major.	.216
24. Have you had financial problems related to school (e.g., in danger of not having enough money to finish).	.268
25. Have you received a grade that you think was lower than you deserved.	.227
26. Have you received a grade that was unfair compared to the grade received by others in the course.	.191

Note. Cronbach's Alpha=.65 *The strain scale is comprised of 26 variables, which are dichotomous in nature (no=0, yes=1). Given the dichotomous nature of the responses, the KR-20 statistic represents the alpha level for the scale.

Given the above inter-item total correlations, it was noted that items numbered 12, 18 and 19 were below .100. Upon inspection of those items, a second reliability analysis was run without the above-mentioned items to examine the alpha level. The new analysis yielded a similar alpha level (alpha=.6485). Since there was no substantial increase in the alpha level, the items remained in the scale. The 26 item scale was used for analysis purposes.

The alpha level for this scale was .6484 which DeVellis (1991) considered to be minimally acceptable. This alpha level was higher than a previous study conducted by Capowich et al. (2001), which used this scale as their measure of strain. The Capowich et al. study had an alpha level of .58. Hoffman and Miller (1998) contended that a low alpha level for a strain scale was not surprising, in that, stressful life events often reflect discrete and independent episodes in individuals' lives. Given the above information, all items in the scale were retained for analysis purposes.

In addition to the alpha level, the Kuder-Richardson 20 (KR-20) statistic was used to assess the reliability of the scale. The Kuder-Richardson (1937) coefficient is a special case of the Cronbach alpha, it is interpreted in the same manner as the Cronbach alpha reliability coefficient. This is an overall measure of internal consistency, used for scales with a dichotomous response format. Like alpha, the KR-20 has a normal range between 0.00 and 1.00 with the higher numbers indicating higher internal consistency. The KR-20 essentially is the mean of all possible split-half coefficients. The KR-20 provided only an overall score and gave no information on the individual items.

Statistic	Formula
KR-20	$(N/N\text{-}1)\,[1\text{-}\Sigma p_i q_i / \sigma^2_x]$
Cronbach's Alpha	$\alpha = \dfrac{k}{k\text{-}1}\ \ 1\text{-}\ \dfrac{\Sigma \sigma^2_i}{\sigma^2_{yi}}$

Figure 3. Equations for KR-20 and Cronbach's alpha.

Note. KR-20, k=number of item in the scale; s^2 =square of the standard deviation of the scores of the respondents; apq=product of percent of the group getting an item right (p) times the percent of the group not getting an item right (q) added over all items; the apq term equals σ^2

The formula for the KR-20 is similar to the formula for Cronbach's alpha. See Figure 3 for formulas. When the test format has only one correct answer, KR-20 is algebraically equivalent to Cronbach's alpha. Therefore, the KR-20 reliability estimates may be considered special cases of Cronbach's alpha. Thus, the KR-20 equals .58.

Reliability Analysis for Situational Anger Scale
A reliability analysis was conducted for the seven-item, Situational Anger scale. This newly created scale was intended to capture the construct of situational anger, as a direct response to a particular type of driving incident. The respondent was asked to report his/her level of anger on a four point, Likert scale. The scale ranged from Not at All to Very Angry, with Not at All being coded as 1 and Very Angry coded as 4. The mean for the Situational Anger scale is 18.91 with a standard

deviation of 4.41. Because of incomplete data with respect to items in this particular scale, the number of cases used for the reliability analysis is 629.

Table 14: Item Total Correlations for Situational Anger Scale (N=629)

Item	Item-Total Correlations
1. Being cut in front of on the highway.	.474
2. Being tailgated by another vehicle for more than 1 mile.	.535
3. Being given an obscene due to your driving.	.672
4. Being verbally confronted by another driver due to your driving.	.714
5. Being behind a vehicle moving slowly in the left lane, obstructing you from passing.	.544
6. Being behind a driver who is indecisive at an intersection, thus making you late for an appointment.	.547
7. Being physically confronted by another driver because of your driving.	.591

Note. Cronbach's Alpha=.83

Item-total correlations for these seven items revealed that all correlations were above the .30 standard. According to the internal consistency estimate, the alpha for this scale is .83, which is considered very good by the standards set by DeVellis (1991).

Reliability Analysis for Self-Control Scale
A reliability analysis was conducted for the 24 item, Self Control scale. This scale was developed by Grasmick and his colleagues (1993), and it is one of the most widely used scales to measure an individual's level of self- control. The respondent was asked to assess his/her level of self-control on a four point, Likert scale. The scale ranged from Strongly Disagree (coded as 1) to Strongly Agree (coded as 4). Thus, those who scored higher on the scale are more likely to have lower levels of self-control. The mean for the scale was 51.53 with a standard deviation of 10.26. Because of incomplete data with respect to items in this particular scale, the number of cases used for the reliability analysis was 619.

Table 15: Item Total Correlations for Self-Control Scale (N=619)

Item	Item-Total Correlations
1. I often act on the spur of the moment.	.458
2. I don't devote much thought and effort to preparing for the future.	.472
3. I often do whatever brings me pleasure here and now, even at the cost of some distant goal.	.548
4. I'm more concerned about what happens to me in the short run than in the long run.	.583
5. I frequently try to avoid things that I know will be difficult.	.448
6. When things get complicated, I tend to quit or withdraw.	.354
7. The things in life that are easiest to do bring me the most pleasure.	.358
8. I dislike really hard tasks that stretch my abilities to the limit.	.392
9. I like to test myself every now and then by doing something a little risky.	.308
10. Sometimes I will take a risk just for the fun of it.	.446
11. I sometimes find it exciting to do things for which I might get in trouble.	.523
12. Excitement and adventure are more important to me than security.	.536
13. If I had a choice, I would almost always rather do something physical than something mental.	.468
14. I almost always feel better when I am on the move than when I am sitting and thinking.	.335
15. I like to get out and do thing more than I like to read or contemplate ideas.	.375
16. I seem to have more energy and a greater need for activity than most other people my age.	.331
17. I try to look out for myself first, even it if means making things difficult for other people.	.505
18. I'm not sympathetic to other people when they are having problems.	.397
19. If things I do upset people, it's their problem, not mine.	.365
20. I will try to get the things I want even when I know it's causing problems for other people.	.512
21. I lost my temper pretty easily.	.461

Table 15: Self-Control Scale (continued)

Item	Item-Total Correlations
22. Often, when I'm angry at people I feel more like hurting them than talking to them about why I am angry.	.488
23. When I am really angry, other people better stay away from me.	.398
24. When I have a serious disagreement with someone it's usually hard for me to talk about it without getting upset.	.347

Note. Cronbach's Alpha=.87

Item-total correlations for these 24 items demonstrated that all correlations were above the .30 standard. The item total correlations ranged from .331 to .583. According to the internal consistency estimate, the alpha for this scale is .87, which is considered very good by the standards set by DeVellis (1991). It was also consistent with previous studies that used the Grasmick et al. (1993) scale as a measure of self-control. The Grasmick et al. (1993) study yielded an alpha level of .80. Research conducted by Wood et al. (1993), which used the Grasmick et al. scale had an alpha level of .88. Arneklev et al. (1998) also administered the Grasmick et al. self-control scale at two time intervals to undergraduate populations, and had alpha levels of .86 and .89 respectively.

Reliability Analysis for Peer Behavior Scale
In order to capture the potential influence of peers in relation to aggressive driving and road rage behaviors, questions concerning their closest friend's driving behaviors were asked. This scale is comprised of four items, in which the respondent was asked to assess his/her closest friend's past participation in speeding, giving obscene gestures, verbal confrontations, and physical confrontations in relation to driving. The responses were reported on a three point, Likert scale. The scale ranged from Never (coded as 1), Sometimes (coded as 2) and Always (coded as 3). Thus, higher scores reflect that the respondent's friends were more likely to engage in aggressive driving offenses. The mean for the scale was 6.69, with a standard deviation of 1.84. Because of incomplete data with respect to items in this particular scale, the number of cases used for the reliability analysis was 635.

Table 16: Item Total Correlations for Peer Behavior Scale (N=635)

Item	Item-Total Correlations
1. How often does your closest friend speed.	.434
2. How often does your closest friend use obscene gestures.	.646
3. How often does your closest friend engage in verbal confrontations on the road.	.622
4. How often does your closest friend engage in physical confrontations on the road	.40

Note. Cronbach's Alpha=.73

Item-total correlations for these four items revealed that all correlations were above the .30 standard. The item total correlations ranged from .407 to .646. According to the internal consistency estimate, the alpha for this scale is .73. According to DeVellis (1991) an alpha between .70 and .80 was considered respectable.

Reliability Analysis for STAXI-2 Trait Anger Scale
A reliability analysis was conducted for the STAXI-2 Trait Anger Scale. This scale consisted of ten items, in which the respondent had to answer on a four point, Likert scale. The responses were coded as Almost Never =1, Sometimes=2, Often=3, and Almost Always=4. Due to a few incomplete responses, the N for this scale was 633 students. The mean for the Trait Anger Scale was 19.27, with a standard deviation of 5.78.

An internal consistency analysis of the STAXI-2 Trait Anger scale was conducted. The item-total correlations ranged from .486 (Item 10-"I feel infuriated when I do a good job") to .701 (Item 2- "I have a fiery temper."). The reliability analysis for the STAXI-2 Trait Anger scale resulted in a variance of 33.43 and a standard deviation of 5.78. The Cronbach's alpha for this scale was .87. According to DeVellis (1991), an alpha level between .80 to .90 is very good. The alpha level for this sample was also consistent with prior studies (See Spielberger, 1999).

Reliability Analysis for Total Aggression Expression Scale (TAE)
A reliability analysis was conducted for the Total Aggression Expression (TAE) subscale of the Driving Anger Expression Scale (DAX) (Deffenbacher et al., 2002). This scale represented the dependent variable (aggressive driving and road rage behaviors). This

scale was comprised of three subscales (i.e., Verbal Aggressive Expression subscale, Personal Physical Expression Scale, and use of Vehicle to Express Aggression Scale) within the overall Driving Anger Expression scale. The Total Aggression Expression scale consisted of 34 items, which the respondent was asked to answer on a four point, Likert scale. The responses were coded as Almost Never =1, Sometimes=2, Often=3, and Almost Always=4. Due to a few incomplete responses, the N for this scale was 633 students. The mean for the Total Aggression Expression Scale was 57.29, with a standard deviation of 14.93.

Table 17: Item Total Correlations for TAE (N=633)

Item	Item-Total Correlations
1. I give the other driver the finger.	.543
2. I drive right up on the other driver's bumper.	.568
3. I drive a little faster than I was.	.551
4. I try to cut in front of the other driver.	.471
5. I call the other driver names aloud.	.604
6. I make negative comments about the other driver.	.649
7. I follow right behind the other driver for a long time.	.506
18. I try to get out of the car and tell the other driver off.	.404
9. I yell questions like "Where did you get your license."	.556
10. I roll down the window to help communicate my anger.	.515
11. I glare at the other driver.	.639
12. I shake my fist at the other driver.	.527
13. I stick my tongue out at the other driver.	.198
14. I call the other driver names under my breath.	.393
15. I speed up to frustrate the other driver.	.671
16. I purposely block the other driver from doing what he/she wants to do.	.573
17. I bump the other driver's bumper with mine.	.291
18. I go crazy behind the wheel.	.541
19. I leave my brights on in the other driver's rear view mirror.	.523
20. I try to force the other drivers to the side of the road.	.322
21. I try to scare the other driver.	.502
22. I do to other drivers what they did to me.	.606
23. I drive a lot faster than I was.	.558
24. I swear at the other driver aloud.	.681

Table 17: TAE (continued)

Item	Item-Total Correlations
25. I swear at the other driver under my breath.	.471
26. I flash my lights at the other driver.	.504
27. I make hostile gestures other than giving the finger.	.540
28. I shake my head at the other driver.	.565
29. I yell at the other driver.	.677
30. I make negative comments about the other driver under my breath.	.543
31. I give the other driver a dirty look.	.638
32. I try to get out of the car and have a physical fight with the other driver.	.287
33. I think things like "Where did you get your license".	.496
34. I slow down to frustrate the other driver.	.630

Note. Cronbach's Alpha=.93

Item-total correlations for these 34 items revealed that all but three correlations were above the .30 standard. The item total correlations ranged from .198 to .681. The items that were below the .30 standard were the items numbered 13, 17, and 32. These individual items that yielded correlations below the .30 level were inspected to determine if their exclusion would more fully reflect the construct. However, merely raising the alpha level was only one consideration in deciding which items should be excluded. The other consideration was to carefully examine if the item truly represented the underlying construct of aggressive driving.

All three of the items (i.e., items 13, 17, and 32) were represented in the Personal Physical Expression subscale. Two of these items had a correlation close to the .30 standard (.291, and .287 respectively). The item number 13 (i.e., "I stick my tongue out at the other driver," item total correlation=.198) is more problematic with respect to its correlation magnitude. However, the alpha level for the Personal Physical Expression subscale is .82. If item number 13 were removed from the scale, the alpha level would only increase to .83. Upon reviewing the underlying construct of the scale, using personal attributes to make the other driver aware that you are angry, sticking one's tongue out does fit with the meaning of the construct. Thus, taking into account both the correlative magnitude and the content validity, all three items were retained in the scale.

Table 18: TAE Subscales Alpha Levels

Total Aggression Expression (TAE) subscales	Items (see above TAE chart)	Cronbach's Alpha (TAE scale=.93)
Verbal Aggressive Expression	5, 6, 9, 11, 14, 24, 25, 28, 29, 30, 31, 33	Alpha=.90
Personal Physical Expression	1, 8, 10, 12, 13, 17, 18, 20, 21, 27, 32	Alpha=.82
Use of Vehicle to Express Anger	2, 3, 4, 7, 15, 16, 22, 23, 26, 34	Alpha=.88

In terms of the above-noted subscales, the Verbal Aggression Expression subscale had an alpha level of .90, the Personal Physical Expression subscale yielded an alpha level of .82, and the Use of Vehicle to Express Aggression had an alpha level of .88. These alpha levels were consistent with prior research. The Deffenbacher et al. (2002) study conducted a reliability analysis of the subscales of the Total Aggression Expression scale and found that the Verbal Aggressive Expression scale yielded an alpha level of .88, Personal Physical Aggressive Expression scale had an alpha level of .81, and use of vehicle to express anger yielded an alpha level of .86.

According to the internal consistency estimate, the alpha for this Total Aggression Expression (TAE) scale was .93, which was considered very good by the standards set by DeVellis (1991). It was also consistent with a previous study that used the Deffenbacher et al. (2002) scale as a measure of aggressive driving. The Deffenbacher et al. scale (2002) yielded an alpha level of .90.

<u>Reliability Analysis for the Driving Survey (DS)</u>
The second measure of the dependent variable, the Driving Survey, was also subject to reliability analysis. This was a 28 item scale, in which the participant reported his/her participation in various aggressive driving acts. The response format allowed the participant to report the number of times (i.e., 0 to 5+, with 5+ being treated as a 5 for analysis purposes) he/she engaged in the specific driving incident. The mean

for the scale was 33.67, and the standard deviation was 23.51. Because there were incomplete responses for this particular scale, the valid N for this scale is 622.

Table 19: Item Total Correlations for Driving Survey Scale (N=622)

Item	Item-Total Correlations
1. Broken or damaged a part of a vehicle (e.g., pulled knob of the radio, kicked a fender).	.335
2. Had an argument with a passenger while you were driving.	.496
3. Had a verbal argument with the driver of another vehicle.	.399
4. Had a physical fight with the driver of another vehicle.	.282
5. Made an angry gesture at another driver or pedestrian.	.575
6. Swore at or called another driver or pedestrian names.	.476
7. Flashed your headlights in anger.	.521
8. Have you honked your horn in anger.	.522
9. Yelled at another driver or pedestrian.	.588
10. Drove while being very angry.	.553
11. Lost control of your anger while driving.	.484
12. Drove up close behind another driver in anger.	.627
13. Cut another driver off in anger.	.593
14. Driven without using your seat belt.	.357
15. Drank alcohol and driven.	.438
16. Been drunk and driven.	.449
17. Driven 10 to 20 miles over the limit.	.381
18. Drive 20+ mph over the limit.	.505
19. Passed unsafely.	.633
20. Tailgated or followed another vehicle too closely.	.613
21. Changed lanes unsafely.	.671
22. Drifted into another lane.	.537
23. Switched lanes to speed through slower traffic.	.522
24. Gone out of turn at a red light or stop sign.	.603
26. Driven Recklessly.	.627
27. Run a red light or stop sign.	.507
28. Entered an intersection when the light was turning red.	.535

Note. Cronbach's Alpha=.92

Item-total correlations for these 28 items demonstrated that all but one correlation was above the .30 standard. The item total correlations ranged from .282 to .671. The item below the .30 standard was item number 4 (i.e., had a physical fight with the driver of another vehicle). Although this item yielded a correlation below the .30 level, it was an essential part of the construct. However, the item was further scrutinized to determine if its exclusion would more fully reflect the construct, while increasing the alpha level. It was determined that this item represented the very core of road rage behaviors, as it was considered to be the most serious offense. Therefore the item was retained in the scale. The alpha level for this scale was .92, which according to DeVellis' standards (1991) is considered very good.

Guttman Scaling of Road Rage Behaviors

Currently, neither the Total Aggression Expression (TAE) Scale nor the Driving Survey (DS) contained items that progress into a hierarchical, Guttman-style order (nor was there any reason to believe that the surveys' authors intended to do so). However, the above measures of the dependent variable did not take into consideration the seriousness of offenses. It is suggested that the aggressive driving and road rage items may be rank ordered into a format of increasing acts of severity. It was anticipated that these items could be ordered, and thus could be treated as a Guttman scale. As a result of choosing the items to represent road rage and its increase in severity, these items comprised a Guttman scale, which determined how far individuals were willing to participate in more serious acts of road rage.

Guttman scaling, or cumulative scaling, implies a developmental sequence of aggressive driving behaviors (Andrews & Hops, 1991). It assumes that if an individual engages in a particular driving act, the individual also engages in all of the driving acts earlier in the scale. For example, the third item in the scale was, "I give the other driver the finger," and the second item was, "I make negative comments about the other driver under my breath." It was assumed that an individual who gives the finger had also made negative comments about another driver under his/her breath. Therefore, the affirmation of any item on a Guttman scale indicated participation of all prior items on the scale (DeVellis, 1991).

Since there were two measures of the dependent variable (i.e., Total Aggression Expression Scale and the Driving Survey), items were taken from both instruments for the inclusion into the new scale. First, using face validity, the researcher decided to categorize all of the items into constructs (i.e., Speeding, Gestures, Verbal Signals, Vehicle Signals, Property Damage, Verbal Confrontation, and Physical Altercation) that appeared to represent aggressive driving behaviors. Second, after the categories were delineated, items from each category were chosen to represent that particular category. Third, for purposes of rank ordering, it was decided that the level of violence or potential harm against the victim was the most salient aspect of the construct. Therefore, it was suggested that this ordering would result in decreasing frequency of responses as the level of reported violence and damage increased.

Table 20: Guttman Scale of Aggressive Driving Behaviors (N=635)

Item Order/Score	Valid N	%
1. Driven 10 to 20 miles over the limit?	539	84.88%
2. I make negative comments about the other driver under my breath.	483	76.06%
3. I give the other driver the finger?	268	42.20%
4. I swear at the other driver aloud.	257	40.47%
5. I flash my lights at the other driver.	194	30.55%
6. Broken or damaged a part of the vehicle.	45	7.09%
7. I had a verbal argument with the driver of another vehicle?	36	5.67%
8. I had a physical fight with the driver of another vehicle?	18	2.83%

Note. Coefficient of Reproducibility=.8611

This newly created scale has an alpha level of .54. As mentioned previously, since this scale had a dichotomous response format, the KR-20 statistic (.54) was used, which was equivalent to the Cronbach's Alpha. However, it was not expected that these items would yield a high alpha level. The items were then ordered, the number of errors was calculated for each item. Errors were considered to be responses that endorsed higher-level items but did not affirm all preceding items.

A coefficient of reproducibility could be calculated from the formula below.

Coefficient of reproducibility=
1- (total errors/number of scale items x N)

Figure 4. Coefficient of reproducibility.

A coefficient of reproducibility of .8611 was calculated. The number of errors in the scale was 706. There were 8 items in the scale and a total of 635 complete cases. Thus, the denominator equaled 5,080. Although Guttman initially stated that 90 percent was an acceptable cutpoint; he later declared that 80 percent accuracy was also an acceptable cut-off point. The coefficient of reproducibility met the standard. The coefficient of reproducibility was also a measure of reliability, in that, an individual who scored a certain level of aggressive driving would be expected to reproduce the score in other instances.

Table 20 provides a breakdown of the items that were included in this scale as well as the percentage of respondents who participated in each of the driving acts. The chart illustrated that more serious offenses (i.e., items 7 and 8) had lower participation rates than less serious offenses. Therefore, an individual's score on the Guttman scale aided in classifying an individual at the psychometric level. By knowing an individual's score on this scale, it would help to reproduce his/her driving behavior. For example, an individual scored an 8 (out of 8) on the scale. A person who scored an 8, would be considered a highly aggressive driver. Given this information, it was concluded that this person not only would commit serious acts of aggressive driving, but also was likely to have committed less serious acts of aggressive driving as well. Thus, the person was likely to have committed the acts listed in questions one through seven.

Validity of Instruments

It is important to assess the validity of the scale on its face. The content validity of the scales was determined through comparison of the items with the domain measures of behaviors, established in the literature. According to DeVellis (1991), content validity can be evaluated when the domain was well defined.

In terms of validity, it is necessary to revisit the reliability analyses. The reliability analyses of the current study have demonstrated good reliability through the inter-item total correlations as well as the alpha levels of the respective scales. Nunnally (1967) provided a theoretical framework for verifying the validity of scales, he states, "The square root of coefficient alpha is the estimated correlation of a test with errorless scores" (p. 196). This assumption then suggests that an alpha coefficient that correlates highly with an errorless score is measuring the proper latent variable. Guilford (1954, p. 399-400) also contends that validity is indicated by the square root of the proportion of true variance, in other words, the square root of its reliability, or the index of reliability. Using this formula, a test of validity was conducted for each of the variables put forth in the theoretical framework.

Content Validity of Strain
According to GST, strain can arise from situations in which individuals fail to achieve positively valued goals, when individuals are presented with noxious circumstances, and when individuals lose something to which they assign positive value (Agnew, 1992). Failing to achieve positively valued goals includes strain that arises from situations that individuals perceive as inequitable or unjust. Strain as a result of experiencing noxious stimuli involved noxious/negative interactions that individuals may experience at school, at home, and in their neighborhoods. Strain evolving from the loss of positively valued stimuli involves situations in which individuals lose something that they value such as, a close friend, a parent, or a nice place to live and go to school. However, it is important to note that these types of strain may overlap given the perspective of the individual. Some of the items may represent more than one type of strain. The Capowich et al. (2001) scale was used in this study. Table 22 illustrates the content validity of items for the three types of strain.

Table 21: Content Validity Assessment for Strain

Elements of Strain	Corresponding Scale Items
Failure to achieve positively valued goals	100, 101, 102, 103, 111, 112

Table 21: Content Validity Assessment for Strain (continued)

Elements of Strain	Corresponding Scale Items
Presentation of noxious stimuli	81, 82, 84, 86, 89, 90, 91, 104
Removal of positive stimuli	83, 85, 87, 88, 92, 93, 94, 95, 96, 97, 98, 99

In addition to the content validity, the index of reliability was also examined. For this scale, the square root of the alpha level (Alpha=.6484) yielded an index of reliability of .8052. The results of this demonstrate a strong case for a valid measure of strain.

Construct Validity of Situational Anger
Aggressive forms of expression (i.e., aggressive driving and road rage) correlated positively with measures of anger, thus providing evidence of scale validity for Situational Anger. This is evidenced by the high correlation between situational anger and TAE ($\underline{r}$=.507), DS ($\underline{r}$=.390) and GS ($\underline{r}$=.330). This also holds true for the relationship between Trait Anger and the TAE ($\underline{r}$=.515), DS ($\underline{r}$=.422) and GS ($\underline{r}$=.340). Furthermore, the correlation between situational anger and trait anger is .488, thus, demonstrating that they share an underlying construct of anger. The strong relationships with reported aggression further support the validity of measures of expressing anger while driving (i.e., aggressive driving).

For the situational anger variable, the index of reliability was also examined. For this scale, the square root of the alpha level (Alpha=.8336) yielded an index of reliability of .9130. The results of this demonstrate a strong case for a valid measure of situational anger.

Content Validity of Self-Control
Gottfredson and Hirschi (1990) defined people who have low self-control as individuals having personalities predisposing them to criminal acts. Grasmick et al. (1993) used six domains: Impulsivity, Simple tasks, Risk Seeking, Physical Activities, Self-centeredness, and Temper. Each of these domains represent four questions, all of which culminated into the individual's level of self-control. Grasmick et al. (1993) report the corresponding items for each domain, or component of Self-Control. See Table 22 for the items that represent each

category. Prior research (Grasmick et al., 1993) yielded a self-control eigenvalue of 4.7; thus demonstrating unidimensionality of the construct of self-control.

Table 22: Content Validity for Self-Control

Domain	Corresponding Scale Items
Impulsivity	130, 131, 132, 133
Simple tasks	134, 135, 136, 137
Risk Seeking	138, 139, 140, 141
Physical Activities	142, 143, 144, 145
Self-centeredness	146, 147, 148, 149
Temper	150, 151, 152, 153

In addition to the content validity, the index of reliability was also examined. For this scale, the square root of the alpha level (Alpha=.8688) yielded an index of reliability of .9321. The results of this demonstrate a strong case for a valid measure of self-control.

Content Validity of Peer Behavior
In assessing the content validity of peer behavior, it was necessary to review the definition used for investigating peer behavior. For this study, the concept of peer behavior was based on two concerns. The first item asked the respondent to think of his/her closest friend, and the second part asked the respondent to recount how often that person engaged in acts of aggressive driving or road rage. Furthermore, another question asked the respondent to report if his/her closest friend ever influenced him/her to commit a criminal act. These questions taken together constitute the role of peer behavior in the context of whether or not the respondent was likely to engage in the act as well.

In addition to the content validity, the index of reliability was also examined. For this scale, the square root of the alpha level (Alpha=.7262) yielded an index of reliability of .8522. The results of this demonstrate a strong case for a valid measure of peer behavior.

Content Validity of Dependent Variables
Beginning with the measures of the dependent variables, the Total Aggression Expression (TAE) scale, Driving Survey, and the Guttman Scale of Road Rage, each scale had demonstrated its validity. First,

previous research (Deffenbacher et al., 2001; Deffenbacher et al., 2002) has validated both the TAE and DS scale. In the case of the dependent measures of road rage, two of three measures (TAE and the DS) contained items that were taken directly from the literature. These instruments were used because they contained existing scales. Second, the Guttman scale was created from taking items, which have established reliability and validity. Third, the three measures were highly correlated. The correlations between the measures are .635 for the DS and TAE, .685 for the DS and GS, and .633 for the TAE and GS. Each of these correlations was significant at the p< .001 level.

In addition to using prior research as a guide, the researcher also asked independent raters to assess whether the items contained in the survey (i.e., those items geared to represent aggressive driving and road rage behavior) were representative of the definition of road rage. Each agreed that the items represented the domain of aggressive driving and road rage behaviors. In addition to the independent raters, a pre-test was administered to undergraduate students. The students were asked to note any questions/concerns with the items representing road rage, yet none of the returned surveys indicated that there was a problem with the domain items.

In assessing the content validity of the Total Aggression Expression scale, the elements of aggressive driving as defined by Deffenbacher et al. (2002) were compared to both the individual scale items and the entire scale. Furthermore, the definitions and research contained in the literature review were taken into consideration. Given this, the specific items were matched to the subcategories of the scale. The sub-categories of the scale were highly correlated with the overall scale (i.e., verbal aggression and TAE=.885, Personal Physical Aggression and TAE=.773, and use of Vehicle to Express Anger =.875). Overall, the TAE scale appears to have good content validity. See Table 23.

Table 23: Content Validity Assessment for TAE

Elements of Road Rage	Corresponding scale items
Verbal Aggressive	22, 23, 26, 28, 31, 41, 42, 45, 46, 47, 48, 50

Table 23: Content Validity Assessment for TAE (continued)

Elements of Road Rage	Corresponding scale items
Personal Physical Aggressive	18, 25, 27, 29, 30, 34, 35, 37, 38, 39
Use of Vehicle to Express Anger	19, 20, 21, 24, 32, 33, 36, 39, 40, 43, 51

In addition to the content validity, the index of reliability was also examined for the TAE. For this scale, the square root of the alpha level (Alpha=.9342) yielded an index of reliability of .9665. The results of this demonstrate a strong case for a valid measure of the TAE.

The Deffenbacher et al. Driving Survey (2001) contained two subscales in which the items reflect driving related anger and risky driving behavior. In assessing content validity, the elements of aggressive driving were defined and compared to both the individual scale items and the entire scale. Given the above information and prior research in which the Driving Survey was utilized, the DS scale appears to have good content validity. See Table 24.

Table 24: Content Validity Assessment for Driving Survey (DS)

Elements of Road Rage	Corresponding Scale Items
Driving-Related Anger	52, 53, 54, 55, 56, 57, 58, 59, 60,. 61, 62, 63 64
Risky Driving Behavior	65, 66, 67, 68, 69, 70, 71, 72, 73, 74, 75, 76, 78, 79, 80

In addition to the content validity, the index of reliability was examined. For this scale, the square root of the alpha level (Alpha=.9154) yielded an index of reliability of .9568. The results of this demonstrate a strong case for a valid measure of strain.

In terms of assessing the validity of the Guttman version of the aggressive driving and road rage scale, it is important to note that the Guttman scale was created from taking items from the existing TAE scale and the DS, both of which have established validity and reliability. Furthermore, the items to be included in the Guttman scale were scrutinized for their representativeness of the domain as well as inspected by two independent raters, who agreed that the items reflect the content of the construct.

Bivariate Correlations

The next step in the analysis process consisted of conducting bivariate procedures. The bivariate correlations were presented between each of the independent variables and between the independent and dependent variables. Bivariate correlations do not imply cause and effect relationships; however, they were used to determine if any significant associations exist between the variables. This procedure also was used to test for multicollinearity among the independent variables in this study. The absence of multicollineary is necessary in order to meet one of the assumptions for regression analysis (Schroeder, Sjoquist, & Stephan, 1986). Perfect multicollinearity occurs when one independent variable is perfectly correlated with another independent variable. High multicollinearity creates estimation problems by producing high variances for the slope estimates and large standard errors. See Table 25 for bivariate correlations.

Correlations, or the Pearson's r, were examined for the independent variables, the independent and dependent variables, and the two measures of the dependent variable. Correlations were also discussed in terms of their magnitude, direction, and significance. The association was displayed as a correlation coefficient that ranged from −1.00 to +1.00. If there was a positive association, the coefficient was between zero and +1.00. If there was a negative association, the coefficient was between zero and −1.00. As a general rule, correlations between +/- .20 were considered weak, +/- .20 to .40 were considered moderate, +/- .40 to .60 were considered moderately strong, and greater that +/- .60 were considered strong (DeVellis, 1991). The direction of the correlation was also helpful in interpreting the association between the variables. Lastly, the level of significance is reported for the correlations between the variables (See Table 25).

Table 25: Bivariate Correlations Among Variables

Variable	(1)	(2)	(3)	(4)	(5)	(6)	(7)	(8)	(9)	(10)	(11)	(12)	(13)	(14)	(15)	(16)
Age (1)	1															
	(638)															
Gender (2)	-.067															
	(638)															
Race (3)	.077	-.084*														
	(638)	(638)														
Commuter (4)	.369**	-.031	.021													
	(638)	(638)	(638)													
Miles Daily (5)	.112**	.001	-.044	.234**												
	(594)	(594)	(594)	(594)												
Driver's Class (6)	-.059	.126**	-.104	-.051	.031											
	(638)	(638)	(638)	(638)	(594)											
Police Stops (7)	.010	-.218**	.098*	-.008.	.088*	.056										
	(638)	(638)	(638)	(638)	(594)	(638)										
Traffic Cit. (8)	.031	-.146**	.062	.016**	.106**	.056	.521**									
	(638)	(638)	(638)	(638)	(594)	(638)	(638)									
Speeding (9)	.067	-.147**	.086*	.092*	.130**	.041	.506**	.588**								
	(638)	(638)	(638)	(638)	(594)	(638)	(638)	(638)								
Prior Acc. (10)	-.005	-.013.	.098*	.012	.091	.018	.248**	.260**	.265**							
	(638)	(638)	(638)	(638)	(594)	(638)	(638)	(638)	(638)							

Table 25: Bivariate Correlations Among Variables (continued)

Variable	(1)	(2)	(3)	(4)	(5)	(6)	(7)	(8)	(9)	(10)	(11)	(12)	(13)	(14)	(15)	(16)
Trait Anger (11)	-.063	-.014	.036	-.057	.167**	.003	.128**	.182**	.163**	.175**						
	(633)	(633)	(633)	(633)	(589)	(633)	(633)	(633)	(633)	(633)						
Strain (12)	-.199**	-.020	.093*	-.147**	.115**	-.038	.193**	.164**	.152**	.130**	.245**					
	(637)	(637)	(637)	(637)	(593)	(637)	(637)	(637)	(637)	(637)	(632)					
Sit. Anger (13)	-.167**	.018	-.053	-.092*	.065	.016	.039	.095*	.028	.117**	.488**	.131**				
	(629)	(629)	(629)	(629)	(586)	(629)	(629)	(629)	(629)	(629)	(624)	(628)				
SC (14)	-.173**	-.223**	.101*	-.137**	.083*	-.029	.149**	.168**	.157**	.131**	.516**	.249**	.333**			
	(619)	(619)	(619)	(619)	(576)	(619)	(619)	(619)	(619)	(619)	(614)	(618)	(610)			
Peer Beh. (14)	-.137**	-.211**	-.041	-.101*	.135**	.039	.179**	.113**	.095*	.084*	.297**	.242**	.226**	.364**		
	(635)	(635)	(635)	(635)	(592)	(635)	(635)	(635)	(635)	(635)	(630)	(634)	(626)	(616)		
TAE (15)	-.120**	-.152**	.011	.070	.156**	.004	.242**	.183**	.156**	.210**	.515**	.236**	.507**	.428**	418**	
	(633)	(633)	(633)	(633)	(589)	(633)	(633)	(633)	(633)	(633)	(628)	(632)	(624)	(614)	(630)	
DS (16)	-.043	-.276**	-.040	.026	.152**	-.045	.217**	.208**	.163**	.166**	.422**	.191**	.390**	.440**	.455**	.635**
	(622)	(622)	(622)	(622)	(581)	(622)	(622)	(622)	(622)	(622)	(617)	(621)	(613)	(603)	(619)	(617)

Note. Correlation between DS and TAE is .635** (617)
** Correlation is significant at the p<.01 level
* Correlation is significant at the p<.05 level (N) Valid N

Variables in the Correlation Matrix

The independent variables derived from the theoretical model include: strain, situational anger, self-control, and past peer behaviors. The control variables for this study included: age, gender, race/ethnicity, commuter status, miles driven daily, driver's education class, number of times stopped by police for vehicle violation, number of traffic citations, number of speeding tickets, number of prior accidents, and trait anger. The dependent variables included two measures of road rage. The first measure of the dependent variable included the Total Aggression Expression Inventory (Deffenbacher et al., 2002) and the second measure included the Driving Survey (Deffenbacher et al., 2001). It is important to clarify that other variables were considered for placement in the model but have been ruled out for the following reasons. Although data were collected on the respondent's class standing, this information was not used for analysis purposes. The class standing variable was used initially to determine the representativeness of the sample to the population; however, since the person's class standing is closed tied to the individual's age, the age variable was included in the analysis. The driving experience variable was calculated to determine the length of time that the respondent has experience driving behind the wheel of a vehicle, however, this variable was also excluded from the matrix.

Initially, both age and driving experience variables were included in the correlation matrix. The "age" variable represented an individual's chronological age in years, thus reflecting a natural progression of time. The "driving experience" variable reflected the length of time that a person has held a driver's license (i.e., variable age at which he/she received his/her driver's license was subtracted from variable of current age); thus representing the amount or length of time a person has behind the wheel of a vehicle.

Since both variables are based on time, they both demonstrated similar correlations with the dependent and independent variables. Furthermore, they were highly correlated with each other ($r=.967$, $p=.000$). When initially placed in the model, the Variance Inflation Factor for age was 18.769; and for driving experience it was 18.627. Both numbers are greater than 4.0, which is typically the cut off point for ruling out collinearity (Mertler & Vannatta, 2002). Also, the tolerance statistics for age was .053, and for driving experience was

.054. Both numbers are less than .20, which is the typical cut off point for ruling out collinearity as well (Mertler & Vannatta, 2002). In addition to these statistical justifications, the prior research has cited age as a significant predictor of road rage behaviors. Given these factors, the variable of age was used in the model.

Correlations Among the Independent Variables
As mentioned previously, the independent variables for this study included: strain, situational anger, self-control, and peer behaviors. The control variables included: age, gender, race/ethnicity, miles driven daily, commuter status, driver's education class, number of times stopped by police for vehicle violation, number of traffic citations, number of speeding tickets, number of prior accidents, and trait anger.
Upon investigating the correlation coefficients for multicollinearity, it appeared that the highest correlation among the independent variables was between the Self-Control scale and the Trait Anger scale (r = .516, p< .01). The 24-item scale used to measure an individual's level of self-control included a 4-item subscale, which reflected an individual's temper. Thus, one small component of trait anger was being assessed by the self-control measure and also by a separate measure. Although these variables are highly correlated, it did not constitute a collinearity problem. Furthermore, it is argued that both trait anger and self-control are stable personality characteristics, therefore, it was expected that they would be correlated to some degree.

It is important to note that this study used the Trait Anger scale from the STAXI-2 (Spielberger, 1999) to assess trait anger. However in previous strain literature, (see Mazerolle & Piquero, 1994) the trait anger variable was assessed using the 4-item temper subscale from Grasmick et al. (1993). For this study it is acknowledged that the self-control variable is based on other indicators (i.e., impulsivity, simple tasks, risk seeking, physical activities, and self-centeredness) in addition to trait anger. Although the items are similar, none of the items are identical to those items in the Grasmick et al. scale (1993). Therefore, both scales tap into dispositional anger, so it came as no surprise that this is the case.

Among the remaining independent variables, the next highest correlation coefficient is between Trait Anger and Situational Anger variables (r=.488; p<.01). The Trait Anger scale is comprised of items that assess an individual's dispositional level of anger, while the

Situational Anger scale taps into a person's level of anger given a specific circumstance. Thus, both scales measure the construct of anger yet do so from different perspectives.

It is also important to note, that among the control variables there are high correlations between number of police stops and number of traffic citations (r=.521, p<.01), number of police stops and number of prior speeding tickets (r=.506, p<.01), and number of traffic citations and prior speeding tickets (r=.588, p<.01). Each of these variables was concerned with driving behaviors which have been acknowledged by police.

Given the above cases, it is important to revisit the concept of multicollinearity. Multicollinearity arises whenever two or more independent variables used in regression are not independent but are correlated. A frequent practice is to examine the bivariate correlations among the independent variables, looking for a coefficient of about .8 or larger. None of the correlates between independent variables reached beyond the .6 level. However, this does not take into account the relationship of an independent variable with all the other independent variables (Lewis-Beck, 1980). Therefore, other tests were conducted to assess the existence of multicollinearity among the variables.

Tolerance statistics and variance inflation factors (VIF) were conducted to examine potential problems with mulitcollinearity in the model. According to Mertler and Vannatta, (2002), tolerances should exceed .1 and variance inflation factors should be less than 4. The variables were not affected by multicollinearity as their tolerance scores ranged from .608 - .904 and variance inflation factors were below 1.6.

Correlations between the Independent and Dependent Variables

Upon investigation of the bivariate correlations among the independent variables (i.e., strain, situational anger, self-control, peer behavior) and the dependent variables (i.e., TAE and DS,), it was found that all of the coefficients were significant at the .01 level. Furthermore, all of the correlations were positive. The highest correlation occurred with the Situational Anger and TAE (r=.507, p<.01). This suggested that students with high levels of situational anger may also engage in road rage behavior. The lowest correlation, yet statistically significant, was between Stain and the Driving Survey (r=.191, p<.01). This suggested that students with high levels of strain may also engage in road rage behaviors.

The independent variables also were examined separately with the two measures of the dependent variable. In response to the TAE scale, each of the independent variables was significant at the .01 level. The correlations with the TAE were situational anger (r=.507), self-control (r=.428), peer behavior (r=.418), and strain (r=.236). With respect to the DS scale, each of the independent variables was significant at the .01 level. The correlations with the DS was peer behavior (r=.455), self-control (r=.440), situational anger (r=.390), and strain (r=.191). Although the magnitudes of the above relationships differ, all of the associations were statistically significant. It is important to note that the relationship between strain and each of the dependent variables was weak yet significant.

The interpretations for each relationship between the independent and dependent variables were the same. Individuals who experience strain may also engage in road rage. Individuals who have experienced situational anger also participate in road rage. Persons who have low levels of self-control may also participate in road rage behaviors. Individuals who have friends that engaged in road rage behaviors also have engaged in road rage behaviors.

In addition to the main independent variables, the control variable "trait anger" had demonstrated significant relationships to both the independent and dependent variables. Trait anger, an individual's disposition toward anger, was significantly correlated with each of the dependent variables. Trait anger and the TAE had a strong, positive correlation (r=.515, p<.01). Trait anger and the DS had a strong, positive correlation (r=.422, p<.01).

The relationships between the gender variable and the dependent variables were also examined. Prior literature indicated that gender may affect whether a person is likely to engage in road rage behaviors. Gender had negative moderate correlations with all three of the measures of the dependent variable. There is a moderate negative correlation between Gender and the DS (r= -.276, p<.01) and a weaker correlation exists between gender and TAE (r= -.152, p<.001). Gender is a dichotomous variable, where 0 represents males and 1 is coded as female. These initial results suggest that women may be less likely to participate in road rage.

Correlations among the Dependent Variables

The research question "Is there a correlation between the Total Aggression Expression Inventory (TAE) and the Driving Survey (DS)" was examined. The results indicated that there was a strong positive correlation (r=.635, p<.01) between the two measures of the dependent variable that assessed the participation in road rage. Correlations were examined among the measures of the dependent variable. The resulting correlation was positive, strong, and significant. The above correlation demonstrates that both measures of the dependent variable assessed the same overall construct: road rage behaviors. The corroboration of measures also provides evidence of the validity and reliability of the construct. Furthermore, these measures of the dependent variable have been used in prior studies and have proven to be reliable and valid.

In addition to the above measures of the dependent variable, it was previously mentioned that a Guttman scale was devised from the survey data. Although this scale could be treated as another measure of the dependent variable for analysis purposes, it was not used in the path analysis. The justification for not using the Guttman scale version was two fold. First, the Guttman scale was created by taking specific items from the above preexisting scales. Second, the Guttman scale and the above scales are highly correlated. The correlation between the TAE and the Guttman (r=.635, p<.01) and the correlation between the DS and the Guttman (r=.685, p<.01) were strong. Therefore, only the TAE and the DS dependent variables were used for analysis purposes.

Summary of Correlations

All of the correlation coefficients between the independent variables and the dependent variables were found to be significant at the .01 level (2-tailed tests). The independent variables that are significantly correlated with the dependent variables included: Strain, Situational Anger, Self-Control, and Peer Behavior. The independent variables were correlated with each other; however, they did not constitute multicollinearity. The two dependent variables were also correlated with each other (r=.635), thus demonstrating that they were measuring the same underlying construct through the use of similar questions.

Analysis of the Research Questions and Hypotheses

The purpose of this study was to gain an understanding of road rage behaviors by examining relationships between control variables, strain, situational anger, self-control, peer behavior, and road rage. In order to view these relationships within the proper context, path analysis was used to delineate the relationships between and among the variables. At this time it is important to revisit the research questions this study posed.

1. To what extent do college students participate in road rage?

2. Is there a correlation between the Total Aggression Expression (TAE) subscale of the Driving Anger Expression Inventory and the Driving Survey?

3. To what extent does a person's level of strain influence road rage?

4. To what extent does strain have an effect on situational anger?

5. Is anger a mediating variable in the strain model?

6. To what extent is situational anger associated with coping mechanisms?

7. To what extent do coping mechanisms (self-control and peer behaviors) mediate the effects of strain on road rage?

In addition to each of these research questions, there were corresponding hypotheses, which will provide evidence to support or refute the research questions.

1. To what extent do college students participate in road rage?

In order to assess the level of participation in road rage by college students, descriptive statistics were examined. These descriptive statistics included the mean scores on the Total Aggression Expression

Inventory (TAE) and the Driving Survey (DS). It is necessary to revisit the descriptive statistics of the dependent variables. As seen below, the mean score for the TAE was 57.29 and the mean score for the DS was 33.67. Generally, these scores show that students were participating in behaviors that range from roadway annoyances to traffic violations to outright assaultive behaviors. Recall from the descriptive statistics provided earlier in the chapter, that 98.1% of the participants had participated in at least one act of aggressive driving.

Table 26: Descriptive Statistics for the Dependent Variables

Variable	Mean	Std. Dev.	Minimum Score	Maximum Score	N*
TAE	57.29	14.931	34	126	633
Driving Survey	33.67	23.511	0	140	622

Note. *The N for the study is 638.

To further delineate the extent of participation, the following table presents selected frequencies from the items in the TAE scale. The selected frequencies from the TAE scale represent the reported participation in these acts. The items were chosen to reflect a wide array of the types of questions that the survey asked. Some of the items represent aggressive driving behaviors while others reflect road rage behaviors. Although most respondents did not report frequent involvement in aggressive driving and road rage, those that did report participation in these acts pose a threat to public safety. Furthermore, since aggressive driving and road rage behaviors are committed against anonymous individuals, these statistics demonstrate that anyone is subject to victimization. However, this does not suggest that college students are more likely to engage in road rage than other segments of the population.

Table 27: Frequencies of Selected Items from the TAE

Behavior	Almost Never	Sometimes	Often	Almost Always
I call the other driver names aloud	149 (23.4%)	218 (34.2%)	168 (26.3%)	103 (16.1%)

Table 27: Frequencies of Selected Items from the TAE (continued)

Behavior	Almost Never	Sometimes	Often	Almost Always
I swear at the other driver aloud	188 (29.5%)	239 (37.5%)	130 (20.4%)	81 (12.7%)
I give the other driver the finger	369 (57.8%)	202 (31.7%)	46 (7.2%)	21 (3.3%)
I shake my fist at the other driver	468 (73.4%)	114 (17.9%)	38 (6.0%)	18 (2.8%)
I leave my brights on in the other driver's rear view mirror.	510 (79.9%)	100 (15.7%)	18 (2.8%)	10 (1.6%)
I speed up to frustrate the other driver	283 (44.4%)	224 (35.1%)	88 (13.8%)	43 (6.7%)
I drive right up on the other driver's bumper	294 (46.1%)	240 (37.6%)	81 (12.7%)	23 (3.6%)
I bump the other driver's bumper with mine	600 (94.0%)	27 (4.2%)	9 (1.4%)	2 (.3%)
I try to force the other driver to the side of the road.	610 (95.6%)	21 (3.3%)	4 (.6%)	3 (.5%)
I try to get out of the car and tell the other driver off	587 (92.0%)	33 (5.2%)	10 (1.6%)	8 (1.3%)
I try to get out of the car and have a physical fight with the other driver	581 (91.1%)	39 (6.1%)	11 (1.7%)	4 (.6%)*

Note. * This row does not equal 100%; denotes missing data.

With respect to the Driving Survey, the frequencies of reported behavior are listed below in Table 28. Most of the items clearly show that many people refrain from acts of road rage. Furthermore, it was found that the most frequent acts reported are also less serious in nature. However, one item in particular increased in its frequency. The item concerning speeding showed that over half of the individuals reported speeding at least 5 times or more. Thus, those who reported speeding, speed often.

Table 28: Frequencies of Selected Items from the DS

Behavior	0	1	2	3	4	5
Broken or damaged a part of a vehicle	521 (81.7%)	72 (11.3%)	28 (4.4%)	6 (.9%)	3 (.5%)	8 (1.3%)
Had a verbal argument with the driver of another vehicle	553 (86.7%)	49 (7.7%)	22 (3.4%)	6 (.9%)	3 (.5%)	5 (.8%)
Had a physical fight with the driver of another vehicle	608 (95.3%)	12 (1.9%)	6 (.9%)	4 (.6%)	3 (.5%)	5 (.8%)
Lost control of your anger while driving	522 (81.8%)	52 (8.2%)	26 (4.1%)	18 (2.8%)	4 (.6%)	15 (.2.4%)
Driven 10 to 20 miles over the speed limit	51 (8.0%)	46 (7.2%)	64 (10.%)	71 (11.1%)	46 (7.2%)	360 (56.4%)
Driven recklessly	427 (66.9%)	82 (12.9%)	49 (7.7%)	36 (5.6%)	13 (2%)	30 (4.7%)

Research question one posited the hypothesis "How much of a problem is road rage among college students?" First, it must be noted that it is difficult to compare the findings of this study to prior studies on road rage. This study is unique in that only select items from the preexisting scales DAX and the DS have been used, therefore, there is no comparative data with similar populations. It can be stated that the majority of individuals have noted that they have engaged in what is deemed aggressive driving. Furthermore, some respondents have reported engaging in outright road rage (i.e., 18.3% engaged in vehicle vandalism). It can be suggested that any infringement on public safety can be seen as problematic. Consequently, this statement does not in any way conclude that college students demonstrate more road rage than other segments of the population. This study does not include a control group nor is there similar data available for comparison purposes.

2. Is there a correlation between the Total Aggression Expression (TAE) subscale of the Driving Anger Expression Inventory and the Driving Survey?

As mentioned previously in the correlation matrix, the two measures of the dependent variable, namely, the Driving Survey and the Total Aggressive Expression scale were highly correlated (r=.635, p<.01).

Table 29: Correlation of Dependent Variables

Variable	TAE
DS	.635**
	(617)

Note. ** Correlation is significant at the .01 level
(N) Valid N

A strong correlation between the two measures was expected due to the nature of the questions in the survey. Both of the measures required the respondent to report his/her participation in various driving situations. The response categories for the TAE required the respondent to note his/her reaction behind the wheel of the vehicle when angered by other drivers. The categories included: almost never, sometimes, often and almost always. The DS required the respondent to report the exact number of times he/she engaged in aggressive driving or road rage. Therefore, a strong correlation between these measures also acted as a validity check for the domain of aggressive driving and road rage behaviors.

Path Models

Research questions three through seven were answered via path analysis. In order to properly investigate the nature of the relationships between the control variables, independent variables, and dependent variables, path analysis was employed. Path analysis is considered to be an extension of the regression model, as it uses a number of regression models for purposes of including all proposed relationships in the theoretical explanation (Agresti & Finlay, 1997). Path analysis searches for both associations among variables as well as for causal relationships. It is important to note, that association is not sufficient to imply causation. In other words, path analysis was a useful tool for testing a theory.

The primary advantage of path analysis was that the path was based on a theoretical framework, which presumed causal relationships among the variables in the model. At the same time the path diagram graphically displays the pattern of causal relations among a set of variables (Kerlinger & Pedhazur, 1973). As outlined in Kerlinger and Pedhazur (1973, p. 309), the assumptions that underscore the application of path analysis include:

(1) The relations among the variables in the model are linear, additive, and causal. Consequently, curvilinear, multiplicative, or interaction relations are excluded.

(2) Residuals are not correlated with variable preceding them in the model, nor are they correlated among themselves. The implication of this assumption is that all relevant variables are included in the system.

(3) There is a one-way causal flow in the system.

(4) The variables are measured on an interval scale.

Specifically, Wright (1934, p. 134) stated that:

...the method of path coefficients is not intended to accomplish the impossible task of deducing causal relations from the values of the correlation coefficients. It is intended to combine the quantitative information given by the correlations with such qualitative information as may be at hand on causal relations to give a quantitative interpretation.

The following figure was based on an explicit theoretical framework, as specified in the previous chapters. In order to answer each of the research questions and corresponding hypotheses, this model will be modified as per the variables entered into the path specified.

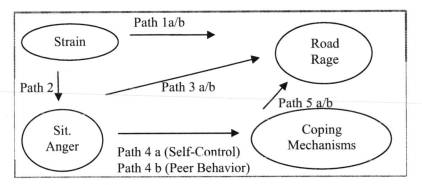

As an initial step in the path analysis process, the control variables were delineated to include: age, gender, race, commuter status, number of miles driven daily, driver's education course, number of times stopped by police for a traffic violation, number of traffic citations, number of speeding tickets, number of accidents, and trait anger. Each of these control variables was used in the following path analyses. The theoretical variables included strain, situational anger, self-control and peer behavior. The dependent variables included both the Total Aggressive Expression Inventory (TAE) and the Driving Survey (DS). Research questions three through seven are presented in response to the path analysis findings.

3. To what extent does a person's level of strain influence road rage?
Given this research question, the corresponding hypothesis included: Individuals who experience higher levels of strain are more likely to experience higher levels of road rage. In order to assess this research question and test this hypothesis, path model 1 was examined. It is important to note that the results yielded in the path model 1 are preliminary. The final results will not be realized until path model 5, which includes the complete theoretical model.

Table 30: Strain and Total Aggressive Expression (N=582)

Independent Variables	Unstd..Slope (b) (Std. Error)	Standardized Coefficients (β)	t
Age	-.298 (.146)	-.076*	-2.045
Gender	-3.660 (1.067)	-.121**	-3.429
Race/Ethnicity	-4.025 (1.868)	-.076*	-2.155
Commuter status	-.871 (1.330)	-.025	-.655
Miles driven daily	.037 (.021)	.062	1.724
Driver's educatio	.147 (1.177)	.004	.125
Police stops	1.348 (.339)	.169**	3.979
Traffic citations	-.201 (.566)	-.016	-.356
Speeding tickets	-.923 (.819)	-.051	-1.127
Accidents	1.514 (.565)	.098**	2.680
Trait Anger	1.155 (.096)	.438**	12.095
Strain	.411 (.182)	.084*	2.266

Note. R^2=.343
F=24.788, p<.000
S_e = 12.258
**p<.01, *p<.05

As an initial step in the analysis process, multiple regression was conducted to determine R^2 and the standardized betas were investigated for the strength of association between the variables. Given the above model, strain and the control variables explained 34.3 percent of the variance in the dependent variable, TAE. Therefore, by taking the independent and control variables into consideration, the error in predicting road rage was reduced by 34.3 %. Because this is the initial path model, it is expected that the R^2 will increase as additional theoretical variables are added to the model.

According to the unstandardized slopes of the regression model, age, gender, race/ethnicity, police stops, accidents, trait anger, and strain were all statistically significant. Of these variables, trait anger appeared to have the greatest impact on road rage (β=.438, p<.01). Trait anger had a positive coefficient, indicating that those who have a high level of trait anger are also more likely to engage in road rage. Trait anger is an important variable in the theoretical model. It is being used as a control variable in this model as prior research would suggest that trait anger is a stable personality characteristic. Furthermore, the strain literature suggests that an individual's disposition (as evidenced by the trait anger level) plays a role in how the individual internalizes strain. Given the above preliminary findings, this was congruent with the theoretical literature.

In terms of strength of the relationship, the remaining variables included the number of times stopped by police, gender, number of accidents, age, race/ethnicity, and strain, all of which are statistically significant. According to the police stops variable, the more times that a person was pulled over by the police for a traffic stop, the greater his/her participation in road rage. Gender had a significant negative relationship with road rage, which suggests that females are less likely to engage in road rage than males. The number of accidents, in which the respondent was the driver, had a positive correlation with road rage, indicating that individuals who have more accidents are also likely to engage in road rage at a higher rate. Race also is a significant variable. In terms of race, the data suggest the Caucasians are more likely to engage in road rage. Age also played a role in road rage, as younger individuals were more likely to engage in road rage.

Lastly, the theoretical variable, strain, also played a role in road rage. As the hypothesis stated: Individuals who experience higher levels of strain are more likely to experience higher levels of road rage. Strain had a positive relationship with road rage ($\beta=.084$, $p<.05$), indicating that those who experienced higher levels of strain also experienced higher levels of road rage. It must be noted that although the strain variable was significant in comparison to other variables, it did not have a strong effect based on the standardized coefficient. Thus, the standardized coefficient suggested a relatively weak relationship. From this particular model, there was preliminary evidence to demonstrate that while controlling for the above variables, strain did have a direct effect on road rage as evidenced by the TAE. However, caution must be used with these results. The final results for the model will be provided in path model 5.

It is important to note that each of the figures that correspond to the regression analyses (e.g., Table 30) depict only the theoretical link being examined. However, for each figure the control variables are taken into account, yet due to space these variables as well as the residual error terms are denoted in the text and not shown in the model. The residual error term for this model is .81031. The residual error term for the model is calculated by taking the square root of one minus

R^2. The residual error term is used to indicate the effect of variables not included in the model, in other words, the unmeasured variables.

As mentioned previously, there were two measures of the dependent variable of road rage. The same hypothesis as above was tested using the Driving Survey as the dependent variable. The results are as follows.

Table 31: Strain and Driving Survey (N=574)

Independent Variables	Unstd..Slope (b) (Std. Error)	Standardized Coefficients (β)	t
Age	-.134 (.236)	-.022	-.566
Gender	12.254 (1.741)	-.258**	-7.039
Race/Ethnicity	-8.730 (3.000)	-.107**	-2.910
Commuter status	-.922 (2.170)	-.017	-.425
Miles driven daily	.075 (.036)	.079*	.104
Driver's education	-1.733 (1.918)	-.033	-.903
Police stops	.808 (.553)	.065	1.461
Traffic citations	1.395 (.937)	.069	1.489
Speeding tickets	-1.050 (1.351)	-.036	-.777
Accidents	1.907 (.922)	.079*	2.069
Trait Anger	1.467 (.155)	.355**	9.477
Strain	.689 (.296)	.089*	2.327

Note. R^2=.300
F=20.051, p<.000
S_e = 19.865
*p<.01, **p<.05

Similar to the above analysis, the preliminary evidence demonstrated that strain, while taking the control variables into consideration, has a direct effect on road rage as evidenced by the Driving Survey. By using this model, the error is reduced in predicting road rage by 30.0 percent (R^2=.300). The significant variables in this model included: trait anger, gender, race, strain, number of miles driven, and accidents.

Of these variables and congruent to the above model, trait anger appeared to have the greatest impact on road rage (β=.355, p<.01). Trait anger had a positive coefficient, indicating that among those who have a high level of trait anger, they are also more likely to engage in road rage. Gender had a negative coefficient, and a significant influence on road rage (β= -.258, p<.01). This indicated that males were more likely to experience road rage than women.

In terms of strength of the association, the remaining variables included race, miles driven, accidents, and strain. The race variable (β =-.107, p<.01) indicated that minorities were less likely to engage in road rage than whites as Whites were coded as zero and minorities were coded as one. The number of miles (β=.079, p<.05) driven also has a significant impact on road rage. This suggested that individuals who drive more miles per day were more likely to experience road rage. The number of accidents (β=.079, p<.05) had a positive coefficient, which demonstrated that individuals who had a higher number of accidents in which they were the driver were more likely to experience road rage.

Lastly, the theoretical variable, strain, as suggested in the above model as well, played a role in road rage. As the research question stated: does strain influence road rage behavior? Yes, strain had a positive relationship with road rage (β=.089, p<.05), indicating that those who experience higher levels of strain also experienced higher levels of road rage. From this particular model, there was preliminary evidence to demonstrate that while controlling for the above variables, strain did have a direct effect on road rage as evidenced by the DS. However, caution must be used with these results. The final results for the model will be provided in path model 5.

The residual error term for this model is .83648. The residual error term for the model is calculated by taking the square root of one minus R^2. The residual error term is used to indicate the effect of variables not included in the model, in other words, the unmeasured variables.

4. To what extent does strain have an effect on situational anger?
This research question concerns the relationship between strain and situational anger. The corresponding hypotheses is: Individuals who experience higher levels of strain are more likely to experience higher levels of situational anger.

Table 32: Strain and Situational Anger (N=579)

Independent Variables	Unstd..Slope (b) (Std. Error)	Standardized Coefficients (β)	t
Age	-.136 (.045)	-.119**	-3.031
Gender	.133 (.331)	.015	.403
Race/Ethnicity	-1.032 (.572)	-.067	-1.804
Commuter status	-.143 (.410)	-.014	-.348
Miles driven daily	-.002 (.007)	-.011	-.276
Driver's education	-.037 (.366)	-.004	-.101
Police stops	.021 (.105)	.009	.202
Traffic citations	.192 (.175)	.052	1.099
Speeding tickets	-.339 (.253)	-.063	-1.341
Accidents	.152 (.175)	.034	.869
Trait Anger	.375 (.029)	.488**	12.776
Strain	-.001 (.056)	-.001	-.020

Note. R^2=.273
F=17.785, p<.000
S_e = 3.790
**p<.01
*p<.05

The purpose of path model 2 was to determine the relationship between strain and situational anger, while accounting for all of the control variables. In this model, strain did not yield a significant value (β=-.001, p=.984). Furthermore, the path coefficient was negative. Thus, since the regression coefficient was so close to zero, it suggested that there is no relationship between the two variables. Given this finding, this preliminary evidence is in opposition to Agnew's General Strain Theory. This finding did not support the relationship between strain and situational anger as purported by Agnew (1992).

However, there were two significant variables in the model. Both the trait anger and age variables were significant. The trait anger variable was a measure of an individual's predisposition to anger. This was an expected relationship since, both variables were essentially measuring anger, just the root of the anger is different. In reference to trait anger, the model indicated that as trait anger increased, situational anger increased (β=.488, p<.01). In reference to age, (β= -.119, p<.01), the model indicated that as age increases, situational anger decreases.

Therefore, older respondents were less likely to experience situational anger (as portrayed in the driving circumstances). Given the above information, the research hypothesis did not support the assertion that strain, while controlling for other variables, impacts situational anger in this model.

The residual error term for this model is .85233. The residual error term is used to indicate the effect of variables not included in the model, in other words, the unmeasured variables.

5. Is anger a mediating variable in the strain model?
The fifth research question assessed the role of anger as a mediating variable in the model. The corresponding hypothesis was: Individuals who experience higher levels of situational anger are more likely to engage in road rage. This hypothesis was tested with both measures of the dependent variable: TAE and DS.

Table 33: Situational Anger and TAE (N=574)

Independent Variables	Unstd..Slope (b) (Std. Error)	Standardized Coefficients (β)	t
Age	-.145 (.139)	-.037	-1.047
Gender	-3.761 (1.015)	-.124**	-3.704
Race/Ethnicity	-2.950 (1.770)	-.056	-1.667
Commuter status	-.563 (1.265)	-.016	-.445
Miles driven daily	.038 (.020)	.064	1.852
Driver's education	.446 (1.120)	.013	.399
Police stops	1.307 (.320)	.165**	4.081
Traffic citations	-.414 (.535)	-.033	-.774
Speeding tickets	-.573 (.775)	-.031	-.739
Accidents	1.355 (.535)	.088*	2.534
Trait Anger	.742 (.102)	.282**	7.247
Strain	.443 (.173)	.090*	2.561
Situational Anger	1.092 (.128)	.321**	8.506

Note. R^2=.418
F=31.044, p<.000
S_e = 11.579
**p<.01, *p<.05

The preliminary evidence in the above model suggested that the error in predicting road rage was reduced by 41.8 percent by taking the independent and control variables into consideration. This is an increase in R^2 from the first path model. The increase in R^2 is due to the addition of situational anger as a variable.

The purpose of path model 3 was to determine the relationship between situational anger and road rage, while accounting for all of the control variables. In this model, situational anger yielded a positive coefficient and had a significant impact on road rage as measured by the TAE ($\beta=.321$, p<.01). Thus, it is suggested that as an individual's level of situational anger increases, one's participation in road rage increased. This finding supported the relationship between situational anger and road rage.

In addition to situational anger, there are other significant variables in the model. Trait anger, number of police stops, gender, strain, and number of accidents each significantly impact road rage. The trait anger variable is a measure of an individual's predisposition to anger. In this model, the relationship between trait anger and road rage is evident. The model indicates that as trait anger increases, road rage increases ($\beta=.282$, p<.01). Thus far in the building of the path model, trait anger had consistently been shown as a significant variable.

The number of police stops was also a significant variable. The slope of the police stops variable ($\beta= .165$, p<.01) indicated that an individual with a higher number of police stops was more likely to engage in road rage activities. Furthermore an individual's gender is a significant factor in road rage behavior. The gender variable ($\beta= -.124$, p<.01) suggested that females are less likely to engage in road rage than males. This finding was consistent with prior research on the likelihood of women as being road rage offenders. The number of accidents that an individual had also was a significant indicator of road rage. The accident variable ($\beta=.088$, p<.01) indicated that individuals who had higher numbers of accidents were more likely to engage in road rage.

The strain variable remained significant in this model. The strain variable ($\beta=.090$, p<.01) suggested that individuals with higher levels of strain were more likely to engage in road rage behaviors. In this model, the effect of strain was similar to the effect that the strain variable had in path model 1a, here it was actually slightly stronger. This means that situational anger did not mediate its effect as predicted by the theory. Given the above preliminary information, the research hypothesis was supported: Individuals who experience higher levels of situational anger are more likely to experience higher levels of road rage.

The residual error term for this model is .76249. The residual error term for the model is calculated by taking the square root of one minus R^2. The residual error term is used to indicate the effect of variables not included in the model, in other words, the unmeasured variables.

In addition to the above results, the path model also was assessed using the Driving Survey as the dependent variable.

Table 34: Situational Anger and DS (N=566)

Independent Variables	Unstd..Slope (b) (Std. Error)	Standardized Coefficients (β)	t
Age	.045 (.233)	.007	.191
Gender	-12.398 (1.716)	-.259**	-7.227
Race/Ethnicity	-7.459 (2.946)	-.091*	-2.532
Commuter status	-.787 (2.138)	-.014	-.368
Miles driven daily	.076 (.035)	.080*	2.166
Driver's educatio	-1.631 (1.890)	-.031	-.863
Police stops	.768 (.542)	.062	1.418
Traffic citations	1.196 (.917)	.059	1.304
Speeding tickets	-.653 (1.324)	-.022	-.493
Accidents	1.695 (.904)	.070	1.876
Trait Anger	1.014 (.172)	.245**	5.901
Strain	.684 (.292)	.088*	2.341
Situational Anger	1.232 (.216)	.230**	5.692

Note. R^2=.338
F=21.701, p<.000
S_e = 19.434
**p<.01, *p<.05

The preliminary evidence in the above model as demonstrated in Table 34 suggested that the error in predicting road rage was reduced by 33.8 percent by taking the independent and control variables into consideration. This was an increase in R^2 from the first path model.

The increase in R^2 was from the addition of situational anger as a variable.

The purpose of path model 3 was to determine the relationship between situational anger and road rage, while accounting for all of the control variables. In this model, situational anger yielded a positive coefficient and had a significant impact on road rage as measured by the Driving Survey ($\beta=.230$, $p<.01$). Thus, it was suggested that as an individual's level of situational anger increased, one's participation in road rage increased. This finding supported the relationship between situational anger and road rage.

In addition to situational anger, there were other significant variables in the model. In order of greatest impact to least impact, the variables gender, trait anger, situational anger, race, strain, and miles driven each significantly impacted road rage. In terms of gender ($\beta=-.259$, $p<.01$), there was a negative coefficient. Thus, indicating that females were less likely to engage in road rage behaviors. This was an expected relationship as the literature on road rage has indicated women were less likely to participate in the behavior.

The trait anger variable was a measure of an individual's predisposition to anger. In this model, the relationship between trait anger and road rage was evident. The model indicated that as trait anger increases, road rage increased ($\beta=.245$, $p<.01$). Thus far in the building of the path model, trait anger had consistently been shown to be a significant variable with respect to the Driving Survey.

Race was also a significant variable. The race variable ($\beta=-.091$, $p<.01$) indicated that minorities were less likely to engage in road rage activities. To recall the coding of this variable, zero was coded for Caucasian, and one was coded for minorities. In this case, the strain variable remains significant in this model. The strain variable ($\beta=.088$, $p<.05$) suggests that individuals with higher levels of strain are more likely to engage in road rage behaviors. These results were very similar to the previous model and in path 1, where situational anger did not mediate strain. Lastly, the number of miles driven variable ($\beta=.080$, $p<.05$) indicated that individuals who drive a high number of miles were more likely to engage in road rage.

The residual error term for this model is .81390. The residual error term for the model is calculated by taking the square root of one minus R^2. The residual error term is used to indicate the effect of variables not included in the model, in other words, the unmeasured variables.

Given the above preliminary information, the research hypothesis was accepted and the null hypothesis is rejected: Individuals who experience higher levels of situational anger are more likely to experience higher levels of road rage.

6. To what extent is situational anger associated with coping mechanisms?

There were two corresponding hypotheses with this research question. The first hypothesis stated: Individuals with high levels of situational anger are more likely to have low levels of self-control. The second hypothesis stated: Individuals with high levels of situational anger are more likely to have close peers who have engaged in past road rage behaviors.

Table 35: Situational Anger and Self-Control (N=561)

Independent Variables	Unstd..Slope (b) (Std. Error)	Standardized Coefficients (β)	t
Age	-.287 (.101)	-.108**	-2.829
Gender	-4.851 (.746)	-.232**	-6.504
Race/Ethnicity	2.179 (1.316)	.059	1.656
Commuter status	-1.745 (.924)	-.072	-1.889
Miles driven daily	.010 (.015)	.024	.654
Driver's educatio	-.240 (.824)	-.010	-.292
Police stops	.003 (.234)	.000	.011
Traffic citations	.002 (.391)	.000	.004
Speeding tickets	.532 (.569)	.043	.936
Accidents	.111 (.389)	.011	.286
Trait Anger	.761 (.075)	.427**	10.186
Strain	.216 (.128)	.064	1.693
Situational Anger	.173 (.096)	.073	1.813

Note. R^2=.353
F=22.962, p<.000;
S_e = 8.408
**p<.01, *p<.05

As an initial step in the model, multiple regression was conducted to determine the R^2 and the standardized betas were investigated for the strength of association between the variables. Given the above model

(Table 35), the control variables, strain and situational anger explain 35.3 percent of the variance in self-control. Therefore, by taking the independent and control variables into consideration, the error in predicting self-control was reduced by 35.3 percent.

According to the standardized slopes of the regression model, only trait anger, gender, and age were statistically significant. Of these variables, trait anger appeared to have the greatest impact on self-control (β=.427, p<.01). Trait anger had a positive coefficient, indicating that individuals who have higher levels of trait anger were also more likely to have low self-control. (Recall, that self-control was coded so that individuals who scored high actually have low self-control). Furthermore, trait anger was an important variable in the theoretical model. It was being used as a control variable in this model as prior research (Gottfredson & Hirschi, 1990) would suggest that trait anger is a stable personality characteristic. Furthermore, the strain literature suggests that an individual's disposition (as evidenced by the trait anger level) plays a role in how the individual internalizes strain.

In terms of strength of the relationship, the remaining variables included gender and age, each of which was statistically significant. Gender (β= -.232, p<.01) had a significant negative relationship with low self-control, which suggested that females had higher self-control than males. Age (β= -.108, p<.01) also played a role in self-control; the model indicates that younger individuals had lower self-control.

It should be noted that the theoretical variables strain and situational anger were not significant in this particular model. Although both variables were in the direction of the expected relationship, they did not reach the .05 significance level for a two tailed test. The strain variable (β=.064, p<.090) was approaching significance, moreover, if the significance level was set at .10, it would be significant. The same holds true for the situational anger variable (β=.073, p<.070). The variable was approaching significance, however it does not meet the .05 threshold. If the sample size were larger, both of these variables may have reached the .05 significance level. However, the relationship is significant with using a one tailed test as indicated by the hypothesis.

The residual error term for this model is .80446. The residual error term for the model is calculated by taking the square root of one minus R^2. The residual error term is used to indicate the effect of variables not included in the model, in other words, the unmeasured variables. Given the above evidence, the research hypothesis "Individuals with high levels of situational anger are more likely to have low levels of self-control" was not supported. Although situational anger has a positive coefficient (β=.073, p<.070) and is approaching significance, the variable does not hold up in this particular model.

As mentioned previously the coping mechanisms consisted of both self-control and peer behaviors. This hypothesis measures the extent that situational anger is associated with peer behavior.

Table 36: Situational Anger and Peer Behavior (N=577)

Independent Variables	Unstd..Slope (b) (Std. Error)	Standardized Coefficients (β)	t
Age	-.042 (.020)	-.087*	-2.098
Gender	-.791 (.146)	-.210**	-5.414
Race/Ethnicit	-.565 (.253)	-.087*	-2.234
Commuter status	-.244 (.181)	-.056	-1.343
Miles driven daily	.007 (.003)	.094*	2.368
Driver's education	.212 (.162)	.050	1.314
Police stops	.088 (.046)	.090	.911
Traffic citations	-.037 (.077)	-.024	-.483
Speeding tickets	-.066 (.112)	-.029	-.591
Accidents	-.007 (.078)	-.004	-.096
Trait Anger	.067 (.015)	.206**	4.548
Strain	.095 (.025)	.157**	3.834
Situational Anger	.027 (.019)	.065	1.471

Note. R^2=.212
F=11.668, p<.000;
S_e = 1.671
**p<.01, *p<.05

Given the above model (Table 36), the control variables, strain and situational anger explain 21.2 percent of the variance in peer behavior. The variable peer behavior represents the respondent's closest friend and his/her participation in past road rage behaviors. Therefore, by taking the independent and control variables into consideration, the error in predicting the association with peer behavior is reduced by 21.2%.

According to the standardized slopes of the regression model, gender, trait anger, strain, miles driven, race, and age were statistically significant. Of these variables, gender (β=-.210, p<.01) appeared to have the greatest impact on associating with peers who had engaged in past road rage activities. Therefore, it was suggested that females were less likely to associate with deviant peers. This association has been substantiated in the strain literature.

Trait anger (β= .206, p<.01) had a positive coefficient, indicating that individuals who have higher levels of trait anger are also more likely to associate with deviant peers. Trait anger was an important variable in the theoretical model. It was being used as a control variable in this model as prior research (Gottfredson & Hirschi, 1990) would suggest that trait anger is a stable personality characteristic. Prior research indicated that people with similar personality traits tend to spend time with others of the same personality traits. Lastly, the primary theoretical variable strain (β=.157, p<.01) had a positive coefficient, suggesting that individuals who have higher levels of strain were more likely to associate with deviant peers.

The remaining variables included miles driven, race, and age. The variable, miles driven, (β=.094, p<.018) is associated with deviant peers. This variable suggested that the more miles one drives the more likely he/she was to associate with deviant peers. A possible explanation for this relationship was if a person is friends with an individual initially, he/she is more likely to spend time together and, in turn, they more likely to travel together in a vehicle.

In terms of the race variable (β= -.087, p<.05), the data suggested that nonwhites are less likely to associate with deviant peers. It was also found that nonwhites are less likely to engage in road rage as well. Given the small percentage of nonwhites in the college sample, a possible explanation is that minority and international students are more concerned with their education than spending time with individuals who may jeopardize their academic enrichment. Another alternate explanation is that they are more likely to spend time with other international or minority students. Age (β= -.087 p<.05) also plays a role in the association with deviant peers. The model indicated that older individuals were less likely to associate with deviant peers. The literature on crime in the life span as well as literature on maturity, demonstrated that older individuals tend to "age out" of crime and deviant associations (Gottfredson & Hirschi, 1990).

The residual error term for this model is .88792. The residual error term for the model is calculated by taking the square root of one minus

R^2. The residual error term is used to indicate the effect of variables not included in the model, in other words, the unmeasured variables.

Given the above evidence, the research hypothesis: Individuals with higher levels of situational anger are more likely to associate with deviant peers was assessed. The research hypothesis is not supported. Although situational anger had a positive coefficient (β=.065, p<.142), it was not a significant indicator of the association between anger and deviant peers.

7. To what extent do coping mechanisms mediate the effects of strain and anger on road rage?

The corresponding hypothesis was: Individuals with higher levels of strain, higher levels of anger, low levels of self-control, and high levels of peer behavior are more likely to engage in road rage. Both measures of the dependent variable are used. Furthermore, a detailed interpretation of the full model and a comparison of the findings of each model with the respective dependent variable was examined.

Table 37 Full Model with TAE (N=554)

Independent Variables	Unstd..Slope (b) (Std. Error)	Standardized Coefficients (β)	t
Age	.027 (.137)	-.007	-.198
Gender	-1.564 (1.054)	-.051	-1.483
Race/Ethnicity	-2.151 (1.785)	-.040	-1.205
Commuter status	-.113 (1.251)	-.003	-.090
Miles driven daily	.027 (.020)	.046	1.349
Driver's educatio	.203 (1.105)	.006	.184
Police stops	1.160 (.313)	.148**	3.703
Traffic citations	-.306 (.522)	-.024	-.585
Speeding tickets	-.627 (.760)	-.035	-.826
Accidents	1.382 (.523)	.090**	2.640
Trait Anger	.494 (.110)	.189**	4.500
Strain	.357 (.173)	.072*	2.060
Situational Anger	1.064 (.128)	.311**	8.295
Self-Control	.153 (.058)	.104**	2.610
Peer Behavior	1.482 (.295)	.182*	5.020

Note. R^2=.461
F=30.728, p<.000 S_e = 11.207 **p<.01, *p<.05

Path model 5a includes all of the important theoretical and control variables as dictated by the theoretical framework. Given the above model (Table 37), the control variables, strain, situational anger, self-control and peer behavior explain 46.1% of the variance in road rage as evidenced by the TAE. As a result, by taking the independent and control variables into consideration, the error in predicting road rage is reduced by 46.1 percent. Furthermore, it is important to note the increase in the R^2 from earlier models that examined road rage. This R^2 included all of the control variables in addition to all of the salient theoretical variables as purported in the theoretical framework.

According to the unstandardized slopes of the regression model, seven variables, including all of the theoretical variables, were statistically significant. The significant variables included: situational anger, trait anger, peer behavior, times stopped by police, self-control, number of accidents, and strain. Situational anger, while controlling for other variables, appeared to have the greatest impact on road rage ($\beta=.311$, $p<.01$). Thus, individuals who experienced higher levels of situational anger were more likely to experience higher levels of road rage. This relationship was expected given the nature of road rage activities. Situational anger was a key concept in Agnew's model, thus demonstrating that individuals could experience anger within given contexts and have an outlet to express that anger on the road.

Trait anger had a significant positive coefficient, indicating that individuals who have higher levels of trait anger ($\beta=.189$, $p<.01$) are more likely to engage in road rage. Furthermore, trait anger was an important variable in the theoretical model. It was used as a control variable in this model as prior research (Gottfredson & Hirschi, 1990) would suggest that trait anger is a stable personality characteristic. Furthermore, the strain literature suggested that an individual's disposition (as evidenced by the trait anger level) plays a role in how the individual internalizes strain. Throughout all of the path models, trait anger consistently had been a significant variable in the model. It was apparent that trait anger influenced many of the other variables in the model.

Peer behavior played a significant role in the strain model. Peer behavior refers to the respondent's closest friend and his/her past deviant behaviors specific to road rage. The model yielded a positive coefficient for peer behavior ($\beta=.182$, $p<.01$), demonstrating that individuals who had deviant peers were more likely to engage in road rage behavior. This relationship had been substantiated in the literature on strain as well as with differential association.

As per the model, an individual's level of self-control influenced his/her level of road rage. The self-control variable ($\beta=.104$, p<.01) suggested that individuals with low levels of self control were more likely to participate in road rage. There is a vast amount of literature that purports the concept of self-control as being a stable personality trait. Furthermore, the components that comprise self-control included characteristics such as: impulsivity, risk seeking, temper, self-centeredness, physical activities, and simple tasks. It would be easy to contend that the act of road rage is an impulsive reaction to another driver infringing on one's "right" on the road or as risk seeking behavior exemplified by speeding.

Just as the preliminary evidence suggested in path model 1, strain remained a significant variable in this model. When taking all of the control variables, situational anger, and coping mechanisms into account, strain still remained significant. Therefore, since strain ($\beta=.072$, p<.05) had a positive coefficient, it indicated that individuals with high levels of strain were more likely to participate in road rage. However, strain was a relatively weak variable in comparison to other significant variables in the model. In addition to the direct effect of strain on road rage, it was evident from the models that strain also operated through the coping mechanism of peer behavior to influence road rage. This relationship was evidenced by the significant relationship between strain and peer behavior in path model 4b as well as in the full path model demonstrating the significant relationship between peer behavior and road rage.

The variables, number of times stopped by police and number of accidents, were also significant indicators of road rage in this model. The number of times stopped by police ($\beta=.148$, p<.01) suggested that individuals who have been stopped by police were more likely to engage in road rage. In reference to accidents ($\beta=.090$, p<.01), individuals who had been in an accident were more likely to engage in road rage.

There are two residual error terms for this model. The residual error term for peer behavior variable is .88792. The residual error term for road rage as evidenced by the TAE is .73414. The residual error term is calculated for endogenous variables in the model by taking the square root of one minus R^2 from the corresponding regression analyses.

Given the above evidence, the research hypothesis: Individuals with higher levels of strain, higher levels of situational anger, lower levels of self-control, and higher associations with deviant peers are more likely to engage in road rage was supported. The research hypothesis was accepted and the null hypothesis was rejected. Therefore, the data fit the model as specified. There were certain theoretical associations that reached significance. Strain, situational anger, peer behavior, and self-control were all associated with road rage (TAE). The strain variable had both direct and indirect effects on road rage (TAE). The direct effect of strain with road rage revealed a positive, significant relationship (β=.072, p<.05). The indirect effect of strain showed that strain was operating through peer behavior to influence road rage. Thus, strain was associated with a coping mechanism (i.e., peer behavior), which was associated with the dependent variable of road rage.

The situational anger variable demonstrated a direct, positive, significant effect (β=.311, p<.01) on road rage, while accounting for other variables. The peer behavior variable revealed a direct, positive, significant effect (β=.182, p<.01) on road rage. The self control variable yielded a direct, positive, significant effect (β=.104, p<.01) on road rage. As shown in the previous models, the trait anger variable maintained significance in the full model.

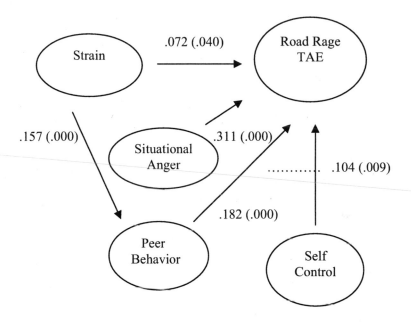

Figure 5. Path model 5a: Full Path Model (TAE).
The residual error term for the Peer Behavior variable is .88792. The residual error term for the Road Rage (TAE) variable is .73414.

Lastly, to complete the assessment of the theoretical framework, path model 5 was also examined in relation to the Driving Survey as its dependent variable. In addition to providing the analysis of this model, the two full models (TAE and DS) are compared.

Table 38: Full Model with DS (N=546)

Independent Variables	Unstd..Slope (b) (Std. Error)	Standardized Coefficients (β)	t
Age	.275 (.226)	.046	1.218
Gender	-7.790 (1.754)	-.162**	-4.442
Race/Ethnicity	-6.528 (2.914)	-.078*	-2.240
Commuter status	.600 (2.073)	.011	.290
Miles driven daily	.056 (.034)	.060	1.662
Driver's educatio	-2.430 (1.831)	-.045	-1.328
Police stops	.388 (.520)	.031	.745
Traffic citations	1.526 (.879)	.076	1.736
Speeding tickets	-.557 (1.276)	-.019	-.436
Accidents	1.628 (.868)	.067	1.875
Trait Anger	.502 (.182)	.122**	2.754
Strain	.408 (.287)	.052	1.421
Situational Anger	1.129 (.212)	.209**	5.323
Self-Control	.3462 (.097)	.151**	3.581
Peer Behavior	3.102 (.490)	.241**	6.332

Note. R^2=.410
F=24.622, p<.000
S_e = 18.458
**p<.01, *p<.05

    This model (Table 38) also included all of the important theoretical and control variables as dictated by the theoretical framework in relation to the Driving Survey (DS). Given the above model, the control variables, strain, situational anger, self-control and peer behavior explained 41.0% of the variance in road rage as evidenced by the DS. As a result, by taking the independent and control variables into consideration, the error in predicting road rage is reduced by 41.0 percent. Furthermore, the R^2 had increased from the earlier models that examined road rage. This R^2 included all of the control variables in addition to all of the salient theoretical variables as purported in the theoretical framework.

    According to the unstandardized slopes of the regression model, six variables were statistically significant. All of the theoretical variables, except the strain variable reached significance in relation to the dependent variable. The significant variables, beginning with the variables with the greatest impact, included: peer behavior, situational anger, self-control, gender, trait anger, and race.

Peer behavior (β=.241, p<.01) while controlling for all variables, had the greatest impact on road rage as evidenced by the Driving Survey. This relationship demonstrated that individuals whose close friends had participated in road rage were also more likely to participate in road rage. This relationship was an expected association given the findings from prior literature.

Situational anger, while controlling for other variables, had an impact on road rage (β=.209, p<.01). Thus, individuals who experienced higher levels of situational anger were more likely to experience higher levels of road rage. This relationship was expected given the nature of road rage activities. Situational anger was a key concept in Agnew's model, thus demonstrating that individuals can experience anger within given contexts and that they have an outlet to express that anger on the road.

As per the model and consistent with the previous model, an individual's level of self-control influences his/her level of road rage. The self-control variable (β=.151, p<.01) suggested that individuals with low levels of self control were more likely to participate in road rage. There is an abundance of literature which purports self-control as being a stable personality trait. Furthermore, the components that comprise self-control include characteristics such as: impulsivity, risk seeking, temper, self-centeredness, physical activities, and simple tasks. It would be easy to contend that the act of road rage was an impulsive reaction to another driver infringing on one's "right" on the road or as risk seeking behavior exemplified by speeding. Gender played a significant role in this model. The gender variable (β=-.162, p<.01) purported that females were less likely to engage in road rage. This was consistent with prior research on female criminality; and, specifically, participation in acts of road rage.

Trait anger had a significant positive coefficient, indicating that individuals who had higher levels of trait anger (β=.122, p<.01) were more likely to engage in road rage. Furthermore, trait anger was an important variable in the theoretical model. Throughout all of the path models, trait anger consistently had been a significant variable in the model. It was apparent that trait anger influences many of the other variables in the model. Race was also a significant variable. In this model, nonwhites (β=-.078, p<.05) were less likely to engage in road rage. This was consistent with the previous models

Contrary to the preliminary evidence suggested in path models 1b and 3b, the strain variable did not reach significance. Strain, when taking all of the control variables, situational anger, and coping mechanisms into account, did not reach a level of significance. However, strain (β=.052, p<.156) did yield a positive coefficient, meaning that the relationship was in the expected direction. Therefore, strain did not have a significant direct effect on road rage when taking all the independent variables into consideration. However, it is also important to point out that the strain variable was significant in the relationship between strain and peer behavior. Thus is it suggested that strain is operating through the coping mechanism as opposed to having a direct effect (See path model 4b).

There are two residual error terms for this model. The residual error term for peer behavior variable is .88792. The residual error term for road rage as evidenced by the DS is .76838. The residual error term is calculated for endogenous variables in the model by taking the square root of one minus R^2 from the corresponding regression analyses.

Given the path findings, the research hypothesis: Individuals with higher levels of strain, higher levels of situational anger, lower levels of self-control, and higher associations with deviant peers are more likely to engage in road rage is not supported. However, there were certain theoretical associations that reached significance. Situational anger, peer behavior, and self-control were all associated with road rage (DS). The situational anger variable demonstrated a direct, positive, significant effect (β=.209, p<.01) on road rage, while accounting for other variables. The peer behavior variable revealed a direct, positive, significant effect (β=.241, p<.01) on road rage. The self control variable yielded a direct, positive, significant effect (β=.151, p<.01) on road rage. There was also an indirect effect that materialized in this model; it revealed that strain operated through the peer behavior variable. As shown in the previous models, the trait anger variable maintained significance in the full model. However, given the above associations, the research hypothesis was not fully supported.

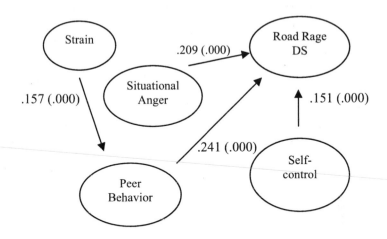

Figure 6 Path model 5b: Full Path Model (DS).
The residual error term for the Peer Behavior variable is .88792. The
residual error term for the Road Rage (DS) variable is .76838.

In addition to the results given in path models 5a and 5b, stepwise
regression was conducted. Stepwise regression is was used to
determine the subsets of predictor variables that most adequately
predict responses on a dependent variable by linear regression. All of
the control and theoretical variables were placed in the model, and the
two measures of the dependent variables (i.e., TAE and the DS) were
interchanged for analysis purposes.

The stepwise regression results from TAE as the dependent
variable reveal that six of the variables in the model explain
approximately half (45.0%) of the variance in the dependent variable.
These six variables include: Situational Anger, Peer Behavior, Trait
Anger, Police Stops, Self-Control, and Accidents. These six variables
were significant and together raised the R^2 from.262 to .450. Similar
results occurred with the DS as the dependent variable. The stepwise
regression results from DS as the dependent variable reveal that 7 of
the variables in the model explain 39.6 percent of the variance in the
DS. These seven variables include: Peer Behavior, Trait Anger,
Gender, Situational Anger, Self-Control, Traffic Citations, and Miles

Driven Daily. In this case, these seven variables were significant and together raised the R^2 from .201 to .396.

Conclusion

To conclude, the results of the path analyses, specifically with respect to the dependent variable TAE, provided qualified support for Agnew's GST. Given the path models with TAE as the dependent variable, there was a significant direct effect of strain on road rage. This direct effect remained after taking into account all control and theoretical variables. There was also an association between strain, peer behavior, and road rage. This relationship was evidenced by the increase in strain that an individual experienced, the increase in peer behavior as indicated by the number of deviant acts their friends have committed, and an increase in road rage. Therefore, this model suggested that there was a significant relationship between strain and peer behavior, thus providing qualified support for strain theory and its association with coping mechanisms. Because this was a cross-sectional study as opposed to longitudinal study, a causal inference should not be made in this case.

It is also important to point out that each of these variables had a significant independent effect, while accounting for the control variables, on road rage. Consequently, as Agnew contends that strain may lead to a negative affect, namely anger; this model did not support that contention. In this model the relationship between strain and anger (i.e., strain influences situational anger) was not significant (β= -.001, p< .984). Essentially, it was a zero slope or it had no effect. Furthermore, this model suggests that as an individual's level of strain increased, his/her level of anger decreased, which is contrary to Agnew' assertion.

It is necessary to note that there were variables that were significant with the TAE but did not reach significance with the DS in the full model. The full model with respect to the DS, provides less support for strain theory. The strain variable was not significant in this full model (β=.052, p<.156); however, the association was in the expected direction. With respect to the strain variable, there was an association between strain and the peer behavior variables in the path model. There was an indirect effect of strain through the peer behavior variable. The situational anger, self-control, and peer behavior variables were all significant in this model. Furthermore, there were control variables that were significant as well, namely, gender, race, and trait anger. Despite the results of the DS full model, the TAE model does demonstrate qualified support for strain theory.

Another important finding that materialized was the role of trait anger in the path models. In each of the models, trait anger was found to have a significant effect on the dependent variables as well as on some of the independent variables. As stated previously, an individual's level of trait anger reflects the person's disposition toward anger in general situations. Thus, it was considered to be a stable personality characteristic, which may affect other facets of the individual's personality as well as how he/she handled certain situations. In these models, trait anger appeared to influence the situational anger, peer behavior, self-control, and road rage (with both the TAE and the DS). This is consistent with Agnew, in that, he contends that one's disposition is a major factor in one's ability to handle strainful situations as well as its ability to give rise to a negative affect. At the same time this is consistent with Gottfredson and Hirschi (1990) self-control theory in that one's disposition is a stable personality trait that influences behavior.

CHAPTER 6

Discussion and Conclusions

As evidenced by previous research and this current project, roadways and highways are dangerous places (Blake, 1998; Blanchard et al., 2000; Deffenbacher et al., 2000; Murray, 2000; Willis, 1997; Wrightson, 1997). Recall from Chapter Two that road rage is defined (for this project) as an incident in which a motorist commits various infringements on the road that act to annoy, endanger, threaten to injure, injure, or damage the property of another motorist or passenger, in response to a traffic dispute, altercation, or grievance. Although many of the acts reported in this study were of a less serious nature (e.g., speeding, gesturing, unlawful passing, yelling obscenities), there were individuals who reported verbally and physically confronting other drivers. Road rage remains a salient public safety issue.

In addition, this study also collected information on General Strain Theory (GST) (Agnew, 1992). It was hypothesized that individuals who experienced greater amounts of strain would engage in aggressive driving or road rage. It was further hypothesized that if an individual experienced strain, he/she would also experience a negative affect (i.e., anger, anxiety, depression), which may or may not be tempered by certain coping mechanisms. If the conditions were ripe they would succumb to a deviant adaptation, in this case road rage. A change in or lack of any of these elements had an effect on overall participation in acts of aggression and/or road rage. This study tested the theory by examining the sources of strain (i.e., failure to achieve positively valued goals, presentation or anticipated presentation of noxious stimuli, and removal or anticipated removal of positively valued stimuli) the role of situational anger, the role of self-control and the role of peer behaviors on aggressive driving and road rage. While there has been considerable research testing GST, this is the first known test of GST with aggressive driving and road rage as the dependent variable.

The purpose of the study was to examine the role of GST on college students' participation in aggressive driving and road rage. This research contributes to the body of knowledge concerning deviance, by exploring a rarely studied type of crime (road rage) with

181

an existing criminological theory. Furthermore, the criminological theory tested in this study was usually used with an adolescent population, and the data for this project were collected from a college student sample. The researcher administered a self-report questionnaire to students, which asked them to report their level of strain, anger, self-control, peer, deviant peer relationships, and participation in acts of aggressive driving and road rage. The analysis phase examined whether GST predicted reported aggressive driving and road rage.

This study sheds light on the prevalence of aggressive driving and road rage acts committed by college students in Pennsylvania. By providing a further test of GST (Agnew, 1992), a better understanding of the nature of aggressive driving and road rage incidents was obtained. The major findings of the study are discussed below, along with the policy implications, limitations, and directions for future research.

Discussion of Research and Theoretical Findings

The primary purpose of this study was to add to the theoretical and empirical body of knowledge about road rage and GST. The first research question measured the extent of road rage among college students. By examining the data it was suggestive that students were participating in behaviors that ranged from roadway annoyances to traffic violations to vehicle vandalism to assaultive behaviors. Although most respondents did not report frequent involvement in road rage, those who do report participating in these acts pose a threat to public safety. As mentioned previously in the literature, some minor driving infractions escalate into more serious incidents of aggressive driving and road rage.

Even though many of the reported acts were minor in nature, the frequency of these acts was high. For example, the item "I call the other driver names aloud" is a less serious form of aggressive driving, yet 42.4 percent of respondents say they engage in this behavior "often" or "almost always." Recall that many incidents begin as a verbal altercation and escalate into a more serious incident (Luckenbill, 1977). Since acts of road rage are committed against anonymous individuals, these statistics demonstrate that anyone is subject to victimization on the roadways. At this time, it is important to reiterate that these data do not suggest that college students are more likely to engage in road rage than other segments of the population. Consequently, there is no control group to compare these data.

The second research question examined the association between the two measures of the dependent variable road rage. The Total Aggressive Expression (TAE) scale and the Driving Survey (DS) were highly correlated (r= .635, p<.01). Although there were some similarities and differences in the scales, the correlation of the two demonstrated that a variety of acts was considered to be aggressive driving and road rage.

The remaining research questions tested the theoretical model for GST. The major theoretical variables in the path models included: strain, situational anger, self-control, peer behavior, and road rage. The control variables included: age, gender, race/ethnicity, commuter status, miles daily, driver's education, police stops, traffic citations, speeding tickets, prior accidents and trait anger. The first path model measured the impact of strain on road rage (i.e., TAE and the DS), while accounting for the control variables. This analysis used only strain as the independent variable; no additional theoretical variables were included in the model. This was done to achieve a baseline understanding of the nature of the relationship between strain and road rage. In path models 1a and 1b, (TAE and DS respectively), strain yielded a direct, positive, significant relationship with road rage. Thus, there was initial support for strain's direct association with road rage. This finding is consistent with previous research that demonstrated a direct link between strain and delinquency (Agnew & White, 1992; Hoffman & Cerbone, 1999; Hoffman & Miller, 1998; Mazerolle et al., 2000; Paternoster & Mazerolle, 1994; Piquero & Sealock, 2000, Baron, 2004).

The second path model examined the relationship between strain and situational anger. As Agnew (1992) purported in the theory, individuals who experience higher levels of strain were more likely to experience a negative affect. For Agnew, negative affect included anger, anxiety, frustration, and depression (1992). The study did not include variables representing anxiety, frustration and/or depression. However, this study did not find support for the relationship between strain and situational anger. Therefore, it is possible that one of these negative affects may have been operating, yet this study did not measure these alternatives. The extremely small regression coefficient between strain and situational anger is in opposition to research demonstrating the relationship between strain and anger (Brezina,

1996; Broidy, 2001; Mazerolle & Piquero, 1998). However, these studies have used a measure of trait anger as a mediating variable, whereas, this study used a situational anger variable as a mediating variable in the model.

Path models 3a and 3b focused on the relationship between situational anger and road rage (i.e., TAE and DS, respectively). In both models the relationship between situational anger and road rage was direct, positive, and significant. Thus, these results added support to Agnew's theory. In these models, the results indicate that situational anger significantly predicts participation in road rage. This finding is consistent with the Mazerolle et al., (2003) research using situational anger as a predictor of behavioral intentions. At the same time, other research is inconclusive concerning the linkage between anger and deviance. Although Broidy (2001) found anger and other negative emotions to be related to general crime among college students, others have found such a relationship to be relatively weak and limited only to violent or aggressive acts (Mazerolle & Piquero, 1998; Piquero & Sealock, 2000). Mazerolle et al. (2000) demonstrated no direct link at all between anger and violent delinquency, drug use, or school deviance.

Path models 4a and 4b are unique in that the role of coping mechanisms is introduced into the models. As Agnew (1992) contended, individuals who experience strain may or may not engage in deviant adaptations due to the coping mechanisms they have at their disposal. Agnew specifically suggests that an individual's disposition is an important determinant to whether the individual will choose a deviant or nondeviant coping strategy. Disposition takes into account the temperament of the individual, the previous learning history of the individual, the belief system of the individual, and the person's attributions regarding the cause of the adversity (Agnew, 1992). He further suggests that individuals who associate with delinquent peers are more likely to be exposed to deviant models and beliefs, and to receive reinforcement for delinquency. There has been relatively little research on the role of coping mechanisms with respect to GST.

Two path models examined the association between situational anger and coping mechanisms. Path model 4a examined the association between situational anger and self-control, whereas, path model 4b focused on the association between situational anger and peer behaviors. The control variables and strain were included in each of these models. Path model 4a did not support the contention that situational anger is associated with self-control. In this case the relationship was found to be positive yet not significant; however, it was approaching significance. It is important to note that in this case, the relationship to be tested was that of situational anger and the coping mechanism.

Path model 4b examined the association between situational anger and peer behavior. For this research, peer behavior refers to the notion that if the respondent's closest peer engaged in road rage there is a higher likelihood of the respondent also becoming involved in road rage. Theoretically, the stronger the association a person has with individuals who engage in road rage, the more likely he/she is to engage in road rage. This model did not support the contention that situational anger is associated with peer behavior. It is important to note that, in this case, the relationship to be tested was that of situational anger and the coping mechanism.

However, an interesting finding was discovered. From this model it was found that strain, when accounting for the control variables, yielded a significant positive relationship with the coping mechanism (i.e., peer behavior). This gave qualified support for strain theory and its association with coping mechanisms, as Agnew purported in his research (1992).

The final path models included all of the theoretical and control variables. Path model 5a used the TAE as its dependent variable and path model 5b used the DS as its dependent variable. Although there are many similarities between the models, there were also some differences. Both of the models yielded peer behavior, self-control, situational anger, and trait anger as significant variables. However, path model 5a revealed that strain was also a significant variable, as well as the number of police stops, and the number of accidents. Path model 5b indicated that gender and race were significant variables. Both of the models were able to explain a similar amount of the variance in the dependent variable. Path model 5a explained 46.1 percent of the variance in the TAE, whereas, path model 5b explained 41.0 percent of the variance in the DS.

Path model 5a suggested support for GST. In this model the direct relationship between strain and road rage was supported even with the addition of other theoretical variables. The relationship between strain and peer behavior also held up in this model. Furthermore, the indirect relationship between strain, peer behavior, and road rage was supported in this model. The independent effects of situational anger and self-control on road rage were seen in the model. Overall, this model provides support for Agnew's GST; strain has both direct and indirect effects on deviance. This direct effect of strain on deviance (i.e., road rage) is consistent with previous research (Agnew & White, 1992; Paternoster & Mazerolle, 1994; Hoffman & Miller, 1998; Hoffman & Cerbone, 1999; Mazerolle et al., 2000; Piquero & Sealock, 2000, Baron, 2004). At the same time, there are many studies that have failed to demonstrate the sort of conditioning effects predicted by the theory (Paternoster & Mazerolle, 1994; Hoffman & Miller, 1998; Mazerolle & Piquero, 1998).

Path model 5b, reveals qualified support for GST. In this model there is an indirect relationship between strain and road rage as mediated by peer behavior. Therefore, the relationship suggests that strain is associated with coping mechanisms, which, in turn, is associated with the deviant adaptation of road rage. However, the direct relationship between strain and road rage was eliminated due to the addition of other theoretical variables. The independent effects of self-control and situational anger remain significant in the model.

In addition to these theoretical variables, one control variable in particular, trait anger, was found to be an important variable in all of the paths. As Agnew (1992) proposed, there are various management strategies, such as personal and social support mechanisms, which may attenuate the effects of stress on adolescents. A constraint on one's behavior depends upon the individual's own coping resources, such as temperament, problem-solving skills, self-esteem, and other dispositional characteristics (Agnew, 1992). The traits that a person has effects the adaptation strategy he/she chooses to employ. The Baron (2004) study also demonstrated that trait anger is a significant predictor of crime. Furthermore, Gottfredson and Hirschi (1990) suggested that trait anger is a stable personality characteristic. Stable attributes have the ability to influence decisions and behaviors of individuals.

Policy Implications

There are two overriding policy implications associated with General Strain Theory (GST); both of which elicit suggestions for programs. According to Agnew (1995) a way to relieve strain is to introduce family, school, and peer group programs that teach prosocial skills. Thus, if the individual is exhibiting prosocial behaviors, he/she will be less likely to provoke a negative reaction from others (Agnew, 1995).

Another proposal is to "reduce the likelihood that people will respond to negative events with delinquency [deviance]" by providing them with social support and teaching better coping skills (Agnew, 1995, p. 43). Given these guidelines, there are programs which can be implemented that may be helpful in alleviating road rage.

The first suggestion is to reduce the adversity in the individual's environment by providing him/her with more participation in the decisions that affect his/her life; thus increasing the person's sense of "distributive justice" (Agnew, 1995, p. 64). Many of the questions in this study asked the respondent to report if the following events had occurred in his/her home. (i.e., "I started attending a new school?" ; "Have you or someone in your family divorced?"; "Separation?"; "Have you or someone in your family been in trouble with the law?" ; "Have you had any school problems?"). Each of these questions as well as the life situations they represent may be perceived as aversive in nature. Therefore, to overcome these adverse environments, academic and social monitoring, support, and rewards for prosocial behavior could be provided. These services could be provided by the counseling center on campus. Furthermore, counselors should not only be aware of the implications that these situations present, but also how the individual may cope with these events.

Another policy implication would be to "provide social support such as advocates or counselors and mediation programs to increase [individuals'] ability to solve problems legitimately, particularly in stressful times of transition" (Agnew, 1995). There are many critical points in an individual's college career that can evoke stress. From the questions in the survey as well as real life situations, many individuals have had a significant other break up with him/her, had a friendship end, and have transferred to a new school at the same or higher academic level. Given these events, there is a considerable amount of stress associated not only with the event itself, but also how to cope with the event in a positive way. In this case, there should be counseling programs that are available on campus to students who have experienced these situations. In the case of students transferring to a new school, there should be a mandatory orientation to the individual's program and the school's academic and counseling resources. Having a social support network may be beneficial for the individual in terms of problem solving and academic achievement.

Another similar policy implication would be to "increase social skills training and problem-solving and anger control programs to increase the ability of youths to cope with adversity without resorting to delinquency [deviance] (Agnew, 1995, p. 64). This particular implication is congruent with the dependent variable of road rage, since road rage maintains an element of anger. Recall from the definition of road rage that the act itself refers to an individual committing various infringements on the road that act to annoy, endanger, threaten to injure, injure, or damage the property of another motorist or passenger, in response to a traffic dispute, altercation, or grievance. Thus, campus programs should be in place that serve to counsel students, specifically focusing on acknowledging one's anger issues before he/she acts upon them. These sessions should provide techniques to reduce anger, to increase positive outlets for anger, and to enhance ways to cope with anger. This policy recommendation should be viewed cautiously, as the research on anger management is still mixed as per its effectiveness. However, Sharkin (1988) has suggested that counseling is effective in helping people manage maladaptive anger in a general sense as well as in managing driving anger and road rage tendencies. While there has been research support for anger management programs, it is not the panacea to angry behavior.

Agnew (1995) put forth these policy recommendations for the purposes of curbing the effects of strain on delinquency and deviance. Although these policy implications may be effective for certain samples, they might not be the most appropriate for this particular study. As pointed out in the research findings, trait anger was found to be a strong predictive indicator as well as consistently significant in the path models. Consequently, strain was a weaker predictive indicator, yet it remained significant in many models. Therefore, policy implications may be better apt to focus on programs that target dispositional characteristics that individuals possess. Perhaps, the interventions should begin earlier than college.

There are steps that can be taken prior to entering college. Although there are many high schools with drivers' education programs, many of these programs only offer the lecture-based portion of drivers' education, and not the hands-on driving component. Therefore, driver's education programs should include a component that deals specifically with driving while angry. Many times students do not know how to handle certain road situations effectively, especially when another driver does something that annoys the driver. Thus, if the individual behind the wheel of the vehicle is angry or stressed while driving, then dangerous consequences may arise.

Students should learn proper techniques to deal with driving while angry and also how to effectively respond to drivers on the road who infringe on other drivers.

Education and prevention programs that focus on stressors while driving may also be beneficial in reducing road rage. Relaxation techniques can be practiced while driving, especially when drivers are caught in slow moving traffic or when experiencing other forms of impeded travel. Listening to soothing music or audiobooks, drinking herbal tea, aromatherapy, and other ways to promote relaxation while driving could be encouraged (Sharkin, 2004). Time management strategies may also be helpful in countering driver stress and anger in individuals who do not manage their time well.

Not only should these types of programs be offered as a prerequisite for young drivers (in high school) but also for drivers whose driving record is less than stellar. As the study found, many individuals have been stopped by police, received traffic citations for speeding or other driving infractions, and have been involved in an accident. Given these statistics, driver's education classes should be suggested by police or deemed mandatory by the magistrate. Again these courses should include a component of driving while angry and how to effectively respond to other's driving infractions.

Since many of the individuals surveyed reported being stopped by police, yet an equal number did not receive traffic citations, it may prove beneficial for law enforcement to pay more attention to speeders and other traffic violators. Furthermore, once the offender is pulled over, officers should have available to them a mechanism to note (e.g., a box on the citation to check if this is aggressive driving or an incident of road rage) if the offense stemmed from a driving incident. As mentioned in Chapter One, there is currently no mechanism for police to uniformly gather information on the extent of aggressive driving and road rage in Pennsylvania. Due to the expense of recruiting, training, and hiring law enforcement personnel, another option is to utilize red-light cameras at intersections. If the cameras catch traffic violators, a citation would be sent to the offending motorist. This may act as a deterrent to future aggressive driving.

Society must acknowledge that acts of aggressive driving and road rage amount to a serious public safety issue. Awareness of one's own and others' driving is the first step in changing the attitudes and behaviors of drivers in this country. For this reason, public service announcements should focus on the consequences of aggressive driving and road rage as they relate to one's own safety and the safety of others. These public service announcements could come in the form of a 30 second commercial on television and radio, which communicate the message to a large audience. Another format of the public service announcement is to place signs along the roadways warning individuals of aggressive drivers (e.g., "Beware of Aggressive Drivers" "Do Not Tailgate"). These may serve as a reminder to the driver to (1) not participate in aggressive driving, and/or (2) to be aware that others may be engaging in aggressive driving. These signs should be placed in areas in which there have been known cases of road rage.

Limitations of the Study

The goal of this research project was to determine the extent of road rage among college students while at the same time provide a viable explanation for this behavior through Agnew's General Strain Theory (GST). While every effort was made to ensure a sound research project, there are some limitations. These limitations concentrate on sampling and instrumentation concerns.

<u>Sampling</u>
The institutions of higher education that were chosen for this study were institutions to which the researcher had access. While there were concerns with using availability samples (Babbie, 1998), these samples have been the accepted mode for much of the cited research. Furthermore, the use of college-aged youth as respondents for empirical research has been widely exercised in criminology and other social sciences (Nagin & Paternoster, 1993; Piquero & Tibetts, 1996; Tibbetts & Herz, 1996). Nagin and Paternoster (1993) contend that a sample of university students is likely to contain a number of marginal deviants. As pointed out in the literature and previously, road rage behaviors are not uncommon to university-aged respondents.

Although a carefully devised single-stage, cluster sample was used to draw the samples from both institutions, this method was not without its limitations. First, both institutions that were chosen for the study were comprised of predominantly Caucasian participants; therefore, the role of race and ethnicity may not be adequately represented in this sample. Second, the majority of the students in these samples were from middle-class backgrounds. These two limitations may mask any socioeconomic and ethnic influences that may affect aggressive driving and road rage behaviors.

Since an individual's level of self-control was being taken into account, the utilization of university students poses another possible problem. In order for students to excel in academia, students must demonstrate a certain amount of diligence and tenacity. It has been noted in the literature that students who are in college may have reached a certain threshold of self-control, especially with respect to task persistence and future time orientation. This is contrary to the characterization of one who has a low level of self-control. In their research, Gottfredson and Hirschi (1990) purported that university students were most likely to be characterized by high levels of self-control, consequently, they were relatively restricted in deviance involvement. Although these concerns were relevant, based on previous research, variation in offending was not a problem. This study found sufficient variation in deviance among university students.

Lastly, a limitation of this study related to external generalizability. This sample was restricted to undergraduate students. Since the college undergraduates may not be typical of all undergraduate students or the public at large, the results of the study cannot be generalized beyond the population of the particular institutions being studied. Thus this limits the usefulness of the findings, in that, college samples might vary significantly from community samples in age, racial composition, education, socioeconomic status, and other variables.

Instrumentation

The individual scales that comprise the survey instrument used in this study were expected to work well or be appropriate for this population. As noted in Chapter 5, the strain scale, which yielded a Cronbach's alpha level of .65, is considered to be minimally acceptable by DeVellis standards (1991). This strain scale (Alpha= .58) was used in a prior study (Capowich et al, 2001); however, it is important to note that this study yielded a higher alpha level than the previous study. Although the alpha level is below acceptable standards, the primary justification for using this strain scale was for theoretical purposes. Because this study examined the role of strain in explaining road rage behaviors, a strain scale was necessary. Many of the strain studies have used such scales pertaining to stress, negative life events, neighborhood problems, school and peer hassles, and life hassles as measures of strain (Agnew & White, 1992; Aseltine et al., 2000; Paternoster & Mazerolle, 1994).

Directions for Future Research

It would appear that based on the findings, more testing of Agnew's General Strain Theory should be conducted. The concept of strain, specifically the three sources of strain, is difficult to operationalize. It has been argued that the sources of strain measured in previous research may also be interpreted as variables measuring concepts from other theories, specifically social learning and social bonding theories (Akers & Sellers, 2004). Therefore, the variables used to measure strain should be better delineated as well as tap into the motivational processes of strain.

The sources of strain stem from different arenas (i.e., school, work, family, and home). Agnew suggested (2001) future research should focus on the types of strain most likely to lead to criminal or delinquent coping, which may include strains that are seen as unjust, are high in magnitude, emanate from situations in which social control is undermined, and pressure the individual into criminal or delinquent associations. Agnew recommends measuring types of strain that meet these criteria, including, but not limited to, parental rejection, negative school experiences, abusive peers, and criminal victimization (Agnew, 2001).

Although many researchers have tested the direct link between strain and deviance (Agnew & White, 1992; Paternoster & Mazerolle, 1994; Hoffman & Miller, 1998; Hoffman & Cerbone, 1999; Mazerolle et al., 2000; Piquero & Sealock, 2000), few studies have examined the strain, negative affect, and deviance linkage or the strain, negative affect, coping mechanisms, and deviance linkage. The research studies that have focused on the link between strain and negative affect, in most cases, have used a dispositional measure of anger as the theoretical variable (Brezina, 1996; Mazerolle & Piquero, 1997, 1998: Mazerolle et al., 2000). Future research should focus on situational anger as the theoretical variable mediating strain and deviance or strain and the coping mechanisms and deviance, since situational anger appears to be more consistent with the context of GST as purported by Agnew.

The link between strain and coping mechanisms should be further examined. Although Agnew (1992) contends that coping mechanisms play a role in whether or not individuals will succumb to a deviant adaptation, there are few research studies that include coping mechanisms in their models. Thus, there is little empirical evidence to date on the role that they play in the model. Furthermore, if coping mechanisms are included in the model, more than one coping mechanism should be included; thus indicating which mechanisms are more pivotal in relation to others.

In addition to the further testing of strain theory, the results of this study provide a platform for examining the viability of Gottfredson and Hirschi's self-control theory as an explanation for aggressive driving and road rage. As suggested in the findings, dispositional characteristics may be able to better explain why individuals participate in aggressive driving and road rage. It was noted in the literature that both trait anger and self-control are stable personality characteristics or are considered to be enduring traits. Each of these variables was revealed to be significant indicator of aggressive driving. Given this information, self-control theory should be tested as an alternate explanation for the behavior.

Because aggressive driving and road rage can be subjective in nature, concerning what constitutes it and how to respond to it, qualitative studies should be conducted to decipher what specific acts are the most troublesome to others. These studies should attempt to ascertain how minor acts of aggressive driving escalate into more serious acts or road rage. These studies could also focus on the car atmosphere that may precipitate acts of aggressive driving or road rage. For example, does the type of music factor into how one drives or what role does alcohol play in aggressive driving or does the type of car one drives factor into one's participation in road rage. Furthermore, the qualitative study would lend itself to asking the participants open-ended questions concerning under what conditions they would absolutely refrain from aggressive driving.

Conclusion

This study has attempted to fill a gap in the academic literature on deviance. Although road rage has been studied from psychological and sociological perspectives, this is the first known study to examine road rage from a criminological perspective, General Strain Theory (GST). Clearly, this study augments the literature on strain theory.

This study found substantial evidence that college students participate in aggressive driving and road rage. Although many of the acts that individuals participated in were of a minor nature, there were some individuals who engaged in more serious forms of road rage. It further identified reasons associated with why individuals engage in aggressive driving and road rage. Many of these reasons stem from strain, anger, low levels of self-control, and deviant peer relationships. Individuals who participate in aggressive driving and road rage pose a substantial risk to public safety, not only to themselves but also to others on the roadways.

This study has important implications for GST. In using GST as the theoretical framework, the relationships between strain, situational anger, self-control, deviant peers, and road rage were examined. The findings of the study support GST in its direct effects on deviance and provide qualified support for the indirect effects of strain on a specific form of deviance (i.e., road rage) through peer behavior.

Another contribution of this study is that it included measures of both trait anger and situational anger. Situational anger was used as the theoretical variable and trait anger was used as a control variable. This was based on the assumption that high trait anger individuals are more likely to develop situational anger in response to strain. In this study, the assumption that trait anger would have a significant effect on situational anger was supported. Much of the past research examined relationships between strain, anger, and deviant adaptations; and the researchers included measures of trait anger in their models (Brezina, 1996; Mazerolle & Piquero, 1997, 1998; Mazerolle et al., 2000). Thus, findings of previous research might simply be conservative, but not necessarily incorrect because decontextualized measures of anger have been used. Lastly, the findings from this study also indicate that strain operates through the coping mechanism of peer behavior; thus strain also indirectly effects road rage.

Future research should focus on the role of anger (i.e., situational anger versus trait anger) in the strain model. With respect to the role of coping mechanisms, future research should examine multiple coping mechanisms, as proposed by Agnew. These mechanisms should be examined in relation to each other as well as their aggregate effects on participating in a deviant adaptation. Future research should test GST in conjunction with rival theories to assess their strength in explaining deviance. It would also be appropriate to examine road rage from a self-control perspective. Lastly, the findings from this study illustrate that there are various policy recommendations that can be implemented that may curb aggressive driving and road rage.

References

AAA Foundation for Traffic Safety. (1997a). Road rage on the rise, AAA Foundation Reports. Retrieved November 7, 1998 from http:www.aaafts .org/Text/research/roadrage.htm.

AAA Foundation for Traffic Safety. (1997b). *Aggressive driving: Three studies.* Washington, DC: AAA Foundation for Traffic Safety. Author.

Academic Schedule. (2003, Spring term). Independent College Admissions Office.

Adams, J. R. (1970). Personality variables associated with traffic accidents. *Behavioral Research in Highway Safety, 1,* 3-18.

Admissions. (2002). *Breakdown of undergraduate students on main campus.* [Electronic data file]. PA: Independent College. Admissions Office.

Aggressive driving now a crime on Arizona highways. (1998). *State Legislatures, 24,* 8.

Agnew, R. (1984). Goal achievement and delinquency. *Sociology and Social Research, 68(*4), 435-451.

Agnew, R. (1985). A revised strain theory of delinquency. *Social Forces, 64* (1), 151-167.

Agnew, R. (1989). A longitudinal test of the revised strain theory. *Journal of Quantitative Criminology, 5*(4), 37-387.

Agnew, R. (1991). Strain and subcultural crime theories. In J. F. Sheley (Ed.), *Criminology: A contemporary handbook.* (pp.273-292). Belmont, CA: Wadsworth.

Agnew, R. (1992). Foundation for a general strain theory of crime and delinquency. *Criminology, 30*(1), 47-87.

Agnew, R. (1994). The techniques of neutralization and violence. *Criminology, 32,* 555-580.

Agnew, R. (1995). Controlling delinquency: Recommendations from general strain theory. In H. Barlow (Ed.). *Crime and public policy: Putting theory to work.* (pp. 43-70). Boulder, CO: Westview Press.

Agnew, R. (2001). Building on the foundation of general strain theory: Specifying the types of strain most likely to lead to crime and delinquency. *Journal of Research in Crime and Delinquency, 38,* 319-361.

Agnew, R., & Brezina, T. (1997). Relational problems with peers, gender, and delinquency. *Youth & Society, 29*(1), 84-111.

Agnew, R., Brezina, T, Wright, J. P., & Cullen, F. T. (2002). Strain, personality traits, and delinquency: Extending general strain theory. *Criminology, 40*, 43-72.

Agnew, R., & White, H. R. (1992). An empirical test of general strain theory. *Criminology, 30*(4) 475-499.

Agresti, A., & Finlay, B. (1997). *Statistical methods for the social sciences.* Upper Saddle River, NJ: Prentice Hall.

Akers, R. L. (1985). *Deviant behavior: A social learning approach.* Belmont, CA: Wadsworth.

Akers, R. L. (1991). Self-control as a general theory of crime. *Journal of Quantitative Criminology, 7*(2), 201-211.

Akers, R., Krohn, M., Lanza-Kaduce, L., & Radosevich, M. (1979). Social learning and deviant behavior: A specific test of a general theory. *American Sociological Review, 44*, 636-655.

Akers, R.L., & Sellers, C. S. (2004). *Criminological theories: Introduction, evaluation, and application.* (4th ed.). Los Angeles, CA: Roxbury Publishing Company.

Alm, H., & Nilsson, L. (1995). The effects of a mobile telephone task on driver behaviour in a car following situation. *Accident Analysis and Prevention, 27*(5), 707-715.

Altman, K. (1997). Road rage runs rampant in high-stress United States Society. U.S. News [On-line] Retrieved November, 8, 1998 from *http://www.cnn.com/US/9707/18/aggressive.driving/index.html.*

Anderson, C. A., & Anderson, D. C. (1984). Ambient temperature and violent crime: Tests of the linear and curvilinear hypotheses. *Journal of Personality and Social Psychology, 46*, 91-97.

Andrews, J., & Hops, H. (1991). The construction, validation, and use of a Guttman scale of adolescent substance use: An investigation of family relationships. *Journal of Drug Issues, 21*, 557-573.

Aneshensel, C. S. (1992). Social stress: Theory and research. *Annual Review of Sociology, 18*, 15-32.

Archer, S. L. (1989). Gender differences in identity development: Issues of process, domain, and timing. *Journal of Adolescence, 12*, 117-138.

Arneklev, B. J., Cochran, J.K., & Gainey, R.R. (1998). Testing Gottfredson and Hirschi's "low self-control" stability hypothesis: An exploratory study. *American Journal of Criminal Justice, 23*(1), 107-127.

Arneklev, B. J., Grasmick, H. G., Tittle, C. R., & Bursik, Jr., R. J. (1993). Low self-control and imprudent behavior. *Journal of Quantitative Criminology, 9*(3), 225-247.

Arnett, J. J., Offer, D., & Fine, M. A. (1997). Reckless driving in adolescence: "State" and "Trait" factors. *Accident Analysis and Prevention, 29*, 57-63.

Aseltine, R. H., Jr., Gore, S., & Gordon, J. (2000). Life stress, anger and anxiety, and delinquency: An empirical test of general strain theory. *Journal of Health and Social Behavior, 41*, 256-275.

Attar, B. K., Guerra, N. G., & Tolan, P. H. (1994). Neighborhood disadvantage, stressful life events, and adjustment in urban elementary school children. *Journal of Clinical Child Psychology, 23*, 391-400.

Averill, J. R. (1982). *Anger and aggression.* New York: Springer-Verlag.

Babbie, E. (1998). *The practice of social research* (8th ed.). Belmont, CA: Wadsworth Press.

Babbie, E. (1990). *Survey research methods.* (2nd ed.) Belmont, CA: Wadsworth Publishing Company.

Bachman, R., & Paternoster, R. (1997). *Statistical methods for criminology and criminal justice.* New York: McGraw-Hill-B&P.

Bachman, J. D., Johnston, L. D., & O'Malley, P. (1987). *Monitoring the Future.* Ann Arbor, MI: Institute for Social Research.

Bandura, A. (1973). *Aggression: A social learning analysis.* Englewood Cliffs, NJ: Prentice Hall.

Bandura, A. (1978). Social learning theory of aggression. *Journal of Communication, 28*(3), 12-27.

Bandura, A., Underwood, B., & Fromson, M. E. (1975). Disinhibition of aggression through diffusion of responsibility and dehumanization of victims. *Journal of Research in Personality, 9*, 253-269.

Baron, S. W. (2004). General strain, street youth and crime: A test of Agnew's revised theory. *Criminology, 42*(2), 457-483.

Bartusch, D. R., Lynam, D. R., Moffitt, T. E., & Silva, P. A. (1997). Is age important? Testing a general versus a developmental theory of antisocial behavior. *Criminology, 35*, 13-48.

Beirness, D. J., & Simpson, H. M. (1988). Lifestyle correlates of risky driving and accident involvement among youth. *Alcohol, Drugs, and Driving, 4*(3-4), 193-204.

Beirness, D. J., Simpson, H. M., Mayhew, D. R., & Pak, A. (2001). *The road safety monitor: Aggressive driving.* Ottawa, Ontario: Traffic Injury Research Foundation.

Benson, M., & Moore, E. (1992). Are white-collar and common offenders the same? An empirical and theoretical critique of a recently proposed general theory of crime. *Journal of Research in Crime and Delinquency, 29*, 251-272.

Berkowitz, L. (1982). Aversive conditions as stimuli to aggression. In L.
    Berkowitz (Ed.), *Advances in Experimental Social Psychology.* (Vol. 15).
    (pp. 3-15). New York: Academic Press.

Berkowitz, L. (1986). *A survey of social psychology.* New York: Holt,
    Rinehart & Winston.

Blake, K. (1998). Federal funds for road rage. *Consumers' Research
    Magazine, 81*(11). p. 38.

Blanchard, E. B., Barton, K. A., & Malta, L. (2000). Psychometric properties
    of a measure of aggressive driving: The Larson driver's stress profile.
    Psychological Reports, 87, 881-892.

Braithwaite, L. (1981). The myth of social class and criminality reconsidered.
    American Sociological Review, 46, 36-58.

Brezina, T. (1996). Adapting to strain: An examination of delinquent coping
    responses. *Criminology, 34*(1), 39-60.

Brezina, T. (1998). Adolescent maltreatment and delinquency: The question
    of intervening processes. *Journal of Research in Crime and Delinquency,
    35,* 71-99.

Brezina, T. (1999). Teenage violence toward parents as an adaptation to family
    strain: Evidence from a national survey of male adolescents. *Youth &
    Society, 30*(4), 416-444.

Broidy, L.M. (2001). A test of general strain theory. *Criminology, 39*(1), 9-35.

Broidy, L. M., & Agnew, R. (1997). Gender and crime: A general strain
    theory perspective. *Journal of Research in Crime and Delinquency, 34*(3),
    275-306.

Brownfield, D., & Sorenson, A. M. (1993). Self-control and juvenile
    delinquency: Theoretical issues and an empirical assessment of selected
    elements of a general theory of crime. *Deviant Behavior, 14,* 243-264.

Burkett, S., & Jensen, E. (1975). Conventional ties, peer influence, and the fear
    of apprehension: A study of adolescent marijuana use. *Sociology
    Quarterly, 16,* 522-533.

Burton, V. S., Jr., Cullen, F. T., Evans, T. D., Alarid, L. F., & Dunaway, R. G.
    (1998). Gender, self-control, and crime. *Journal of Research in Crime
    and Delinquency, 35*(2), 123-147.

Burton, V. S., Jr. , Cullen, F. T., Evans, T. D., & Dunaway, R. G. (1994).
    Reconsidering strain theory: Operationalization, rival theories, and adult
    criminality. *Journal of Quantitative Criminology, 10*(3), 213-239.

Cameron, T. L. (1982). Drinking and driving among American youth: Beliefs
    and behaviors. *Drug and Alcohol Dependence, 10,* 1-33.

Capowich, G. E., Mazerolle, P., & Piquero, A. (2001). General strain theory, situational anger, and social networks: An assessment of conditioning influence. *Journal of Criminal Justice, 29,* 445-461.

Cernkovich, S. A., & Giordano, P. C. (2001). Stability and change in antisocial behavior: The transition from adolescence to early adulthood. *Criminology, 39,* 371-410.

Chesney-Lind, M., & Sheldon, R. G. (1992). *Girls, delinquency, and juvenile justice.* Pacific Grove, CA: Brooks/Cole.

Chodorow, N. (1989). *Feminism and psychoanalytic theory.* New Haven, CT: Yale University Press.

Cloward, R. A., & Ohlin, L. E. (1960). *Delinquency and opportunity.* New York: Free Press.

Cochran, J. K., Wood, P. B., Sellers, C. S., Wilkerson, W., & Chamlin, M. B. (1998). Academic dishonesty and low self-control: An empirical test of a general theory of crime. *Deviant Behavior: An Interdisciplinary Journal, 19,* 227-255.

Coddington, R. D. (1972). The significance of life events as etiologic factors in the diseases of children: A study of a normal population. *Journal of Psychosomatic Research, 1,* 205-213.

Cohen, A. (1955). *Delinquent boys.* New York: Free Press.

Coleman, J. (1961). *The adolescent society.* New York: Free Press.

Compas, B. E. (1987). Coping with stress during childhood and adolescence. *Psychological Bulletin, 101,* 393-403.

Compas, B. E., Davis, G. E., & Forsythe, C. J. (1985). Characteristics of life events during adolescence. *American Journal of Community Psychology, 13,* 677-691.

Compas, B. E., Orosan, P. G., & Grant, K. E. (1993). Adolescent stress and coping: Implications for psychopathology during adolescence. *Journal of Adolescence, 16,* 331-349.

Connell, D., & Joint, M. (1996, November). Driver aggression. *In Aggressive Driving: Three Studies.* United Kingdom: The Automobile Association. AAA Foundation for Traffic Safety.

Cook, K. S., & Hegtvedt, K. A. (1992). Empirical evidence of the sense of justice. In R.D. Masters & M. M. Gruter (Eds.). *The sense of justice: An inquiry into the biological foundations of law.* (pp. 187-210). New York: Greenwood Press.

Cullen, F. T., & Wright, J. P. (1997). Liberating the anomie-strain paradigm: Implications from social support theory. In N. Passas & R. Agnew (Eds.), *The future of anomie theory,* (pp. 187-206). Boston: Northeastern University Press.

Daly, K. (1992). Women's pathways to felony court: Feminist theories of lawbreaking and problems of representation. *Review of Law and Women's Studies, 2,* 11-52.

Deffenbacher, J. L. (1992). Trait anger: theory findings, and implications. In C. D. Spielberger & J. N. Butcher (Eds.), *Advances in personality assessment* (Vol. 9, pp. 177-201). Hillsdale, NJ: Erlbaum.

Deffenbacher, J. L., Deffenbacher, D.M., Lynch, R.S., & Richards, T.L. (2003) Anger, aggression, and risky behavior. A comparison of high and low anger drivers. *Behaviour Research and Therapy, 41*(6), 701-718.

Deffenbacher, J. L., Huff, M. E., Lynch, R. S., Oetting, E. R., & Salvatore, N. F. (2000). Characteristics and treatment of high-anger drivers. *Journal of Counseling Psychology, 47*(1), 5-17.

Deffenbacher, J. L., Lynch, R. S., Deffenbacher, D. M., & Oetting, E. R. (2001). Further evidence of reliability and validity for the Driving Anger Expression Inventory. *Psychological Reports, 89,* 535-540.

Deffenbacher, J. L., Lynch, R. S., Filetti, L.B., Dahlen, E.R., & Oetting, E.R. (2003). Anger, aggression, risky behavior, and crash-related outcomes in three groups of drivers. *Behaviour Research and Therapy, 41*(3), 333-349.

Deffenbacher, J. L., Lynch, R. S., Oetting, E. R., & Swaim, R. C. (2002). The driving anger expression inventory: A measure of how people express their anger on the road. *Behaviour Research and Therapy, 40,* 717-737.

Deffenbacher, J. L., Lynch, R. S., Oetting, E. R., & Yingling, D. A. (2001). Driving anger: Correlates and a test of state-trait theory. *Personality and Individual Differences, 31,* 1321-1331.

Deffenbacher, J. L., Oetting, E. R., & Lynch, R. S. (1994). Development of a driving anger scale. *Psychological Reports, 74,* 83-91.

Deffenbacher, J. L., Oetting, E. R., Lynch, R. S., & Morris, C. D. (1996). The expression of anger and its consequences. *Behaviour Research and Therapy, 34,* 575-590.

Deffenbacher, J. L., Oetting, E. R., Huff, M. E., Cornell, G. R., & Dallager, C. J. (1996). Evaluation of two cognitive-behavioral approaches to general anger reduction. *Cognitive Therapy and Research, 26*(6), 551-573.

Deffenbacher, J.L., Oetting, E.R., Thwaites, G.A., Lynch, R.S., Baker, D. A. Stark, P.S., Thacker, S., & Eisworth-Cox, L. (1996). State-trait anger theory and the utility of the Trait Anger Scale. *Journal of Counseling Psychology, 43,* 131-148.

Deffenbacher, J. L., Petrilli, R.T., Lynch, R.S., Oetting, E.R., & Swaim, R. C. (2003). The driver's angry thoughts questionnaire: A measure of angry cognitions when driving. *Cognitive Therapy and Research, 27,* 383-402.

DeVellis, R. F. (1991). *Scale development: Theory and applications*. Newbury Park: Sage Publications.

Donnerstein, E., & Hatfield, E. (1982). Aggression and equity. In J. Greenberg & R. L. Cohen (Eds.). *Equity and justice in social behavior*. (pp. 309-336). New York: Academic Press.

Donovan, D. M., & Marlatt, G. A. (1982). Personality subtypes among driving-while-intoxicated offenders: Relationship to drinking behavior and driving risk. *Journal of Consulting and Clinical Psychology, 50*, 241-249.

Donovan, D. M., Marlatt, G. A., & Salzberg, P. M. (1983). Drinking behavior, personality factors, and high-risk driving: A review and theoretical formulation. *Journal of Studies on Alcohol, 44*, 395-428.

Donovan, D. M., Queisser, H. R., Salzberg, P. M., & Umlauf, R. L. (1985). Intoxicated and bad drivers: Subgroups within the same population of high-risk men drivers. *Journal of Studies on Alcohol, 46*, 375-382.

Donovan, D. M., Umlauf, R. L., & Salzberg, P. M. (1988). Derivation of personality subtypes among high-risk drivers. *Alcohol, Drugs, and Driving, 4*(3-4), 233-244.

Dukes, R. L., Clayton, S. L., Jenkins, L. T., Miller, T. L., & Rodgers, S. E. (2001). Effects of aggressive driving and driver characteristics on road rage. *Social Science Journal, 38*(2), 323-332.

Elliot, D., & Ageton, S. (1980). Reconciling race and class differences in self-reported and official estimates of delinquency. *American Sociological Review, 45*, 95-110.

Elliot, D., Ageton, S., & Canter, R. (1979). An integrated theoretical perspective on delinquent behavior. *Journal of Research in Crime and Delinquency, 16*, 3-27.

Elliot, D., Huizinga, D., & Ageton, S. (1985). *Explaining delinquency and drug use*. Beverly Hills, CA: Sage Publications.

Elliot, D., Huizinga, D., & Menard, S. (1989). *Multiple problem youth: Delinquency, substance use, and mental health problems*. New York: Springer-Verlag.

Elliot, D., & Voss, H. (1974). *Delinquency and dropout*. Lexington, MA: Lexington Books.

Ellison, P. A., Govern, J. M., Petri, H. L., & Figler, M. H. (1995). Anonymity and aggressive driving behavior: A field study. *Journal of Social Behavior and Personality, 10*, 265-272.

Ellison-Potter, P., Bell, P., & Deffenbacher, J. (2001). The effects of trait driving anger, anonymity, and aggressive stimuli on aggressive driving behavior. *Journal of Applied Social Psychology, 31*(2), 431-443.

Evans, L., & Wasielewski, P. (1983). Risky driving related to driver and vehicle characteristics. *Accident Analysis & Prevention, 15*, 121-136.

Flango, V. E.,& Keith, A. L. (2004). The road less angrily traveled: Aggressive driving legislation. *2004 Trends Report: Future Trends in State Courts, 2004:* The National Center for State Courts.

Foss, R. D., Bierness, D. J., & Spratter, K. (1994). Seat belt use among drinking drivers in Minnesota. *American Journal of Public Health, 84*, 1732-1737.

Fumento, M. (1998). Road rage versus reality. *Atlantic Monthly, 282*(2), 12-17.

Furnham, A., & Saipe, J. (1993). Personality correlates of convicted drivers. *Personality and Individuals Differences, 14*, 329-336.

Gersten, J. C., Langer, T. S., Eisenberg, J. G., & Ozek, L. (1974). Child behavior and life events: Undesirable change or change per se. In B. N. Dohrenwend & B. Dohrenwend (Eds.). *Stressful life events: Their nature and effects.* (pp. 159-170). New York: John Wiley & Sons.

Gibbs, J. J., & Giever, D. (1995). Self-control and its manifestations among university students: An empirical test of Gottfredson and Hirschi's general theory. *Justice Quarterly, 12*(2), 233-255.

Gibbs, J. J., Giever, D., & Martin, J. S. (1998). Parental management and self-control: An empirical test of Gottfredson and Hirschi's general theory. *Journal of Research in Crime and Delinquency, 35*(1), 40-70.

Giordano, P.C., Cernkovich, S. A., & Pugh, M. D. (1986). Friendships and delinquency. *American Journal of Sociology, 91*, 1170-1202.

Gold, M. (1963). *Status forces in delinquent boys.* Ann Arbor: Institute for Social Research.

Gottfredson, M. R., & Hirschi, T. (1990). *A general theory of crime.* Stanford, CA: Stanford University Press.

Grasmick, H. G., Tittle, C. R., Bursik, Jr., R. J., & Arneklev, B. J. (1993). Testing the core empirical implications of Gottfredson and Hirschi's general theory of crime. *Journal of Research in Crime and Delinquency, 30*(1), 5-29.

Greenberg, D. F. (1977). Delinquency and the age structure of society. *Contemporary Crises, 1,*189-223.

Grey, E. M., Triggs, T. J., & Haworth, N. L. (1989). *Driver aggression: The role of personality, social characteristics, risk and motivation.* CR 81. Canaberra, Australia: Federal Office of Road Safety.

Guilford, J. P. (1954). *Psychometric methods.* New York: McGraw Hill.

Gulian, E., Glendon, A., Matthews, G., Davies, D. R., & Debney, M. (1990). The stress of driving: A diary study. *Work and Stress, 4*, 7-16.

Halverson, C.F. Jr., (1988). Remembering your parents: Reflections on the Retrospective Method. *Journal of Personality, 56*(2), 435-443.

Harding, R. W., Morgan, F. H., Indermaur, D., Ferrante, A. M., & Blagg, H. (1998). Road rage and the epidemiology of violence: Something old, something new. *Studies on Crime and Crime Prevention, 7*(2), 221-238.

Harris, R. (2001, July 14). Dog killer given 3-year jail term in road-rage crime. *Pittsburgh Post-Gazette,* p. A5.

Hauber, A. R. (1980). The special psychology of driving behaviour and the traffic environment: Research on aggressive behaviour in traffic. *International Review of Applied Psychology, 29*(4), 461-474.

Hegtvedt, K. A. (1990). The effects of relationship structure on emotional responses to inequity. *Social Psychology Quarterly, 53*, 214-228.

Hendricks, D. L., Fell, J. C., & Freedman, M. (2001). *The relative frequency of unsafe driving acts in serious traffic crashes.* Washington D.C.: National Highway Traffic Safety Administration.

Hennessy, D. A., & Wiesenthal, D. L. (1999). Traffic congestion, driver stress, and driver aggression. *Aggressive Behavior, 25*, 409-423.

Hennessy, D. A., & Wiesenthal, D. L. (2001). Gender, driver aggression, and driver violence: An applied analysis. *Sex Roles, 44,*661-676.

Hindelang, M., Hirschi, T., & Weiss, J. (1981). *Measuring delinquency.* Beverly Hills: Sage Publications.

Hirschi, T. (1969). *Causes of delinquency.* Berkeley: University of California Press.

Hodgdon, J. D., Bragg, B. W. E., & Finn, P. (1981). *Young driver risk-taking research: The state of the art.* Report prepared by National Highway Traffic Safety Administration, U.S. DOT HS-805-967.

Hoffmann, J. P., & Cerbone, F. G. (1999). Stressful life events and delinquency escalation in early adolescence. *Criminology, 37*(2), 343-373.

Hoffman, J. P., & Ireland, T. (1995). Cloward and Ohlin's strain theory reexamined: An elaborated theoretical model. In F. Alder and W.S. Laufer (Eds.). *The legacy of anomie theory.* (pp. 247-270). New Brunswick, NJ: Transaction Publishers.

Hoffmann, J., & Miller, A. (1998). A latent variable analysis of general strain theory. *Journal of Quantitative Criminology, 14*, 83-110.

Hoffmann, J. P., & Su, S. (1997). The conditional effects of stress on delinquency and drug use: A strain theory assessment of sex differences. *Journal of Research in Crime and Delinquency, 34*, 46-78.

IIHS Status Report. (1998). Road Rage. *IIHS Status Report, 33*. p. 10.

Institutional Research. (2002). *Enrollment and Persistence.* [Electronic data file]. Public University Institutional Research, Pubic University.

James, L. (1997). Aggressive driving and road rage: Dealing with emotionally impaired drivers. Retrieved November 8, 2000 from *http://www.house.go v/transportation/surface/sthearin/ist717/james.htm.*

James, L., & Nahl, D. (2000). *Road rage and aggressive driving: Steering clear of highway warfare.* Amherst, NY: Prometheus.

Jessor, R. (1987). Risky driving and adolescent problem behavior: An extension of problem-behavior theory. *Alcohol, Drugs and Driving, 3* (3-4), 1-11.

Jessor, R., & Jessor, S. L. (1977). *Problem behavior and psychosocial development: A longitudinal study of youth.* New York: Academic Press.

Johnson, R. E. (1979). *Juvenile delinquency and its origins: An integrated theoretical approach.* Cambridge: Cambridge University Press.

Johnson, R. E., Marcos, A. C., & Bahr, S. J. (1987). The role of peers in the complex etiology of adolescent drug use. *Criminology, 25*(2), 323-340.

Johnson, J. H., & McCutcheon, S. (1980). Assessing life events in older children and adolescents: Preliminary findings with the life events checklist. In I.G. Sarason & C. C. Spielberger (Eds.). *Stress and Anxiety.* (pp. 111-125). Washington DC: Hemisphere.

Joint, M. (1995, November). Road rage. In AAA Foundation for Traffic Safety (Ed.) *Aggressive Driving: Three Studies.* pp.15-24.

Jonah, B. A. (1986). Accident risk and risk-taking behaviour among young drivers. *Accident and Analysis & Prevention, 18*(4), 255-271.

Keane, C., Maxim, P. S., & Teevan, J. J. (1993). Drinking and driving, self-control, and gender: Testing a general theory of crime. *Journal of Research in Crime and Delinquency, 30*(1), 30-46.

Kerlinger, F. N., & Pedhazur, E. J. (1973). *Multiple regression in behavioral research.* New York: Holt, Rinehart, and Winston, Inc.

Kessler, R. C., & McLeod, J. D. (1984). Sex differences in vulnerability to undesirable life events. *American Sociological Review, 49*, 620-631.

Kornhauser, R. R. (1978). *Social sources of delinquency.* Chicago: University of Chicago Press.

Kostyniuk, L. P., Molnar, L. J., & Eby, D. W. (2001). Are women taking more risks while driving? A look at Michigan Drivers. University of Michigan. Retrieved on December 10, 2001 from *http://www.fhwa.dot. gov/ohim/womens/chapter26.pdf.*

Kowalski, K. M. (1998). How to rein in rage. *Current Health, 25*(3), 6-8.

Kuder, G., & Richardson, M.E. (1937). The theory of the estimation of test reliability. *Psychometrika,2,* 151-160.

LaGrange, T. C., & Silverman, R. A. (1999). Low self-control and opportunity: Testing the general theory of crime as an explanation for gender differences in delinquency. *Criminology, 37*(1), 41-72.

Larson, J. A. (1996). *Steering clear of highway madness: A drivers guide to curbing stress and strain.* Wilsonville, OR: BookPartners, Inc.

Leadbeater, B. J., Blatt, S. J., & Quinlan, D. M. (1995). Gender-linked vulnerabilities to depressive symptoms, stress, and problem behaviors in adolescents. *Journal of Research on Adolescence, 5,* 1-29.

Lewis-Beck, M. (1980). *Applied regression. An introduction.* Thousand Oaks, CA: Sage Publishing.

Linsky, A. S., & Strauss, M. A. (1986). *Social stress in the United States.* Dover, MA: Auburn House.

Liska, A. (1971). Aspirations, expectations, and delinquency: Stress and additive models. *Sociological Quarterly,12,* 99-107.

Longshore, D. (1998). Self-control and criminal opportunity: A prospective test of the general theory of crime. *Social Problems,45*(1), 102-114.

Longshore, D., Stein, J. A., & Turner, S. (1998). Reliability and validity of a self-control measure: Rejoiner. *Criminology, 36* (1), 175-182.

Longshore, D., & Turner, S. (1998). Self-control and criminal opportunity: Cross-sectional test of the general theory of crime. *Criminal Justice and Behavior, 25*(1), 81-98.

Longshore, D., Turner, S., & Stein, J. A. (1996). Self-control in a criminal sample: An examination of construct validity. *Criminology, 34*(2), 209-228.

Luckenbill, D. (1977). Criminal homicide as a situated transaction. *Social Problems, 25,* 176-186.

Lundesgaarde, H. F. (1997). *Murder in Space City: A cultural analysis of Houston homicide patterns.* New York: Oxford University Press.

Marsh, P., & Collett, P. (1986). *Driving passion: The psychology of the car.* Boston: Faber and Faber.

Marsh, P., & Collett, P. (1987). The car as a weapon. *Etc, 44*(2), 146-151.

Martinez, R. (1997). Testimony before the House Committee on Transportation and Infrastructure Subcommittee on Surface Transportation. Washington D.C.: National Highway Traffic Safety Administration. Retrieved on December 10, 2001 from *http://www.house.gov/transportation/surface/sthearin/ist717/martinez.htm.*

Matsueda, R. L. (1982). Testing control theory and differential association: A causal modeling approach. *American Sociological Review, 47,* 489-504.

Mayer, R. E., & Treat, J.R. (1977). Psychological, social, and cognitive characteristics of high-risk drivers: A pilot study. *Accident Analysis and Prevention, 9,* 1-8.

Mayhew, D. R., Donelson, A. C., Beirness, D.J., & Simpson, H. M. (1986). Youth, alcohol, and relative risk of crash involvement. *Accident Analysis and Prevention, 18,* 273-287.

Mazerolle, P., Burton, V. S., Jr., Cullen, F. T., Evans, T. D., & Payne, G. L. (2000). Strain, anger, and delinquent adaptations: Specifying general strain theory. *Journal of Criminal Justice, 28,* 89-101.

Mazerolle, P., & Piquero, A. (1998). Linking exposure to strain with anger: An investigation of deviant adaptations. *Journal of Criminal Justice, 26*(3), 195-211.

Mazerolle, P., & Piquero, A. (1997). Violent responses to strain: An examination of conditioning influences. *Violence and Victims, 12,* 323-343.

Mazerolle, P., Piquero, A. R., & Capowich, G. E. (2003). Examining the links between strain, situational and dispositional anger, and crime: Further specifying and testing general strain theory. *Youth and Society,35*(2), 131-157.

McCord, J. (1984). Drunken drivers in longitudinal perspective. *Journal of Studies on Alcohol, 45,* 316-320.

McDonald, P. J., & Wooten, S. A. (1988). The influence of incompatible responses on the reduction of aggression: An alternative explanation. *Journal of Social Psychology, 128*(3), 401-406.

McFarland, R. A. (1968). Psychological and behavioral aspects of automobile accidents. *Traffic Safety Research Review, 12,* 71-80.

McGuire, F. L. (1976). Personality factors in highway accidents. *Human Factors, 18,* 433-442.

Meadows, R. J. (2001). *Understanding violence and victimization.* (2nd ed.). Upper Saddle River, NJ: Prentice Hall.

Mears, D. P., Ploeger, M., & Warr, M. (1998). Explaining the gender gap in delinquency: Peer influence and moral evaluations of behavior. *Journal of Research in Crime and Delinquency, 35*(3), 251-266.

Merlo, A. V., & Benekos, P. J. (2000). *What's wrong with the criminal justice system: Ideology, politics, and the media.* Cincinnati, OH: Anderson Publishing Co.

Mertler, C. A., & Vannatta, R. A. (2002). *Advanced and Multivariate Statistical Methods.* (2nd ed.). Los Angeles: Pyrczak Publishing.

Merton, R. (1938). Social structure and anomie. *American Sociological Review, 27,* 672-682.

Miethe, T. D., & McCorkle, R. C. (2001). *Crime profiles: The anatomy of dangerous persons, places, and situations.* (2nd ed.). Los Angeles, CA: Roxbury Publishing Company.

Mirowsky, J., & Ross, C. (1995). Sex differences in distress: Real or artifact. *American Sociological Review, 60,* 449-468.

Mizell, L. R., Jr. (1997, November). Aggressive driving. *In Aggressive Driving: Three Studies.* Maryland: Mizell & Co. International Security. AAA Foundation for Traffic Safety.

Mueller, C. W. (1983). Environmental stressors and aggressive behavior. In R. G. Geen & E. I. Donnerstein (Eds.). *Aggression: Theoretical and empirical reviews.* (Vol. 2). (pp. 51-76). New York: Academic Press.

Murray, D. (2000). Identifying aggressive drivers. *Safety & Health,161*(3), 70.

Nagin, D. S., & Paternoster, R. (1993). Enduring individual differences and rational choice theories of crime. *Law & Society Review, 27(3),* 467-496.

Naatanen, R., & Summala, H. (1976). *Road user behavior and traffic accidents.* Amsterdam and New York: North-Holland/American Elsevier.

National Highway Traffic Safety Administration (2000). *Aggressive Driving Enforcement for Implementing Best Practices.* Washington, D.C: NHTSA.

Newcomb, M. D., Huba, G. J., & Bentler, P. M. (1981). A multi-dimensional assessment of stressful life events among adolescents: Deviations and correlates. *Journal of Health and Social Behavior, 22,* 400-415.

Novaco, R. W. (1991). Aggression on roadways. In G. E. Stelmach & P.A. Vroon (Vol. Eds.). *Advances in Psychology* (Vol. 76). In. R. Baenninger *Targets of violence and Aggression* (pp.253-326). New York: North Holland Elsevier Science Publishers B.V.

Novaco, R. W., Stokols, D., Campbell, J., & Stokols, J. (1979). Transportation, stress, and community psychology. *American Journal of Community Psychology, 7*(4), 361-380.

Novaco, R. W., Stokols, D., & Milanesi, L. (1990). Objective and subjective dimensions of travel impedance as determinants of commuting stress. *American Journal of Community Psychology, 18*(2), 231-257.

Nunnally, J. C. (1978). *Psychometric theory* (2nd ed.). New York: McGraw-Hill.

Parry, M. (1968). *Aggression on the road.* London: Tavistock.

Parker, D., Lajunen, T., & Summala, H. (2002). Anger and aggression among drivers in three European countries. *Accident Analysis and Prevention, 34,* 229-235.

Paternoster, R., & Brame, R. (1997). Multiple routes to delinquency? A test of developmental and general theorics of crime. *Criminology, 35,* 49-84.

Paternoster, R., & Brame, R. (1998). The structural similarity or processes generating criminal and analogous behaviors. *Criminology, 36,* 633-670.

Paternoster, R., & Mazerolle, P. (1994). General strain theory and delinquency: A replication and extension. *Journal of Research in Crime and Delinquency, 31*(3), 235-263.

Pearlin, L. I. (1983). Role of strains and personal stress. In H. Kaplan (Ed.) *Psychosocial stress: Trends in theory and research* (pp. 3-32). New York: Academic Press.

Piquero, A. R., & Rosay, A. B. (1998). The reliability and validity of Grasmick et al.'s self-control scale: A comment on Longshore et al. *Criminology, 36(*1), 157-173.

Piquero, N., & Sealock, M. (2000). Generalizing general strain theory: An examination of an offending population. *Justice Quarterly, 17,* 449-484.

Piquero, A., & Tibbetts, S. (1996). Specifying the direct and indirect effects of low self-control and situational factors in offenders' decision making: Toward a more complete model of rational offending. *Justice Quarterly,13*(3), 481-510.

Polakowski, M. (1994). Linking self- and social control with deviance: Illuminating the structure underlying a general theory of crime and its relation to deviant activity. *Journal of Quantitative Criminology, 10*(1), 41-79.

Puente, M., & Castaneda, C. J. (1997). Rage starting to rule the nation's roads. *USA Today.* Retrieved November 16, 2000.(*http://www.dialog.carl.org 2030/sgibin/cw.htm.)*

Pratt, T. C., & Cullen, F. T. (2000). The empirical status of Gottfredson and Hirschi's general theory of crime: A meta-analysis. *Criminology, 38*(2), 931-964.

Rasmussen, C., Knapp, T. J., & Garner, L. (2000). Driving-induced stress in urban college students. *Perceptual and Motor Skills, 90,* 437-443.

Rathbone, D. B., & Huckabee, J. C. (1999, June). *Controlling road rage: A literature review and pilot study.* The AAA Foundation for Traffic Safety: The InterTrans Group.

Retting, R. A., Williams, A. F., & Greene, M.A. (1998). Red light running and sensible countermeasures: *Summary of research findings. Transportation Research Record 1640,* 23-26. Washington D.C.: Transportation Research Board.

Rosenberg, M. (1990). Reflexivity and emotions. *Social Psychology Quarterly, 53,* 3-12.

Ross, M., Thibaut, J., & Evenback, S. (1971). Some determinants of the intensity of social protest. *Journal of Experimental Social Psychology, 7*, 401-418.

Schroeder, L.D., Sjoquist, D. L., & Stephan, P. E. (1986). *Understanding regression analysis: An introductory guide.* Newbury Park, CT: Sage Publications.

Selzer, M. L., & Vinokur, A. (1975). Role of life events in accident causation. *Mental Health and Society, 2*, 36-54.

Sharkin, B. S. (1988). The measurement and treatment of client anger in counseling. *Journal of Counseling and Development, 66*, 361-365.

Sharp, S. F., Terling-Watt, T. L., Atkins, L. A., & Gilliam, J. T., (2001). Purging behavior in a sample of college females: A research note on general strain theory and female deviance. *Deviant Behavior, 22*, 171-188.

Shinar, D. (1997). Aggression and frustration in driving: Situational variable and individual differences. Paper presented at the International Symposium on Risk-Taking Behavior and Traffic Safety, Chatham Bars, MA.

Short, J. F., & Strodtbeck, F. L. (1965). *Group process and gang delinquency.* Chicago: University of Chicago Press.

Simons, R. L., & Robertson, J. F. (1989). The impact of parenting factors, deviant peers, and coping style upon adolescent drug use. *Family Relations, 38*, 273-281.

Sorenson, A. M., & Brownfield, D. (1995). Adolescent drug use and a general theory of crime: an analysis of a theoretical integration. *Canadian Journal of Criminology, 37*, 19-37.

Spector, P.E. (1992). *Summated rating scale construction: An introduction.* Newbury Park: CT: Sage Publications.

Spielberger, C. D. (1988). *State-Trait Anger Expression Inventory.* Odessa, FL: Psychological Assessment Resources.

Spielberger, C. D. (1999). *State-Trait Anger Expression Inventory* (2nd ed.) Odessa, FL: Psychological Assessment Resources.

Spielberger, C. D., Jacobs, G., Russell, S., & Crane, R. (1983). Assessment of the anger: the state-trait anger scale. In J.N. Butcher & C.D. Spielberger (Eds.), *Advances in personality assessment,* vol.2 (pp. 161-189). Hillside, NJ: Erlbaum Publishers.

Spielberger, C. D., Johnson, E.H., Russell, S. F., & Crane, R. (1985). The experience and expression of anger. Construction and validation of an anger expression scale. In M.A. Chesney & R.H. Rosenman (Eds.). *Anger and hostility in cardiovascular and behaviors disorders,* (pp. 5-30). Washington, D.C.: Hemisphere.

Spielberger, C. D., Reheiser, E.C., & Sydeman, S.J. (1995). Measuring the experience, expression, and control of anger. In H. Kassinove (Ed.) *Anger disorders: Definitions, diagnosis, and treatment* (pp. 49-67). Washington, D.C.: Taylor & Francis.

Straus, M. (1991). Discipline and deviance: Physical punishment of children and violence and other crimes in adulthood. *Social Problems, 38*, 133-154.

The Economist. (7/26/1997). Mad, bad and on the road. Vol. 344, issue 8027. p. 26.

Thoits, P. (1984). Coping, social support, and psychological outcomes: The central role of emotion. In P. Shaver (Ed.). *Review of personality and social psychology: Emotions, relationships, and health.* (Vol. 5). (pp.219-238). Beverly Hills, CA: Sage Publications.

Thomas, S. (1993). *Women and anger.* New York: Springer Publishing Co.

Tibbetts, S., & Herz, D. (1996). Gender differences in factors of social control and rational choice. *Deviant Behavior, 17*, 183-208.

Tibbetts, S. G., & Myers, D. L. (1999). Low self-control, rational choice, and student cheating. *American Journal of Criminal Justice, 23*, 179-200.

Tittle, C., Villemez, W., & Smith, D. (1978). The myth of social class and criminality. *American Sociological Review, 43*, 643-656.

Tsuang, M.T., Boor, M., & Fleming, J.A. (1985). Psychiatric aspects of traffic accidents. *American Journal of Psychiatry, 142*, 538-546.

Turner, C. W., Layton, J. F., & Simons, L. S. (1975). Naturalistic studies of aggressive behavior: Aggressive stimuli, victim visibility, and horn honking. *Journal of Personality and Social Psychology, 31*(6), 1098-1107.

Turner, R. J., Wheaton, B., & Lloyd, D.A. (1995). The epidemiology of social stress. *American Sociological Review, 60*, 104-125.

Tyler, T. R. (1990). *Why people obey the law.* New Haven, CT: Yale.

Vest, J., Cohen, W., & Tharp, M. (1997, June 2). Road rage. *U.S.News & World Report, 122* , 24-29.

Wald, M. (1997, July 19). Congress studying 'road rage' in U.S. *Toronto Globe and Mail,* (p. A11.).

Warr, M. (1993). Age, peers, and delinquency. *Criminology, 31*(1), 17-40.

Wasielewski, P. (1984). Speed as a measure of driver risk: Observed speeds versus driver and vehicle characteristics. *Accident Analysis & Prevention, 16*, 89-104

Weisburd, D. (1998). *Statistics in Criminal Justice.* Stamford, CT: Wadsworth.

Willis, D. K. (1997). Road rage laid to stress. *Neiman Reports, 51*(4), 43.

Wilson, T., & Greensmith, J. (1983). Multivariate analysis of the relationship between drivometer variables and drivers' accident, and sex exposure status. *Human Factors, 25,* 303-312.

Wolfgang, M. (1958). *Patterns of criminal homicide.* Philadelphia: University of Pennsylvania Press.

Wood, P. B., Pfefferbaum, B., & Arneklev, B. J. (1993). Risk-taking and self-control: Social psychological correlates of delinquency. *Journal of Crime and Justice, 16* (1), 111-130.

Wright, B. R. E., Caspi, A., Moffitt, T. E., & Silva, P. A. (1999). Low self-control, social bonds, and crime: Social causation, social selection, or both? *Criminology, 37,* 479-514.

Wright, B. R. E., Caspi, A., Moffitt, T. E., & Silva, P. A. (2001). The effects of social ties on crime vary by criminal propensity: A life-course model of interdependence. *Criminology, 39,* 321-352.

Wright, S. (1934). The method of path coefficients. *Annals of Mathematical Statistics, 5,* 161-215.

Wrightson, C. (1997). Road rage accelerates. *Health, 11*(6), 62.

Zillman, D. (1979). *Hostility and aggression.* Hillsdale, NJ: Lawrence Erlbaum.

Zimbardo, P. G. (1969). The human choice: Individuation, reason, and order versus deindividuation, impulse, and chaos. In W. J. Arnold & D. Levine (Eds.). *Nebraska Symposium on Motivation. Current Theory and Research in Motivation.* Vol 17. (pp. 237-307). Lincoln, Nebraska: University of Nebraska Press.

Zuckerman, M. (1979). *Sensation seeking: Beyond the optimal level of arousal.* Hillsdale, NJ: Lawrence Erlbaum.

Appendices

APPENDIX A: PA HOUSE BILLS

The General Assembly of Pennsylvania House Bill 1096 P.N. 1272 Session of 2001

Introduced by Melio, Bebko-Jones, Belardi, Belfanti, Casorio, Corrigan, Cruz, Daley, Frankel, Hennessey, Readshaw, Rooney, Steelman, Wansacz, C. Williams, J. Williams, and Youngblood

Referred to the Committee on Transportation, March 21, 2001 Amending Title 75 (Vehicles) of the Pennsylvania Consolidated Statutes, providing for the offense of aggressive driving.

The General Assembly of the Commonwealth of Pennsylvania hereby enacts as follows: Section 1. Title 75 of the Pennsylvania Consolidated Statutes is amended by adding a section to read: House Bill 1096, §3737 defines aggressive driving as:

A person commits the offense of aggressive driving if the person operates a vehicle in a manner which tends to harass, annoy or alarm another person and in a manner which endangers or is likely to endanger the safety of another person or property when the offense involves the commission of two or more violations of the following sections in a single act or series of acts in close proximity to another vehicle.

Section 3102 (relating to obedience to authorized persons directing traffic)

Section 3111 (relating to obedience to traffic-control devices)

Section 3112 (relating to traffic-control signals)

Section 3114 (relating to flashing signals)

Section 3301 (relating to driving on the right side of the roadway)

Section 3303 (relating to overtaking vehicle on the left)

Section 3304 (relating to overtaking vehicle on the right)

Section 3305 (relating to limitations on overtaking on the left)

Section 3307 (relating to no passing zones)

Section 3310 (relating to following too closely)

Section 3323 (relating to stop signs and yield signs)

Section 3326 (relating to duty of driver in construction and

maintenance areas)
Section 3345 (relating to meeting or overtaking school bus)
Section 3361 (relating to driving vehicle at safe speed)
Section 3362 (relating to maximum speed limits when the violation is more than ten miles per hour higher than the posted speed limit)
Section 3365 (relating to special speed limitations)
Section 3367 (relating to racing on highways)
Section 3702 (relating to limitations on backing)
Section 3703 (relating to driving upon sidewalk)
Section 3710 (relating to stopping at intersection or crossing to prevent obstruction)
Section 3714 (relating to careless driving)
Section 3736 (related to reckless driving)

Penalties

(1)   Except as otherwise provided in this section, any person violating subsection (a) commits a misdemeanor of the third degree.

(2)   Any person who violates this section while in violation of section 3731 (relating to driving under influence of alcohol or controlled substance) and who is convicted of that violation under section 3731 commits a misdemeanor of the first degree.

(3)   Any person who negligently causes serious bodily injury to another person as the result of a violation of this section and who is convicted of violating this section commits a felony of the third degree, and the sentencing court shall order the person to serve a minimum term of imprisonment of not less than 90 days and a mandatory minimum fine of $1,000, notwithstanding any other provision of law.

(c) Definition As used in this section, the term "serious bodily injury" means any bodily injury which creates a substantial risk of death or which causes serious, permanent disfigurement or protracted loss or impairment of the function of any bodily member or organ.

Section 2

This act shall take effect in 60 days.

APPENDIX B: LETTER TO PROFESSORS

Dear Dr./Professor _____,

My name is Maria Garase, I am currently working on a research project and I am requesting your help in the data collection process. Specifically, I would like to distribute an anonymous survey in your class.

The purpose of my research is to examine a public safety issue that affects many people. More specifically this study focuses on aggressive driving and road rage behaviors from a criminological perspective. The present research is designed to determine the types of incidents that precipitate aggressive driving and road rage incidents as well as to examine a possible criminological model that can explain these behaviors.

Please be aware that this project has been approved by the Institutional Review Boards for the Protection of Human Subjects at both institutions where data will be collected and every precaution is being taken to ensure the anonymity of the respondents. There are no known risks or discomforts associated with this research. The class you are currently instructing, ___, was randomly selected from a sampling frame of possible courses. I am therefore seeking your permission to survey all of the students in your class.

As an Instructor, I understand the value of class time and appreciate your consideration of this request. The entire process of introducing the survey and ensuring voluntary informed consent should take approximately 30 minutes. I would like to administer the survey at the beginning of the class period. I am sensitive to the fact that this request is an imposition on your teaching time, and I appreciate your willingness to assist me. Please reply to this request, so that I can be certain that you received this letter.

Please feel free to notify me if you have any questions or concerns. My contact information is provided. I greatly appreciate your attention to this letter. I look forward to hearing from you. Thank you in advance.
Dr. Maria Garase

APPENDIX C: INFORMED CONSENT FORM (PUBLIC
UNIVERSITY)

My name is Maria Garase, and I am conducting research that will be
used to complete my research, and I would like your help. I am
surveying students on both a large university and small independent
college during the Spring of 2003.

You are invited to participate in this research study. The following
information is provided in order to help you make an informed decision
whether or not to participate. If you have any questions please do not
hesitate to ask.

The purpose of this study is to examine a public safety issue that affects
many people. Specifically, this research will examine aggressive
driving and road rage behaviors from a criminological perspective.

If you choose to participate, your consent will be given by handing in a
completed survey. The survey will ask about your own driving
experiences. There are also some questions that deal with your age,
class standing, and major. The survey will also ask you about your
driving habits, traffic citations, and overall driving experiences. Lastly,
the survey contains some questions regarding your personal attitudes
and traits.

Please note that you are not to put your name or any identifying
information on the survey. Your responses are anonymous. There will
be no attempt made to identify who you are. I am only interested in the
overall perspectives of students from this institution—not the
individual's. There are no known personal risks to participating.
Access to the raw data will be available only to my supervisor and me.
The results may be reported in scholarly publications or professional
presentations, and they will be reported only as a group.

It should take you about 30 minutes to complete the entire
questionnaire. Your participation is completely voluntary. You are
free to decide not to participate in this study or to withdraw at any time.
I will distribute the surveys to everyone, but you are not required to
complete it. I appreciate your help. If you do not want to participate,

please remain quietly at your desk until the others are finished and write "discard" on the first page and hand it in as you exit. Questionnaires marked "discard" will be destroyed. If you do not understand any of the instructions, please raise your hand and ask.

This project has been approved by the Institutional Review Board for the Protection of Human Subjects. Thank you very much for your participation and your help in this study. For more information, you may contact me.

If you would like to know the results of the survey, please feel free to contact me. Once the study is completed, I will be happy to share the results with you. Thank you for your participation in this project and assisting in the research.

Sincerely,

Maria Garase

VOLUNTARY CONSENT FORM:
I have read and understand the information on the form and I consent to volunteer to be a subject in this study. I understand that my responses are completely anonymous and that I have the right to withdraw at any time. I have received a copy of this informed consent form to keep in my possession. My consent to participate in this study will be implied when I turn in the completed questionnaire.

APPENDIX D: INFORMED CONSENT FORM (INDEPENDENT COLLEGE)

Dear College Student:

You are invited to participate in a research project, which is a study of aggressive driving and road rage behaviors.

Students who are participating in this study will be administered the same survey during the weeks of April 30 through May 5, 2003, in their regularly scheduled classes. Students enrolled in undergraduate liberal arts courses are invited to participate. There are no known risks associated with your participation in this study and it will take approximately 30 minutes to complete the questionnaire.

Your participation is voluntary and your information is anonymous and confidential. The responses of other students will be aggregated to determine which views are most prevalent among college students. If you chose not participate, please return the survey and wait quietly while your classmates complete the questionnaire. You may withdraw from the study at any time, without penalty. I also ask that if you have already participated in this survey in one of your other classes, that you return the survey and wait quietly while your classmates continue.

Please note that you are not to put any identifying information on this survey. There will be no attempt to identify who you are and no action will be taken to determine which individuals participated. I am only interested in the overall perspectives of students from the College, not your individual views. There are no personal risks to participating. This study has been approved by the Institutional Review Board at the College.

If you would like to know the results of the survey, please feel free to contact me. Once the study is completed, I will be happy to share the results with you. Thank you for your participation in this project and assisting in the research.

Maria Garase

APPENDIX E: DEBRIEFING STATEMENT (INDEPENDENT COLLEGE)

Debriefing Statement

The purpose of this research is to gain knowledge on the aggressive driving and road rage behaviors of college students in Pennsylvania. The purpose of this survey is to gather data regarding college students' road rage behaviors, perceptions of stress, levels of self-control, and peer influences.

If at anytime you have any questions about the research you just participated in, or would like to know the results of the survey, please feel free to contact me. Once the study is completed, I will be more than happy to share the results with anyone who is interested. Thank you for your participation in this project and assisting in the research.

APPENDIX F: SURVEY INSTRUMENT

> Please answer the following questions about your personal characteristics and behaviors honestly. Your participation in this survey is strictly voluntary. This survey is anonymous, and your identity is not known to the researcher. Thank you for your participation. If you are not 18 years of age, you are excused from participation in this survey. Please leave the survey blank, and bring it up to the collection box in the front of the room. Thank you.

1. As of January 1, 2003, what is your age in years?_____

2. What is your gender? Male _____ Female_____

3. As of the end of the Fall 2002 semester, what is your current class standing?
   - Freshman _____
   - Sophomore _____
   - Junior _____
   - Senior _____
   - Graduate _____

4. What is your race/ethnicity?
   - Caucasian _____
   - Black _____
   - Latino _____
   - Asian _____
   - Native American _____
   - Other (please specify)_____

5. Are you a commuter student? No_____ Yes_____

6. As of Spring 2003, what is your CURRENT major?
   _____

7. At what age did you receive your driver's license?
   _____

8. Do you own a vehicle? No_____ Yes_____

9. What type of vehicle do you currently drive most often?
   Year_____
   Model_____

10. How many days per week (out of 7 days) do you drive?

    _____

11. On average, how long do you drive each day?
    _____hours_____ minutes

12. On average, how many miles do you drive on a daily basis?_____

13. Have you ever taken a driver's education class? No_____
    Yes_____
             If yes,13a. What type of driver's education class do you
                 attend:
                 _____School (high-school/college)
                 _____Privately-company or agency
                 _____Court mandated traffic school

    13b. What mode of learning was the class:
                 _____In-class/lecture
                 _____Hands on experience
                 _____Other, please specify_____

For questions 14-17, please answer the questions in terms of the past
one year (March 2002 through March 2003).

14. How many times were you stopped (while driving) by a police
officer? _____

15. How many traffic citations have you received?___ _____

16. How many speeding tickets have you received?_____ _____

17. How many accidents did you have when you were the driver of
the vehicle?_____

Directions for the next 34 questions: Everyone feels angry or furious from time to time when driving, but people differ in the ways that they react when they are angry while driving. A number of statements are listed below which people have used to describe their reactions when they feel angry or furious. Read each statement and then fill in the bubble to the right of the statement indicating how often you generally react or behave in the manner described when you are angry or furious while driving.

(AN)Almost Never (S)Sometimes (O) Often (AA) Almost Always

	AN	S	O	AA
18. I give the other driver the finger.	( )	( )	( )	( )
19. I drive up on the other driver's bumper.	( )	( )	( )	( )
20. I drive a little faster than I was..	( )	( )	( )	( )
21. I try to curt in front of the other driver	( )	( )	( )	( )
22. I call the other driver names aloud.	( )	( )	( )	( )
23. I make negative comments about the other driver	( )	( )	( )	( )
24. I follow right behind the other driver for a long time.	( )	( )	( )	( )
25. I try to get out of the car and tell the other driver off.	( )	( )	( )	( )
26. I yell questions like "Where did you get your license?"	( )	( )	( )	( )
27. I roll down the window to help communicate my anger.	( )	( )	( )	( )
28. I glare at the other driver.	( )	( )	( )	( )
29. I shake my fist at the other driver.	( )	( )	( )	( )
30. I stick my tongue out at the other driver.	( )	( )	( )	( )
31. I call the other driver names under my breath.	( )	( )	( )	( )
32. I speed up to frustrate the other driver.	( )	( )	( )	( )
33. I purposely block the other driver from doing what he/she wants to do. ..	( )	( )	( )	( )
34. I bump the other driver's bumper with mine.	( )	( )	( )	( )
35. I go crazy behind the wheel.	( )	( )	( )	( )

	AN	S	O	AA
36. I leave my brights on in the other driver's rear view mirror.	( )	( )	( )	( )
37. I try to force the other driver to the side of the road.	( )	( )	( )	( )
38. I try to scare the other driver.	( )	( )	( )	( )
39. I do to other drivers what they did to me.	( )	( )	( )	( )
40. I drive a lot faster than I was.	( )	( )	( )	( )
41. I swear at the other driver aloud.	( )	( )	( )	( )
42. I swear at the other driver under my breath.	( )	( )	( )	( )
43. I flash my lights at the other driver.	( )	( )	( )	( )
44. I make hostile gestures other than giving the finger.	( )	( )	( )	( )
45. I shake my head at the other driver.	( )	( )	( )	( )
46. I yell at the other driver.	( )	( )	( )	( )
47. I make negative comments about the other driver under my breath.	( )	( )	( )	( )
48. I give the other driver a dirty look.	( )	( )	( )	( )
49. I try to get out of the car and have a physical fight with the other driver.	( )	( )	( )	( )
50. I think things like "Where did you get your license?"	( )	( )	( )	( )
51. I slow down to frustrate the other driver.	( )	( )	( )	( )

The next questions deal with things that may have happened to you while involved with or driving a vehicle, but do NOT involve auto accidents.

In the **LAST THREE MONTHS**, how many times have you…

	Number of times happened					
	0	1	2	3	4	5+
52. Broken or damaged a part of a vehicle (e.g., pulled knob off the radio, kicked a fender)?	( )	( )	( )	( )	( )	( )
53. Had an argument with a passenger while you were driving?	( )	( )	( )	( )	( )	( )
54. Had a verbal argument with the driver of another vehicle?	( )	( )	( )	( )	( )	( )

	Number of times happened					
	0	1	2	3	4	5+
55. Had a physical fight with the driver of another vehicle?	( )	( )	( )	( )	( )	( )
56. Made an angry gesture at another driver or pedestrian?	( )	( )	( )	( )	( )	( )
57. Swore at or called another driver or pedestrian names?	( )	( )	( )	( )	( )	( )
58. Flashed your headlights in anger?						
59. Honked your horn in anger?	( )	( )	( )	( )	( )	( )
60. Yelled at another driver or pedestrian?	( )	( )	( )	( )	( )	( )
61. Drove while being very angry?	( )	( )	( )	( )	( )	( )
62. Lost control of your anger while driving?	( )	( )	( )	( )	( )	( )
63. Drove up close behind another driver in anger	( )	( )	( )	( )	( )	( )
64. Cut another driver off in anger?	( )	( )	( )	( )	( )	( )
65. Driven without using your seat belt?	( )	( )	( )	( )	( )	( )
66. Drank alcohol and driven?	( )	( )	( )	( )	( )	( )
67. Been drunk and driven?	( )	( )	( )	( )	( )	( )
68. Driven 10-20 mph over the limit?	( )	( )	( )	( )	( )	( )
69. Driven 20+ mph over the limit?	( )	( )	( )	( )	( )	( )
70. Passed unsafely?	( )	( )	( )	( )	( )	( )
71. Tailgated or followed another vehicle too closely?	( )	( )	( )	( )	( )	( )
72. Changed lanes unsafely?	( )	( )	( )	( )	( )	( )
73. Drifted into another lane?	( )	( )	( )	( )	( )	( )
74. Switched lanes to speed through slower traffic?	( )	( )	( )	( )	( )	( )
75. Gone out of turn at a red light or stop sign?	( )	( )	( )	( )	( )	( )
76. Made an illegal turn (e.g., illegal right turn on red light)?	( )	( )	( )	( )	( )	( )
77. Driven recklessly?	( )	( )	( )	( )	( )	( )
78. Run a red light or stop sign?	( )	( )	( )	( )	( )	( )
79. Entered an intersection when the light was turning red?	( )	( )	( )	( )	( )	( )

> Please indicate if any of the following events have occurred in your home, or to members of your
> family, **during the past year.**

81. My family had serious money problems.
No_____
Yes_____

82. My mother or father remarried.
No_____
Yes_____

83. An immediate family member died.
No_____
Yes_____

84. I, or a member of my immediate family, had a serious illness.
No_____
Yes_____

85. A close friend died.
No_____
Yes_____

86. I started attending a new school.
No_____
Yes_____

87. Divorce
No_____
Yes_____

88. Separation
No_____
Yes_____

89. Serious accident
No_____
Yes_____

90. You or someone in your family in trouble with the law.
    No_____
    Yes_____

91. Father/Mother, or both, unemployed
    No_____
    Yes_____

92. Family move
    No_____
    Yes_____

93. During the past year, has a significant other (i.e., boy/girlfriend) broken up with you?
    No_____
    Yes_____

94. During the past year, have you had any school problems (e.g., been kicked out of school, caught cheating)?
    No_____
    Yes_____

95. During the past year, have you been dismissed from a job?
    No_____
    Yes_____

96. During the past year, has a friend broken off a friendship with you?
    No_____
    Yes_____

97. During the past year have you begun a new school experience at a higher academic level than before?
    No_____
    Yes_____

98. During the past year have you transferred to a new school at the same academic level as before?
    No_____
    Yes_____

99. During the past year have you been dismissed from a dormitory or other residence?
No_____
Yes_____

100. During the past year have you failed an important exam?
No_____
Yes_____

101. During the past year have you failed a course?
No_____
Yes_____

102. During the past year have you dropped a course?
No_____
Yes_____

103. During the past year, have you changed your major?
No_____
Yes_____

104. During the past year have you had financial problems related to school (in danger of not having enough money to finish)?
No_____
Yes_____

Answer each of the following by circling the number on the scale that best describes you.

105. How important is it to you to get a college degree?
0   1   2   3   4   5   6   7   8   9   10
Not   Somewhat   Very
Important   Important   Important

106. How likely is it that you will receive a college degree?
0   1   2   3   4   5   6   7   8   9   10
Not   Somewhat   Very
Likely   Likely   Likely

107. How likely that you will get the job you want after graduation?

0 1 2 3 4 5 6 7 8 9 10
Not   Somewhat   Very
Likely   Likely   Likely

108. What do you think your chances are for completing a college degree?

0 1 2 3 4 5 6 7 8 9 10
Very   O.K.   Very Good
Bad Chance Chance   Chance

109. In school, I am getting the grades I think I should be getting (that is, you are living up to your potential)?

0 1 2 3 4 5 6 7 8 9 10
Not   Somewhat   Very
At All   Much So

110. I am having trouble meeting the demands of college finances.

0 1 2 3 4 5 6 7 8 9 10
None   Some   A Lot

111. During the past year, have you received a grade that you think was lower than you deserved?

_____No _____Yes

112. During the past year, have you received a grade that was unfair compared to the grade received by others in the course?

_____No _____Yes

A number of statements that people use to describe themselves are given below. Read each statement and then check the appropriate response to indicate how you generally feel or react.

** For ten items numbered 113-122, See the STAXI-2 Trait Anger Scale in Spielberger, C. D. (1999) *State-Trait Anger Expression Inventory* (2nd ed.). Odessa, FL: Psychological Assessment Resources.

Given the following situations, rate your level of anger. Place a check mark on the line which best describes your anger level.

(NA) Not at All (S) Sometimes (M) Moderately (VM) Very Much

Given this situation, how angry are you?:

	NA	S	M	VM
123.Being cut in front of on the highway.	___	___	___	___
124.Being tailgated by another vehicle for more than 1 mile.	___	___	___	___
125.Being given an obscene gesture due	___	___	___	___
128.Being behind a driver who is indecisive at an intersection, thus making you late for an appointment.	___	___	___	___
129.Being physically confronted by another driver because of your driving.	___	___	___	___

The following questions ask you about your personality/behaviors. Place a check mark in the blank that best suits your personality/behaviors.

(SD) Strongly Disagree (DS) Disagree Somewhat (AS) Agree Somewhat (SA) Strongly Agree

	SD	DS	AS	SA
123. Being cut in front of on the highway.	___	___	___	___
130. I often act on the spur of the moment.	___	___	___	___
131. I don't devote much thought and effort to preparing for the future.	___	___	___	___

	SD	DS	AS	SA

132. I often do whatever brings me
pleasure here and now, even at the
cost of some distant goal.

133. I'm more concerned about what
happens to me in the short run than
in the long run.

134. I frequently try to avoid things
that I know will be difficult.

135. When things get complicated, I tend to
quit or withdraw.

136. The things in life that are easiest to do
bring me the most pleasure.

137. I dislike really hard tasks that stretch
my abilities to the limit.

138. I like to test myself every now and then
by doing something a little risky.

139. Sometimes I will take a risk just for the
fun of it.

140. I sometimes find it exciting to do
things for which I might get in trouble.

141. Excitement and adventure are more
important to me than security.

142. If I had a choice, I would almost
always rather do something physical
than something mental.

143. I almost always feel better when
I am on the move than when I am

sitting and thinking.

	SD	DS	AS	SA

144. I like to get out and do things more
than I like to read or contemplate ideas. ___ ___ ___ ___

145. I seem to have more energy and a
greater need for activity than most
other people my age. ___ ___ ___ ___

146. I try to look out for myself first, even
if it means making things difficult for
other people. ___ ___ ___ ___

147. I'm not very sympathetic to other
people when they are having problems. ___ ___ ___ ___

148. If things I do upset people, it's their
problem, not mine. ___ ___ ___ ___

149. I will try to get the things I want
even when I know it's causing
problems for other people. ___ ___ ___ ___

150. I lose my temper pretty easily. ___ ___ ___ ___

151. Often, when I'm angry at people I
feel more like hurting them than
talking to them about why I am angry. ___ ___ ___ ___

152. When I am really angry, other people
better stay away from me. ___ ___ ___ ___

153. When I have a serious disagreement
with someone it's usually hard for me
to talk about it without getting upset. ___ ___ ___ ___

154.   During the last year, how often does your closest friend
        engage in any of the following acts:

                            Never   Sometimes   Always

        Speeding   _____   _____   _____

        Obscene gestures   _____   _____   _____

        Verbal Confrontations
        on the road   _____   _____   _____

        Physical Confrontations
        on the road   _____   _____   _____

155.   On average, how long have you been friends with the person
        you've identified in question #154: _____ _____

156.   On average, how much time per week do you spend with your
        closest friend identified above?_____

157.   Has your closest friend (that you referred to in the above
        questions) ever influenced you to commit an offense?
        No_____   Yes_____

Index